RED BREAD

RED BREAD

Collectivization in a Russian Village

MAURICE HINDUS

Foreword by Ronald Grigor Suny

INDIANA UNIVERSITY PRESS
Bloomington and Indianapolis

First Midland Book Edition 1988

© 1988 by Indiana University Press
© 1931 by Maurice Hindus

Indiana University Press acknowledges the assistance of Paul O'Dwyer,
Milton Hindus, Deborah Deloria, and Robert Deloria in the preparation
of this edition.

Manufactured in the United States of America

Library of Congress Cataloging-in-Publication Data
Hindus, Maurice Gershon, 1891–1969.
Red bread.
Includes bibliographical references.
1. Bol'she Bykovo (R.S.F.S.R.)—History.   2. Collectivization of
agriculture—Russian S.F.S.R.—Bol'she Bykovo.   3. Hindus, Maurice
Gershon, 1891–1969—Journeys—Russian S.F.S.R.—Bol'she Bykovo.
4. Bol'she Bykovo (R.S.F.S.R.)—Description.   I. Title.
DK651.B595H56   1988   947'.65   88-45100
ISBN 0-253-34953-2
ISBN 0-253-20485-2 (pbk.)
1   2   3   4   5   92   91   90   89   88

CONTENTS

MAURICE HINDUS AND *RED BREAD*
BY RONALD GRIGOR SUNY   vii

I   NADYA'S LETTER   1

II   THE GATHERING OF THE STORM   10

III   THE SPIRIT OF SUNDAY   36

IV   THE COMING OF THE STORM   57

V   MOSCOW MARCHES ON   69

VI   BEYOND THE PALE   86

VII   THE DAILY ORDEAL   104

VIII   "THE RETURN OF THE NATIVE"   135

IX   THE VOICE OF THE MASS   156

X   THE WHITE WEDDING   186

XI   THE KOLHOZ   210

XII   THE NEW AND THE OLD   229

XIII   THE KOOLACK   247

XIV   THE PUZZLED LITTLE FATHER   265

XV   THE LANDLORD HERDSMAN   284

XVI   A NEW GIRL   298

XVII   GIPSY ROSA   320

XVIII   THE FAREWELL VISIT   336

XIX   RED BREAD   355

MAURICE HINDUS AND *RED BREAD*

> To see for the sake of seeing
> and to tell others so that they may
> vicariously share in the seeing: that
> is beyond the reach of the imagi-
> nation of most men in respect of
> Soviet Russia. To them it is not
> a scene to behold, it is a battle to
> take part in. Failure to be an open
> partisan is itself suspect.
> —John Dewey [1]

Maurice Hindus (1891–1969) was a witness to the most profound social change in the early twentieth century—the transformation of peasant Russia into an industrial and urban society. Hindus both stood apart from that revolution, in his own view as an objective observer, and as a sympathetic interpreter to an alien Western world. To his friend, the educator John Dewey, Hindus managed (in the book preceding *Red Bread*) to bring "the most intimate sympathetic response to all the human issues involved in the revolutionary transformation," but at the same time to be "content to see and to report. Nowhere does he assume the divine prerogative of blessing or condemning: nowhere is he the avenging angel of divine wrath nor yet the angel of benediction." [2] To a more cynical age such as our own a posture of objectivity is immediately suspect, even as the attempt may be admired. For without that attempt social science would be impossible.

Born in the Belorussian village of Bolshoye Bykovo, Maurice Hindus writes of his early years as bounded by "a village where time stopped." His father, the head of one of four Jewish families in the hamlet, had once been prosperous but had drunk his inheritance down to a single cow, a horse, and a large house with a shingled roof. Life was precarious for the peasants of western Russia, subject as they were to the vagaries of the weather, unwelcome visits by disease and fire, and fears of the ever-present spirits and demons that lived in the woods and streams nearby. Hindus's village, however, was blessed by a benevolent Polish landlord and a kindly parish priest. It did not know the periodic famines that struck other parts of the empire and was free of anti-Semitism.

The Jewish families engaged a tutor to make certain their children learned Hebrew and Yiddish, as well as Russian, and Maurice was sent to a Russian school in the town of Slutsk. There he first encountered the condescension and scorn directed at peasants, Jew and non-Jew alike. But he "dismissed the matter as just one more example of the incomprehensible ways of city folks, as much a part of the scheme of things as the bitterness of winter and the harshness of muzhik [peasant] life in general."[3] Growing up a peasant, with a deep affection for the simple, hard life of the village, Hindus became, in his words, "a traveler between two worlds," spending much of his adult life as an interpreter of his beloved peasant Russia, with its ageless and unyielding traditions, to the faster-moving, innovative, and individualistic farmers and city dwellers in his adopted America.

In 1905, his father dead and an older brother already in the United States, Maurice, his mother, a brother,

and two sisters left Russia for New York City. Settling
on the Lower East Side, Hindus set about to learn English—first on the noisy streets, later unsuccessfully at
night school, and finally on his own, reading George
Eliot's *Adam Bede*. To escape the squalor and crowding
in New York and improve his health, he moved at age
seventeen to a farm in upstate New York. There as a
hired hand he found a second village home, a classless
society of just folks united by "a genuine sentiment of
friendliness and equality."[4] His love for agriculture re-
kindled, Hindus spent three years on the farm learning
the fundamentals of farming and planning to go on to
agricultural school.

In 1911, however, he entered Colgate University,
where he studied literature. In Carl Baum's tailor shop
he met with other "intellectuals" and discussed politics,
free love, and the humanistic socialism favored by the
immigrant tailor. Hindus was "amused more than en-
lightened" by his reading of the *Communist Manifesto*.
Gradually he gave up the idea of becoming a farmer
and thought more seriously of writing. On graduation
he traveled as a lecturer on the Chatauqua circuit, speaking on the Russian peasantry and meeting the most
popular orators of the day—Helen Keller, Russell
Conwell, and William Jennings Bryan. His warm re-
ception and the evident interest in the subject, even in
small Midwestern towns, convinced Hindus to write
a book on the muzhik. He applied to Harvard University and began intensive study with the Slavicist
Leo Wiener. By the time he completed his book—*The
Russian Peasant and the Revolution* (1920)—Hindus
had produced a monumental treatise welcomed by
reviewers.

His scholarly work, however, was not taken to heart

by a wide reading public, and Hindus turned toward more popular writing to earn a living. After publishing a number of articles for *Century Magazine*—the first on the Dukhobors of western Canada—Hindus was invited by the magazine's editor, Glenn Frank (later the president of the University of Wisconsin), to write a second, less academic book on peasants under Bolshevism. Hindus agreed, and in 1923, after eighteen years away, he returned to Russia and his home village.

His approach to the subject was different from that of many of his contemporaries writing about the Soviet Union. Prevailing opinion in America held that the stated objective of the Leninists to export their revolution made them an international threat to democracy and capitalism. Hindus saw the revolution as a purely Russian phenomenon, generated by internal political and social cleavages, and of little immediate danger to the more prosperous West. Unlike those who relied on Soviet ideological pronouncements or a reading of the Marxist classics as a guide to understanding what was going on in Russia, Hindus chose to "be in the country, wander around, observe and listen, ask questions and digest answers to obtain some comprehension of the sweep and meaning of these events."[5]

His first impression on seeing his village was that nothing had changed—at least for the better. The houses were still wretched, vulnerable to the "red cock," the fire that periodically devastated the wooden buildings. The forest had been cut down by the peasants in a frenzy for timber once the revolution removed all restrictions. And everywhere the eternal mud of rural Russia was as deep and sticky as ever. ("Mud! Mud! Mud! One could write a history of Russia in terms of

mud," he later wrote. [6]) The relatively mild peasants of
Bolshoye Bykovo had joined with peasants throughout
the country in the collective rage against landlords,
even though their kind Polish *pan* had always been
ready to help them in time of need. His fields were
plowed up and thus appropriated by the villagers. His
tiny chapel was ravaged, and when he died "his body
was dragged out of the family vault, stripped of clothes
and jewelry and nailed, naked and feet up, to two adjacent trees. Only when the Bolsheviks arrived did
they bury the body." [7] But first impressions soon passed,
and when Hindus spoke to the villagers he learned that
they were "storming with new passion, new conflicts,
new aspirations. Everyone was bursting with talk. . . .
Never in the old days had the village been so stirred
by conflict or so vehement in its demands on government. Nor did the Soviets at that time interfere with
this surly and boisterous talk." [8] While "older people
wailed that doom was upon them," younger ones, particularly men, felt liberated by the revolution. Now
free of the fears of the Evil One or Rusalka, the water
spirit, no longer attending church, unwilling and not
needing to doff their hats to officials, and free to go to
school, the young muzhiki placed their hopes on the
new *tekhnika* (technology). But when Hindus tried to
show the peasants a better way to tie up grain sheaths for
curing, only the young listened. The older farmers refused to gamble with their crop and preferred the traditional way. "Clearly," Hindus concluded, "coaxing and
persuasion would need to be supplemented by no small
amount of compulsion." [9]

Broken Earth (1926), the book that recorded his return to Russia, was a great success, and by the mid-1920s

Hindus was recognized as an expert on Russia. At a time when the academic study of the USSR hardly existed in the United States outside of Cambridge and Chicago, he was sought as a lecturer and writer. His third book, *Humanity Uprooted* (1929), went through sixteen printings. Now somewhat of a celebrity, he befriended men and women of letters, like John Dewey and George Bernard Shaw (whom he guided through the USSR on a celebrated trip), and he once was prevailed upon by F. Scott Fitzgerald's psychiatrist to allay the novelist's fears of a coming Communist revolution in America. Along with the handful of American correspondents in Moscow, like Walter Duranty and Louis Fischer, Maurice Hindus became one of the most frequently read sources on the Stalin Revolution of the 1930s.

Red Bread remains one of his most valuable works. Hindus visited his home village in 1929, just before the *velikii perelom*, the "Great Breakthrough" that forced the peasants of the Soviet Union to give up their individual farming and join collective farms, and then again in 1930 just after Stalin had called a temporary halt to rapid and forced collectivization. He wandered on foot through the countryside recording conversations with everyone from Communists and priests to simple milk maids, while trying to keep his own views from intruding on his observations. Yet Hindus's preferences come out in his account. For him the Russian revolution (and this includes Stalin's "revolution from above" of the 1930s) was on the whole a powerful force for needed change. He records with great sympathy the heavy human costs, particularly on the so-called kulaks, and wonders if they were required. Communists are seen as severe, often unfeeling, determined to use what

power was needed against elements that they saw as ob-
stacles. As it aimed at changing human society and
human nature, the revolution was cruel, but at the same
time it was "a double-armed power" that stifled and re-
deemed people.[10] He concludes that peaceable methods
alone would not have brought about change at a fast
enough pace. "In Revolution, as in war, it is the objective that counts, and not the price, whether in gold or in
blood."[11]

Hindus's views have been seen by his critics as naive,
apologetic, and even duplicitous. One of his fellow
correspondents, the disillusioned Eugene Lyons, considered Hindus to be one of the most industrious of
Stalin's apologists.[12] More generously, Louis Fischer
wrote that Hindus "understands emotions and ignores
economics. He despised Communist terminology and
Marxist logic and admired the Soviets only for what
they did to uproot and give new life to humanity."[13]
The sociologist Paul Hollander regards Hindus as one
of the "political pilgrims" to socialist societies who ro-
manticize what they see, neglecting the negative and
overemphasizing the beautiful and healthy. Hollander
includes Hindus among those journalists who seemed
to justify as necessary the Ukrainian famine of 1932.[14]
Historian William L. O'Neill deals with the wartime
Hindus, whom he refers to as the "author of numerous
books acclaiming Soviet practices" from which "a generation of progressives learned . . . how to drown the
horrors of Soviet life in a warm bath of sentiment."[15]

Though well equipped for his unusual profession, Hindus
suffered from a condition afflicting all journalists whose ca-
reers were based in the Soviet Union. Reporters who did a tour
of duty in Russia and then moved on could say what they
pleased afterward. But Hindus and others needed to stay. Ac-

cordingly, what they wrote had to pass inspection. . . . They had to accept the fundamental law of Stalinism, which was that the end justified the means, however terrible. For Hindus this law was especially onerous because the peasantry suffered more than most Russians from Stalinism. . . . It fell to Hindus more than any other Westerner to explain away this blunder and this crime [collectivization and dekulakization]. He did so unflinchingly even before the war. [16]

In contrast to his critics, scholars of collectivization have found Hindus's observations valuable as unique sources of evidence on the massive changes in the Soviet countryside. [17] There is general agreement with Hindus that the methods by which peasant agriculture was transformed were wasteful and cruel, that most peasants were resistant to the idea of the collective farm, and that the Communists were insensitive and arrogant in their treatment of the peasants. In *Red Bread* and elsewhere he is clear about Soviet successes, like the erosion of religion and the improvement in the status of women, but is candid about its failures, like the fall in the material standard of living in the 1930s. Yet he remained in all his writings both attached to the memory of the bucolic world of his youth and convinced that that world had to be destroyed so that Russia could enter modern times. In the dark days of the Second World War, inspired by the bitter struggle of the Red Army, Hindus expressed his conviction that without collectivization the Soviet Union would not have been able to industrialize and to survive the Nazi invasion. [18]

Present scholarship is less convinced by the ends–means argument—that the costs of collectivization are more than justified by the rapid industrialization of the USSR—than were many writers of Hindus's generation. In a ground-breaking study of collectivization

Moshe Lewin has shown that the decision to end the mixed economy of the New Economic Policy and embark on the state-administered economy of the Stalinist period was more the product of political infighting, an economic impasse generated by party mismanagement, and the personality of Stalin than it was a rational economic calculation. The country had few tractors with which to mechanize agriculture and no real substitute for the initiative and energy of the productive kulaks. [19] Alternative approaches to industrialization existed within the mixed economy, Lewin argues, that would have been less disruptive economically and less destructive in human terms.

It is true that those years presented a sight which was extolled by many—a huge country transformed quite suddenly into an impressive building site. But it would be a distortion to leave things at that, since those were also years of a national catastrophe of major proportions—of a "severe disruption of economic life," . . . Agriculture was utterly disorganized and huge rural areas plunged into a severe famine; there were inflation, black markets, and a drop in the nation's standard of living, unheard of in conditions of peace. The whole social fabric was shattered, and to keep the kettle from blowing up, the powers of dictatorship were enhanced to an extent which probably could match the extremes of the civil war period. [20]

A Soviet historian, A. A. Barsov, and an American economist, James R. Millar, have made an equally devastating claim against collectivization. The standard argument had been that collectivization had ended peasant discretion over agricultural output and forced a flow of capital from agriculture to industry. But Barsov and Millar maintain that, rather than agriculture supplying goods and services to industry, the flow went the other way. The destruction of livestock and the fall in overall production made agriculture a net importer of material products during the First Five-Year Plan. While the state certainly received grain surpluses from the peasants, it soon had to turn around and use its resources to replace investment in agriculture. Millar concludes that "mass collectivization of Soviet agriculture must be reckoned as an unmitigated economic policy disaster. . . . Agricultural output increased only marginally over the entire period of the 1930s, while labor productivity, yields, and rural and urban consumption per capita declined."[21]

Besides his writings on the Soviet Union, Hindus produced three books on Czechoslovakia, a novel, and a book on the Middle East.[22] He wrote less on the Soviet Union during the years of the Cold War when travel to the USSR was restricted and his particular perspective suspect in the West. After the death of Stalin in 1953 he made two trips to the Soviet Union, one in the summer of 1958, the other in 1960, and produced a prizewinning book, *House Without a Roof: Russia after Forty-three Years of Revolution*. For Hindus the revolution continued, and the best way to understand it was to listen to the people themselves. "I have always believed," he wrote, "that the Soviet Union is a country to hear rather than see."[23] He died in New York City in 1969.

Maurice Hindus developed and popularized a particular form of reporting on the Soviet Union. He did not engage in the abstractions and speculations that scholars with less hands-on experience wove into all-explaining models. He was a founder and practitioner of another tradition in writing on the Soviet Union— one later taken up with enormous success by Alexander Werth, Hedrick Smith, Robert Kaiser, David Shipler, Andrea Lee, Martin Walker, and others. The combination of personal observations, telling anecdotes, and revealing detail in this tradition provided a texture and complexity to the picture of the USSR that shredded the overblown generalizations of the model builders. Real people were central to this school of writing, and while the limitations of anecdote and personal encounter are evident, these journalists and travelers provided a healthy alternative to grand theories and arid abstractions.

Hindus came to Russia with few illusions and therefore avoided disillusionment. Neither a Marxist nor ideologically anti-Soviet, he deliberately worked for a kind of objectivity, though his empathy for the sufferings of his fellow peasants and his hopes for a more humane Russia consistently colored his writing. Complete objectivity was as impossible for Hindus as for any other human observer of the human scene. Yet his perspective was unique and remains valuable. Though his writings have hardly escaped controversy and condemnation, they remain worthy of rereading as a contemporary record of a momentous, complex time still needing understanding and interpretation. His story was perhaps the most important of the twentieth century—the metamorphosis of a peasant country into an industrial giant, its fierce defense against fascism, and its emergence from the darkness of Stalinism. Whether Hindus was an apologist or an honest reporter will be decided by each reader.

Ronald Grigor Suny
The University of Michigan

NOTES

[1] "Introduction," Maurice Hindus, *Humanity Uprooted* (New York: Jonathan Cape and Harrison Smith, 1929), p. xvi.

[2] Ibid.

[3] Maurice Hindus, *A Traveler in Two Worlds*, introduction by Milton Hindus (Garden City: Doubleday, 1971), p. 34.

[4] Ibid., p. 120.

[5] Ibid., p. 311.

[6] Maurice Hindus, *Green Worlds: An Informal Chronicle* (New York: Doubleday, 1938), p. 32.

[7] Ibid., p. 321.

[8] Ibid., pp. 322–323.

[9] Ibid., p. 327.

[10] Maurice Hindus, *Red Bread*, p. 302.

[11] Ibid., p. 357.

[12] Eugene Lyons, *Assignment in Utopia* (New York: Harcourt Brace, 1937).

[13] Louis Fischer, *Men and Politics: An Autobiography* (New York: Duell, Sloan, and Pearce, 1944), pp. 158–159.

[14] All of Hollander's references to Hindus are from a single book, *The Great Offensive* (London: Victor Gollancz, 1933), and do not show the range of his investigations and opinions. (Paul Hollander, *Political Pilgrims: Travels of Western Intellectuals to the Soviet Union, China, and Cuba* [New York: Oxford University Press, 1981; Harper Colophon Books, 1983], pp. 119–120, 126, 134, 145). In his study of the Ukrainian famine, Robert Conquest notes that Hindus, although "a friend of the regime," criticized Soviet misrepresentations of the kulaks and documented the terrible costs of collectivization. (*The Harvest of Sorrow: Soviet Collectivization and the Terror-Famine* [New York and Oxford: Oxford University Press, 1986], pp. 133, 310.)

Hindus visited Ukraine in the summer of 1932 and tells of food shortages and the mismanagement by the party of the grain collections that were leading to hunger. (*The Great Offensive*, pp. 83–84, 95–116.) He traveled with Ralph Barnes of the New York *Herald Tribune*, who defied Soviet censorship and broke the story to the West. Hindus was less bold, though he hinted broadly in his published writings at the time that famine was a reality in parts of the USSR. He later claimed that he learned of the full extent of the famine only in 1934. (*House Without a Roof: Russia after Forty-three Years of Revolution* [Garden City: Doubleday, 1961], pp. 218–221.)

[15] William L. O'Neill, *A Better World. The Great Schism: Stalinism and the American Intellectuals* (New York: Simon and Schuster, 1982), pp. 61, 66.

[16] Ibid., p. 65.
[17] R. W. Davies, *The Industrialization of Soviet Russia, I. The Socialist Offensive: The Collectivization of Soviet Agriculture, 1929–1930* (Cambridge: Harvard University Press, 1980); Lynne Viola, *The Best Sons of the Fatherland: Workers in the Vanguard of Soviet Collectivization* (New York and Oxford: Oxford University Press, 1987).

[18] Maurice Hindus, *Mother Russia* (Garden City, New York: Garden City Publishing Co., 1942); *Russia Fights On* (London: Collins, 1942); *Hitler Cannot Conquer Russia* (Garden City: Doubleday, 1942).

[19] Moshe Lewin, *Russian Peasants and Soviet Power: A Study of Collectivization* (Evanston: Northwestern University Press, 1968). See also his *Political Undercurrents in Soviet Economic Debates* (Princeton: Princeton University Press, 1974) and *The Making of the Soviet System: Essays in the Social History of Interwar Russia* (New York: Pantheon, 1985).

[20] Moshe Lewin, "The Disappearance of Planning in the Plan," *Slavic Review*, XXXII, 2 (June 1973), p. 275.

[21] James R. Millar, "Mass Collectivization and the Contribution of Soviet Agriculture to the First Five-Year Plan: A Review Article," *Slavic Review*, XXXIII, 4 (December 1974), p. 764. See also, James R. Millar and Alec Nove, "A Debate on Collectivization. Was Stalin Really Necessary?" *Problems of Communism*, July–August 1976, pp. 49–62; A. A. Barsov, *Balans stoimostnykh obmenov mezhdu gorodom i derevnei* (Moscow, 1969).

[22] On Czechoslovakia: *To Sing With the Angels* (New York: Doubleday, 1941); *We Shall Live Again* (New York: Doubleday, 1939); *The Bright Passage* (Garden City: Doubleday, 1947). The novel was *Moscow Skies* (New York: Random House, 1936). On the Middle East: *In Search of a Future: Persia, Egypt, Iraq and Palestine* (Garden City: Doubleday, 1949).

[23] *House Without a Roof* (Garden City: Doubleday, 1961), p. xiii.

NADYA'S LETTER

IN the winter of 1930 I received a letter from Russia, from which I quote the following passage:

I am off in villages with a group of other brigadiers organizing *kolhozy*.[1] It is a tremendous job, but we are making amazing progress. It would do you worlds of good to be with us and watch us draw the stubborn peasant into collectivization. Contrary to all your affirmations and prophecies, our *muzhik* is yielding to persuasion. He is joining the *kolhozy*, and I am confident that in time not a peasant will remain on his own land. We shall yet smash the last vestiges of capitalism and forever rid ourselves of exploitation. Come, join us; see with your own eyes what is happening, how we are rebuilding the Russian villages. The very air here is afire with a new spirit and a new energy.

NADYA

I had met Nadya some years ago in a small town on the Volga where she was at work in a museum making maps and geologic pictures. She was short and stocky, with a forest of dark-brown hair always fluffed up at the top; her big gray eyes, in which floated particles of brown, dilated visibly and prettily when she grew animated or excited. She had a round chin, an exquisite mouth, a sharp though pleasant voice, and a winning laugh; and she was a girl of unshakeable

---

[1] Collective or socialistic farms.

convictions. Daughter of a half-Tartar father and a
Polish mother, hers was a mixture of bloods rare even
in a land that is the world's most gigantic melting pot.
Only ten years old when the Revolution broke out,
she was at once swept into its fold, and was one
of the first girls in the city of Kazan to join the
Pioneers, the Communist equivalent of the Boy and
Girl Scouts. She has always been within the party
organization. As soon as she was old enough she joined
the Komsomol,[2] in which she was still an ardent worker
when I last saw her, two years earlier. Throughout
her high school days and later, in the pedagogic institute, where she studied, her one absorbing interest was
the Revolution. It was the dominating passion in her
life, and nothing could supplant it, not even love. When
she was only nineteen she married a young physician,
but left him because he objected to her " wearing herself out with social work."

Now she was giving all her time and energy to the
Revolution. Decisive in her opinions, she was yet free
from the bumptious cocksureness that mars the good
humor of so many revolutionaries and often makes discussion with them futile and disagreeable. However one
might disagree with Nadya's views, one could not help
being impressed with the charm of her manner and the
vigor of her mind.

Often I had discussed with her the destiny of the
peasant in a Soviet society. Again and again she would
insist that my conception of the Russian peasantry
and of farmers the world over — my conviction that
they were so firmly devoted to private property, the
home, the family and other pillars of individualism

[2] Communist youth.

that they would die rather than submit to their forcible disintegration — was only a reflection of the bourgeois ideology which capitalist society had inculcated in me. Would I have cherished these notions had I lived, not in America, but under a Soviet régime? Why did not she share them, she and the hundreds of thousands of young people like her who had their education in revolutionary Russia? She warned me that some day I would remember her words. She would remind me of them, she said. And now as I read her letter I sensed between the lines a dash of malicious joy at the consciousness of triumph.

I was in a Los Angeles hotel when her letter reached me. Sitting there comfortably in a soft chair my thoughts drifted back to the villages in which she and her companions were crusading. I pictured them, youths all, journeying from village to village in peasant carts, on horseback, on foot, in mud and in snow, calling mass meetings, making speeches, engaging in volcanic discussions and forming *kolhozy* — passionately striving in every act to push Russia closer and closer to their ideal of an earthly paradise. I knew that hundreds, thousands, of such Nadyas and their brother revolutionaries all over Russia were embarked on a similar mission, bringing a new gospel and a new mode of social accommodation to the village, in the earnest belief that these would forever end pain and failure in the human world.

It occurred to me that Nadya and those others who shared her faith and her enthusiasm were supremely happy people. Their very work was a source of boundless gratification, for is man ever so exalted as when he is crusading for a cause?

Of course the mere mention of personal happiness would make Nadya chuckle with amusement or fume with indigation. With flushed face and dilated eyes she would deny that she had gone to the villages in search of personal satisfaction. She would deprecate the very suggestion that personal happiness was a basic motive in her life. She would proclaim herself not an adventurer in search of thrills, but a soldier fighting a historic battle.

She would be right, too. She was on the firing line enduring all the hardships and hazards, including possibility of death, that a soldier at the front daily experiences. Will I forget the bony Ukrainian youth with the rattle of death in his lungs confessing that, in spite of the doctor's orders, he dared not keep his windows open at night for fear he would be shot or stabbed? Now and then one reads in the newspapers items that tell their own story. I recall the one about the *Komsomoletz* [3] whom peasants had shut up in a schoolhouse which they then set afire, and, stationing themselves before it with fenceposts, they drove the desperate youth back into the flames whenever he attempted to save himself. I recall another in which peasants seized a Soviet worker, bound him hand and foot, drenched his clothing with kerosene and set fire to him. I was sure that Nadya had a revolver tucked away somewhere in her clothes. She might be working in peaceful territory, but in times of active campaigning, a revolutionary never can tell when or whence a death blow will be leveled at him.

Yet despite discomforts and hazards Nadya was a happy person. Her very letter, brimming with joy and fervor, bore ample evidence of it. Personal satisfaction

---

[3] Member of the Young Communists.

might not have been an objective in her life, but it came in spite of her. Engaged in a task which above all else in the world she loved, happiness was bound to be a by-product of her daily work. No problem of personal maladjustment harassed her. Intellectually and emotionally she was magnificently attuned to the tumult of the times. Indeed, if one were to regard collectivization solely as a means of self-expression for the Nadyas, one could welcome it as a superb gift of the Revolution to Russian youth.

But there was the subject of Nadya's crusade — the many-millioned Russian peasant. Only a few months previous, in village after village, including the one in which I was born, I heard him thunder his protests at the effort to transplant him into a new social soil. Weighted down with inertia and as distrustful of strange ideas as is a wild animal of strange noises, he was confused and baffled. He could not have changed over night — or had he? I wondered. Was such a miracle possible even in Russia?

In Nadya's letter there was not a word on the subject. There was no allusion to the peasant's inner turmoil, as though that were only an incidental trifle. Impassioned revolutionary that she was, she could not and would not be concerned with the hurt of the individual. Not that it had passed her unobserved, but it failed to stir her sympathy. She seemed no more concerned with the peasant's perplexity than is a surgeon with the pain of the patient over whose body he is wielding a scalpel. Her mind and heart were fixed on the glories of tomorrow as she visualized them, not on the sorrows of today. The agony of the process was lost to her in the triumph of achievement.

Yet I could not help being moved by the ordeal that

the peasant was facing. He loomed before me as the central figure in the ever rising Russian drama. Astounding was the double task assigned to him, whether by mere man or by history only time could reveal. With no intermediary halt he was to make a leap from feudalism to the machine age and simultaneously to a mode of social control not only without precedent, but completely out of tune with his heritage and past aims. Was ever a people faced with so epochal a task?

And there was no escaping from it. The Nadyas were barring all avenues of flight. Wherever the peasant turned he found them armed against him. With charts and figures and bursts of eloquence, and sometimes with the powerful arm of the government, they were seeking to bend him to their will. Desperately they were striving to win him to the notion that he had no destiny other than the one they had mapped out for him. Nor were they speaking for themselves only. Official confirmation of their preachments the peasant could read in every issue of the *Pravda,* the official organ of the Communist Party, in that single sentence, heavily underscored and strung out in italics over three columns, which proclaimed that " toward the end of the five-year plan collectivization of the land must in essence be completed."

This was Stalin's pronouncement, and the voice of Stalin was the voice of the Party, which in Russia is the ultimate source of power and authority. Prophecy, boast, threat, the meaning of these words was unmistakable: collectivization would be pushed forward. To Stalin and his cohorts it had come to mean the life or death of the Revolution; moreover, with more than one-fourth of the peasantry already drawn into it, there could be no halt to the movement, still less retreat to the old social forms. The very road backward had been torn up and obliterated. Failure could mean only collapse and chaos.

Whatever the outside world may think of collectivization, henceforth it must be the pivot on which the Revolution is to revolve. Should this pivot give way, the Revolution can only blow to pieces. Nothing can save it. But should it hold together, should collectivization as an economic enterprise prove feasible, however moderately, it will transfigure Russia as nothing else that the Bolsheviks have launched or have planned to launch. I cannot help regarding it as the most colossal revolution that mankind has ever witnessed. Already from a land of puny and ever decreasing landholdings with a distressingly primitive agricultural technic, Russia is rapidly becoming a land of large-scale farms which neither America nor Canada nor the Argentine can rival, farms in which a highly advanced though still incompetently executed method of tillage is crowding out the ancient ways.

It is not, however, the mechanics of farming as much as the social transfiguration it forebodes that makes collectivization so spectacular a force in our age. The thatch-roofed villages which seem rooted in the Russian soil will be torn down and supplanted by rural townships more or less completely socialized. The church will crumble. So, in its present form, will private property. The home, the individualistic family, as we now know it, will be submerged in the new community. Other institutions which have been the sanctities of western civilization will collapse or undergo transmutations which will reduce them to mere skeletons of their former selves. Man, under the impetus of the new changes, is destined to acquire a body of motives, aims, relationships, which in time will make Russia an anomaly among the nations, a real Mars on earth. Limitless and fantastic are the social transmutations inherent in collectivization.

Meanwhile, here is this peasant with his burden of torment and bafflement. He has so much, so very much, to think of and to get excited about and he spills over with talk. His story is, in my judgment, the most momentous in Russia, and it is this story that I have sought to unfold here.

I have travelled far and wide in villages to hear it from his own lips, for no writer living can tell it as eloquently and as movingly as he. Then I journeyed to my native countryside, in the mudlands of Central Russia. My own village there is made up of about a thousand souls, with the older folk still overwhelmingly illiterate. It lies in a hinterland away from the railroad and still knows no telephone, no electricity and no telegraph. I know every house and every gateway in this village. Many of the men and women were once playmates of mine, and it was good to renew old comradeships and to reminisce of the faraway days when together we chased butterflies and gathered cornflowers in the rye fields. I lingered in their homes, in their fields and in other places where they were wont to gather and listened eagerly to their excited talk. Once before, as I have related in *Broken Earth,* I had gone to this part of the country in search of enlightenment, and it was there more than in Moscow or in any other place in Russia that I gained the real feeling of the Revolution, its terror and agony, its power and grandeur. Similarly, this time it was here more than in any other part of the land that I saw the active drama of Russian collectivization.

Nadya, of course, would scorn my method of approach. Absorbed in "socialist construction" she would have no time for the inner turmoil of man or for anything but the perfection of the social mechanism into which he is to fit his destiny. But to me, a mere bystander, the ordeal of the peasant confronted by this momentous parting of the ways, and the transfigurations that await him in the new order, if it ever is realized, make collectivization the most overpowering spectacle in the world.

II

THE GATHERING OF THE STORM

SUMMER, 1929.
Again I am on a pilgrimage to the village of my birth, somewhere in the mudlands of Central Russia. Five years have passed since I last saw it, a brief enough period in the life of a man, even more so in that of a nation. But in present-day Russia, with the fires of Revolution ever aflame, kindling or burning up hope, courage, ambition, five years is a big span of time, an age, an epoch, that scorches its imprint on the soul of man and on the face of the land.

Nature was kind to me this time. The weather was as if made for holidaying, bright skies, clear horizons, immense sunshine. At the market place of the town of S., my last railroad stop, I saw a number of peasants from my old village. They invited me to ride with them, but remembering the rutty roads and the fierce jolting of peasant carts, I decided to walk the twenty-odd miles.

Harvest was in full swing, and on all sides I heard the ripping strokes of sickles as they cut greedy swaths into the rye. Gorgeous rye it was, firm ears without a trace of rust. The tall stalks swayed gently in the flitting breezes or fell with a muffled swish at the stroke of the sickle. Not in a long time had the peasants known such an abundant harvest, nor was it of rye alone.

Potatoes and oats had likewise attained luxurious growth, and the patches of flax, with their puffy little stalks and their heads of shimmering blue, peeping out between stretches of oats and potatoes like the eyes of mischievous children, further attested to nature's bountifulness. It was good to see the earth so handsomely adorned with its own fruitage.

I had no longer any blood ties in the village. The last of our family, a cousin, had moved to a collective farm the previous spring. I felt sad. Father, grandfather, other ancestors as far as I could trace them, lived, toiled and died there. For a long, long time our family had had its roots in the very loam of the land, and now these were plucked up, scattered. Gone we were to all corners of the earth — Europe, Asia, America — to live new lives and build new worlds out of tune with the one out of which we had sprung. Yet memory, association, sympathy drew me close to the old place, as close as any bonds of blood ever could. I felt as though everyone in the village were still my kin.

The nearer I drew to the old place, the greater was my excitement. With a gush of joy I recognized old scenes — the fields, the ponds, the swamps, the brushwood where as a boy I had scampered with other peasant children in search of blackberries, mushrooms, birds' nests or the stray feathers of pasturing geese and ducks which our mothers prized so highly. They stuffed such feathers into the pillows and mattresses which became their daughters' dowries. At last the village itself came into view. At first sight it appeared unchanged; everything seemed to be as it was five, or twenty-five, or perhaps a hundred years ago: there were the humpy barns with umbrella-like roofs of straw; stumpy log huts with their arrow-shaped straw roofs overgrown in places with fat moss; brush fences cracking from dryness; towering sweeps over open wells, the butt ends of the cross-poles weighted down with stones and resting on the ground like dogs on their haunches; unpaved streets with ditches in front of the houses to drain the waters after heavy rains and spring thaws; swells and hollows in the ground, with holes in which the mud never dried out . . . and the same surly dogs, only more of them, as ever leaping and barking furiously as if ready to devour passing strangers.

But as I came closer to the village I paused, startled. At the edge of the swamp, where once flourished a thick forest which the peasants in the early days of the Revolution had vengefully hewed down, there towered the shingled roof of a new building, the tallest and most massive in the village. I hurried thither, and from the inscription above the door I learned that it was a schoolhouse. It seemed unbelievable — yet the inscription glared at me in heavy letters. A huge building it seemed beside the *muzhik* [1] log huts. It had a spacious porch, large windows and folding doors all painted white, city fashion. To the average American, building a schoolhouse in a village of one hundred and eighty families may seem no more exciting an event than putting up a garage or porch or laying a new sidewalk. But for me, with my memories of the old village as it had been in the days of my youth, as it still was five years ago, the sight of this schoolhouse was a supreme adventure. In all the hundreds of years of its existence, the thousands of men and women who had

---

[1] Peasant.

lived and sweltered and died there had never known a schoolhouse. Few, very few of the *muzhiks* there had learned to read and write, or even to sign their names. Not a one had ever subscribed to a newspaper. As a boy I earned barrels of apples and pumpkin seeds signing papers for peasants or writing letters for them. Nor shall I forget that Sunday afternoon during the Russo-Japanese War when a stranger passing through our village collected sacks of rye and hay in return for reading to the people news of the war from journals that were months old. And now a schoolhouse reared its head above the village. Here it was suddenly before me, like an apparition thrust up by the earth.

I walked inside. Though it was vacation time and school had been dismissed for the summer, the two classrooms were not empty. They had been turned into a nursery. A nursery in this mud-encrusted, desolate village! Thirty little wooden beds, with white sheets and white pillows the like of which our peasants never had seen, stood in rows, and little boys and girls from one to four were crawling or dashing about the room in play. Three nurses from a nearby town were in attendance. They spoke freely. It was the first year of the nursery, and happily it had survived all trials. At first the peasants were suspicious. Was it a new trick of the Soviets to mulct fresh levies out of them? Some of the more well-to-do *muzhiks* shook their heads in disdain. No good, they averred, could come from a nursery. The poorer *muzhiks,* chief beneficiaries of the enterprise, though they had been assured that the care of their children would not cost them a copeck, were likewise skeptical. Then someone had loosened a rumor that in a neighboring village children were being starved in the nurseries: they were given only milk, vegetables and cereals instead of potato, sour milk, black bread, pork and cabbage soup, the usual fare of the peasant in these parts. Indeed, in that village one fine morning the people had gone on strike, refusing to send their children to the nursery unless the menu were changed to conform to their dietetic notions.

The nurses, as they narrated this incident, laughed, and so did I. Yet it was no laughing matter. I remembered our old neighbor, Adarya, who bore and buried thirteen children in as many years. Often she would come to our house and sob her heart out to my mother over her ill luck with children. When her blue-eyed Annushka died on the very evening which rounded out her first birthday, Adarya was so mad with grief that she cried herself ill. And could I forget Matrena Kuzlik, once a noted beauty in the village, who at the age of thirty-five looked so drawn and withered that folks spoke of her as a *baba*.[2] On my first visit to the old home she chided me with jolly earnestness for not having brought from America, great miracle-working America, a medicine that would allay fevers and convulsions of children, and save them from death. She had been married fifteen years, she told me, and had borne nine children, but only two had survived, and one of them was having spasms and would, she feared, soon die. There was hardly a mother in the village who was spared the agony of a child's untimely death. They succumbed so easily, these peasant children, to the onslaught of smallpox, croup and all manner of fevers and spasms. It could not be otherwise so long as the people lived in ill-smelling, unventilated one-room huts and

2 An old woman.

shared these with their pigs and chickens and calves. Other things contributed to infant mortality. Mothers, for example, seldom bathed their babies and fed them, with unwashed fingers or through artificial nipples made of dirty linen, their own chewings of black bread and potato or the inevitable *kasha*.[3] And now, here was the nursery, these two sun-flooded rooms with the scrubbed floors, the thirty little beds, with these three bustling nurses and these crawling barefoot tots in clean clothing, each with hair trimmed, face washed, teeth brushed, and with all the toys he could wish.

I sauntered on. On the very spot where our old home had stood since days immemorial was another new building, small but solidly built, with a thatched roof. It was the fire station. Suspended from a projecting beam in the roof hung a piece of rail on which the alarms were clanged. Inside there was nothing so imposing as an engine and the rest of the fire-fighting paraphernalia one finds in an American fire station. A hose, a pump, ladders, half a dozen barrels filled with water in two-wheeled carts and nothing else. Still, it would be more effective in fighting the fire — the " red cock," as the peasants call it — than mere pails of water, their sole weapon heretofore.

Only those who have seen a fire in a Russian village can appreciate what a holocaust it can be. I remembered so well the fires I had seen in my boyhood days, and shuddered as I recalled them. How terribly helpless were these *muzhiks* in the face of the flames flitting from one thatched roof to another and devouring everything before them — houses, barns, woodpiles, trees,

[3] Gruel.

fences, often cows and horses. If lightning struck a building, they believed that milk, not water, must be used to put out the fire. Once, in the seamstress' house, next to ours, a girl was struck down and killed by lightning while she was being measured for her bridal dress. At about the same time, her betrothed, who was plowing in the field, was also struck down by lightning. The village was in an uproar. Surely this was no ordinary accident, but a visitation of some higher power. Meanwhile, from the house of the seamstress, which had caught fire, smoke and flames were puffing their way toward our house. But when some of the men fetched pails of water and poured them over the flames and over our roof, older folks howled with protest and prophesied that only ill luck could come from the use of water instead of milk. Luckily, just then the rain splashed down and put out the struggling flames.

Nothing has been so ruinous to the Russian peasants throughout the ages as fires. Figures which I have before me show that old Russia suffered fifteen times as much damage by flames as did France during the same period, and twenty times as much as Germany. On an average, each village burned once every ten years. As recently as in the year 1925–26 there were more than one hundred thousand fires in Russia, and of these over ninety percent were in the villages. In the old days there was an endless procession of *pogoreltsui* — peasants who had lost their homes through fire — who would make the rounds of villages begging for bread, for straw, for pieces of lumber with which to build new homes for themselves.

A schoolhouse, a nursery, a fire station — all in five years! Surely these were marks of progress, or culture, as the Russians would say. The village, like a plant in moisture and sunlight, was pushing its way to a new growth. It made me feel happy. Five years ago, I heard only talk of impending changes. Then youth alone cherished faith in the possibility of their realization, while the older folk shouted fiercely that there was only doom ahead for their village, for all Russia. And now the beginnings of a new life had flowered into being. I felt sure that this time I should hear only words of satisfaction, that the flood of bitterness which had inundated the *muzhiks* five years previous had ebbed low or had gone entirely. I felt sure, but still . . .

Walking along the meadow past the schoolhouse, I chanced to meet Sergey. He was pasturing a cow in the rich grass of the lowlands. His face had grown broader and thinner; his brush-like beard had visible streaks of gray, and his eyes had widened abnormally, as those of a man afflicted with illness and tribulation. He did not smile, as was his wont, when he greeted me. He was ominously solemn, and no sooner had he replied to my greetings than he launched into a lament. The worst day in his life was now upon him — trouble, trouble, trouble, and no way of escape. Wherever he turned he found himself checked, pushed back. A new policy in the villages — socialization of the land, the *kolhoz* — had I heard of it?

Ah, what a state he had come to! In the early days of the Revolution the Soviets sought to crush him with taxes. He had come to such a pass that at one time he thought of chopping down his fruit trees in order to escape the ruinous taxation. Then the Soviets reversed their position. As a good farmer, capable of becoming a source of culture in the village and serving as an example and stimulus to others to lift their households to a higher plane of productivity, his taxes were lessened and he was encouraged to make the most of his resources. He did. He had struck his stride. He was successful. He was attaining something, getting somewhere, and he was happy. Then the Soviets had gone back to their original policy, only more ruthlessly. And now, because he had recently engaged hired labor for the gathering of his rye, as he had always done, they labeled him *zazhitochny*,[4] just a grade lower than a *koolack*,[5] and levied on him a super-tax. Cows, horses, pigs, hens, every crop he raised, every tree in his orchard, every bee hive he had, they taxed according to a new and crushing schedule. And he would not fool himself as to the purpose of this new attack. It was intended to stifle him. Campaigning for the *kolhoz* as they were, the Soviets wanted to rid the villages of the more successful individual farmer. They did not want him side by side with the *kolhozy*, for fear he would be a menace to the latter. That was clear enough to him. But how could he join a *kolhoz*, he who was accustomed to do all his own planning and thinking and everything? There had been talk of putting him out of his house and taking his land away from him. But he pleaded with the authorities and begged them to have mercy on him, and they finally agreed to allow him to remain on his own premises if he would pay the sum of one thousand roubles. That, then, was the reward he was offered for his lifelong efforts to make something of himself and to prepare for the uncertainties and incapacities of old age. And what could he do now? He

[4] Well-to-do man.
[5] One of the richest members of the peasant class.

had thought of painting his house, but even if he were to remain in it, he would not bother. They would point at him as at a landlord. He was not even mending his fences any more. Once he had five cows, now he had only three; in the fall he would sell one more. Once he owned three horses; now he kept only one, and he would never have more — what the devil was the use, if the political axe was swung down on him every time he made a step forward? The individual did not count. Like an insect he was to be stepped upon and crushed. . . .

A pig had strayed into the path of the pasturing cow and she fled in panic, bellowing frantically. He started after her, and with the help of his dog drove her back to his own land. He approached me again panting heavily and sweating. Removing his hat, he wiped the sweat with his hand and I noted a patch of baldness on the top of his head. His forehead was charted with strips by deep dirt-filled wrinkles; his eyes, deeply sunken, made his broad nose appear enormous, like a clown's. He looked beaten. I said nothing, but he divined my thoughts and added: " Yes, I have grown old in five years. . . . If you come five years hence, I'll be a tottering old man, or else dead. May be it would be better if I were dead. . . . My children are young and they may be able to work into the new system. I do not know. . . . It may be a good system, too. Perhaps people will be happier in a *kolhoz* than they are now as individual farmers — Perhaps. But I am too old to change. God! — " He turned away choking with sobs. In a moment he recovered and apologized for giving vent to his feelings. " Come on Sunday anyway and taste some of my new honey."

I walked on. From the distance I heard someone hailing me. I turned, and saw running toward me a little man wearing a huge cap, his bushy beard flowing over his breast. It was Yekim Lavrentin. " Ah," he spoke as he shook my hand heartily, " countryman of ours, it is so good you came! Have you seen our Miron in America? *Nu,* Miron, the very one with whom you once killed a little animal in your father's cellar — Do you remember? Yes, he has been in America a long, long time, since before the war, and, countryman dear, the other day we got a letter saying that he killed himself. Just imagine! The devil only knows what had possessed him. And think of it — over a woman, yes, a woman! He was living in a place called Meetchigan. He and a friend of his had a room together in a private home, and both of them fell in love with their landlady. But she was married and had a husband and children. So Miron could not stand it, and blew out his brains. Over a woman! — What a fool! If he had come here with his American dollars and his American clothes and his American ways, he could have married the finest girl in this village or in any around here. . . . Ah, what fools some people can be! "

I went with him to his home, a drooping hovel with a dirt floor and unwashed windows, some of them without glass and stuffed with flax husks. The huge coarse table was laden with cucumbers, bread, empty wooden dishes, spoons, round which flocks of flies buzzed viciously. His wife came in with a pail of fresh milk. She strained it into two earthen jars, one of which she set on the table. Fetching a glass, she invited me to help myself to milk. Yekim hurried out to the cupboard and returned with a platter of butter. Placing it beside me and pushing the bread my way, he insisted that I partake of their meager *ugoshtshenye* [6] — meager, indeed, when in Moscow butter and milk were rationed and could be obtained only by long waiting in endless queues! A poor man this Yekim was, but butter and milk he had in greater abundance than any man that I knew in Moscow.

Eagerly Yekim and his wife proceeded to relate the gossip of the village — so and so was married, so and so had died, so and so was beating his wife, so and so was threatening to leave her husband. Women were growing worldly — some of them were even talking of going to the hospital in the city for abortions. They did not want to have many children any more! What was the use, they said, with babies dying so fast? But perhaps the nursery would change things; all were now hoping it would, though at first a lot of folks did not think much of it. There had been a murder in the village for the first time in ages — only last winter, too! Early of an evening Amelko Hrinuk had been visiting in the home of an acquaintance, and as he sat there talking, an unseen person fired at him through the window and shot him dead. The whole town was in an uproar, yet at heart people were glad, because Amelko was a hoodlum. He had organized a secret band which plundered the neighboring villages. He had disgraced the name of the community, for our people had always been honest. Now all was well enough in the village except for this *kolhoz*. All but the young folks were afraid of it, even the *bedniaks*,[7] in spite of all the promises made to them. Some of them

---

[6] Food and drink offered to guests.
[7] Poorest of the peasants.

were signing up; they almost had to; but their hearts were not in it. What did I think of it? Were there *kolhozy* in America? No? Ah, then perhaps they were not a good thing, because if they were, America would have had them, wouldn't she? America had the best of everything. *Nu,* what could a dark, dirty *muzhik* know? He had no mind for anything big or new, and this Revolution with its *kolhozy* and other *ozy* was compelling him to think, think, think, until he had no brains left for anything else.

Neighbors had begun to gather. They had heard of my arrival, and they stopped in on their way home from the fields, sickles on their shoulders, wooden water-buckets on their backs. They were bursting with eagerness to talk — and their chief topic was the *kolhoz*.

" There was a time, my dear," began Lukyan, who had been a blacksmith, and who, despite his seventy-odd years, was upright as a young birch and possessed a head of hair that a man of thirty might envy, " there was a time when we were just neighbors in this village. We quarreled, we fooled, sometimes we cheated one another. But we were neighbors. Now we are *bedniaks, seredniaks,*[8] *koolacks*. I am a *seredniak,* Boris here is a *bedniak,* and Nisko is a *koolack,* and we are supposed to have a class war — pull each other's hair or tickle each other on the toes, eh? One against the other, you understand? What the devil! " And he shrugged his shoulders as though to emphasize his bewilderment at the fresh social cleavage. To him the launching of the class war in his village was an artificially made affair.

[8] So-called " middle " peasants, on an economic plane midway between that of the *bedniak* and the *koolack*.

"They call me a *bedniak*," broke in fat-lipped, freckled Boris Kotlovy, "and there probably is no bigger *bedniak* in the whole of Russia than I am. But think of it: in the old days I would pay my five or seven roubles in taxes, and I would be let alone; not even a dog would look into my private yard. And now I pay no taxes at all, thank you, but I am constantly pestered by this and that — insurance for cow, insurance for horse, insurance for house, insurance for crops. Soon they will be asking insurance for my *lapti* or for my toe-nails."

"In this thing, brother Boris," interposed another flat-faced *muzhik*, "you are indeed wrong. Insurance is not bad. . . ."

"Who says it is bad?" interrupted Boris. "Only why should I have to pay for it?" Laughter greeted his words. But he was in earnest. No peasant, still less a *bedniak*, ever likes to meet a cash obligation, regardless of the worthiness of its purpose.

"But it is other things that worry us," continued the flat-faced *muzhik* as though unconscious of the interruption, "it is this *kolhoz*. That, citizen, is a serious matter — the most serious we have ever encountered. Who ever heard of such a thing — to give up our land and our cows and our horses and our tools and our farm buildings, to work all the time and divide everything with others? Nowadays members of the same family get in each other's way and quarrel and fight, and here we, strangers, are supposed to be like one family. Can we — dark, beastly *muzhiks* — make a go of it without scratching each other's faces, pulling each other's hair or hurling stones at one another?"

"And the worst of it is that it is not for just a certain length of time, but forever," remarked another man. "A soldier may not like to live in barracks with other soldiers, but he knows that it is temporary. In the *kolhoz*, citizen, it means barracks for life. Only death will rescue us from it."

"What is the use of talking," commented a fat-chinned woman, dolefully shaking her head, "we are lost now, by Jove we are; the harder we work the more plague we have on our hearts."

"We won't even be sure," someone else continued the lament, "of having enough bread to eat. Now, however poor we may be, we have our own rye and our own potatoes and our own cucumbers and our own milk. We know we won't starve. But in the *kolhoz*, no more potatoes of our own, no more anything of our own. Everything will be rationed out by orders; we shall be like mere *batraks*[9] on the landlord's estates in the old days. Serfdom — that is what it is — and who wants to be a serf?"

"Yes, and some woman will have ten children and will get milk for all of them; another will have only one child and will get milk for only one, and both will be doing the same work. Where is the justice? Ha!"

"We older folk," protested a bewhiskered graybeard leaning on a heavy staff, "might as well tie a noose around our heads and bid the world goodbye; the young scalawags will tread all over us. It is bad enough even now while we are still masters of our households and our hands yet hold the reins. But in a *kolhoz*, the young scoundrels will put bits into our mouths as though we were horses and steer us around to suit themselves — cursed youth!"

"Dark-minded beasts we may be," wailed another *muzhik* in the hopeless tone which is so habitual to the

[9] Hired help.

peasant whether in real or imaginary distress. "We are not learned; we are not wise. But a little self-respect we have, and we like the feeling of independence. To-day we feel like working, and we work; tomorrow we feel like lying down, and we lie down; the next day we feel like going to town, and we go to town. We do as we please. But in the *kolhoz,* brother, it is do-as-you-are-told, like a horse — go this way and that, and don't dare turn off the road or you get it hard, a stroke or two of the whip on bare flesh. . . . We'll just wither away on the socialist farm, like grass torn out by the roots."

"Hoodlums and loafers," continued still another peasant, "might readily join a *kolhoz.* What have they to lose? But decent people? Their hearts bleed when they see weeds in a field, a leak in a roof. They are *khoziayeva,* masters, with an eye for order, for results. But what could they say in a *kolhoz?* What could they do except carry out the orders of someone else. That's the way I look at it."

"*Nu,*"[10] remonstrated a little man whose cap was pulled down over his ears and who was smoking a pipe shiny with grease, "there is no use in making the thing look so very black. After all, we are not mere cattle. We have not got much culture, and we are backward, but we are not without sense. I can only speak for my-self. If there were only an example of how a *kolhoz* works, so that we could see with our eyes what is what, we wouldn't be so afraid, none of us. . . . Perhaps it is the best thing for us — who knows? But we sit here in this quiet little village, go nowhere, see nothing and know nothing, and here they come with this *kolhoz* so new and so different from anything we have ever heard

[10] Well.

of, and what shall we do? We are just afraid, that's
what we are, all of us."

"It wouldn't be so bad if they would only put three
or four Jews in with us. We don't know how to·run big
things, but Jews are clever, they might make a go of
it," suggested an old *muzhik* in a sheepskin hat and
a huge linen shirt that hung down to his knees.

"But supposing there is a war," broke in the fat-
chinned woman again, "have·you thought of that?"

They stared at one another and at me, transfixed
with anxiety.

"Do you think there will be a war?" The little man
turned to me.

"Why are they shouting so much about it if there
isn't going to be any?" someone speculated.

"Yes, why? Why?" several others repeated almost
in unison.

"And if there is a war, and the invaders come and
find us living on a *kolhoz*, they will say we are Communists and they will cut our throats."

"The Poles will do that anyway."

"They will, they will. Oh, how they will!"

How revealing these open-hearted words of theirs
were! Earnest, simple-minded folk, utterly devoid of a
sense of worldliness, or of a spirit of adventure, they
were actuated solely by the elementary urge of physical self-preservation. The Revolution had shaken them
mightily, but it had failed to implant in them either
the imagination or the social audacity which would
have enabled them to welcome the proposed innova-
tion. They were afraid to break away from their old
fastnesses lest the very earth under them give way and
they tumble into an ugly void.

" But," I said, " is the Soviet actually compelling you to join the *kolhoz?* "

" No, no, no," several voices responded. That, of course, was in the summer of 1929, before the so-called " Great Break."

" But it might as well," answered Boris the *bedniak*. " They have given me no peace of mind since they started the campaign here."

" They make it so hard if we don't join," commented the old man with the long shirt, " that in the end we'll have to join anyway."

Another *muzhik* spoke slowly and thoughtfully, as though he were musing aloud: " Ah, if only we had any assurance that their promises would be fulfilled, that we could really get all the things they say the *kolhoz* will give us. . . . I wouldn't hesitate a minute, *I* wouldn't, even if it is something new and different from what we have been used to."

At this point a new visitor arrived, a tall youth, in boots, in a black blouse and with a shaved head. I had never seen him before. At his appearance the *muzhiks* began to move about restlessly, though they replied to his greeting with promptness and cordiality.

" Here he is," one of the older men began, " our peace-wrecker."

" Peace-maker, grandfather," the youth shot back good-naturedly.

Several men burst into sardonic laughter. But the youth paid no heed to them. A stranger in the village, he was the organizer of the *kolhoz,* therefore a person of stern importance.

" I suppose they have been shedding tears about the

kolhoz," he said to me, and addressing the crowd he continued, " If you have any more tears to shed, you had better not stop now or you'll lie awake all night. Like babies they are," he turned to me again, " they never can fall asleep unless they have had a good cry; and now that you are here — an American — they will be sobbing their hearts out to you all the time. Oh, how they love to sob — "

" What would you expect us to do — dance a jig over the ruination you are planning for us, ha? " remarked a stern-eyed *muzhik* who had not said much all evening, but who was continually puffing at a pipe which had long since gone out.

" Nothing of the sort, no; only it is about time you realized how dark-minded you are."

" That, *tovarishtch,*" [11] a woman broke in angrily, " we know without your reminding us. You had better tell us why you want to take the bread away from us."

" Ingrate, you," sneered Boris the *bedniak,* " you ought to know that he does not want to snatch the bread out of our mouths. He wants to feed us roast pig for breakfast every morning."

" And why not? " fired back the agitator, " must capitalists alone eat roast pig? It won't hurt you if you, too, taste it once in a while."

Laughter, loud and derisive, greeted his words.

" You don't believe it possible," continued the agitator, unperturbed.

" Who said we don't? " sneered the old man with the long shirt. " It must be possible since you Communists are saying it. When we have the *kolhoz* we shall have

[11] Comrade, common form of salutation in Soviet Russia.

a real heaven on earth! No wonder you are against the priests. You don't want to wait for a heaven in the hereafter. Our *babas* will be wearing silks and diamonds, and maybe we shall have servants bringing us tea and pastry to our beds. Haw, haw, haw! I served once as a lackey in a landlord's household. I know how rich people live."

"Everything is possible, grandfather, if we all pool our resources and our powers together," replied the visitor.

More laughter and more derisive comment.

"You Communists are good at making promises. If you would only be half as good at fulfilling them."

"What promises have we failed to fulfill?"

"All, all of them," a number of voices exclaimed.

"*Nu,* be reasonable, citizens. There is a limit to jesting."

"Well, you have promised us a world revolution. Where is it?"

"Yes, where, where?"

"The German workmen were going to send us textiles."

"The American workmen were going to send us machines."

"From every country workmen were going to send us things—that's what you've been promising us."

"*Ekh,* people, quit talking nonsense," shouted someone in the back of the room, "this world revolution's got stuck in the mud on our Russian roads."

A howl of laughter broke loose in which the agitator himself joined.

"It will come yet, this revolution," he said after the roar had subsided.

"Like the devil it will! Other people have more brains than we have."

The agitator remained calm — one has to be when one is among peasants who never hesitate to be frank and cruel in their speech. Counter-revolutionary as this thrust was, the agitator took no occasion to reprimand the speaker. It would have done him no good if he had, and might only have evoked further and more rabid thrusts. But he was beginning to show signs of restlessness. He shifted about and began absentmindedly to thump the table with his fingers.

" Be patient and the revolution will come yet. The bourgeoisie the world over will get it in the neck. Wait. But now let us be sensible. For the twentieth time I am telling you that the *kolhoz* is your only salvation. There is no other for you. Why won't you be reasonable? Think, be sensible. . . ."

"You be sensible," someone countered.

"Yes, you, you!" a host of voices continued.

"I am; we social workers always are."

"So are our cows — they always know enough to bellow when they are hungry and thirsty."

Again laughter.

"Let me talk for awhile, let me say something. . . ."

"Let him, let him, our savior!"

"Savior, savior!" again a chorus of voices jibed gleefully.

"Tell me, you wretched people, what hope is there for you if you remain on individual pieces of land? Think, and don't interrupt. Let us discuss it openly and let the American countryman of yours decide for himself. From year to year as you increase in population you divide and subdivide your strips of land. You cannot even use machinery on your land because no machine man ever made could stand the rough ridges that the strip system creates. You will have to work in your own old way and stew in your old misery. Don't you see that under your present system there is nothing ahead of you but ruin and starvation? "

"We never starved before you wise men of the Party appeared here."

"You came near to starving — why lie? — you *bedniaks* especially. Remember your yesterday. You are just too dark to see the good that we have in store for you. I want this American friend to see you as I see you, as you really are, as you never want to see yourselves. You do not think of a future, of ten, twenty, a hundred years from now, and we do. That's the difference between you and us. The coming generations mean nothing to you. Else you would see a real deliverance in the *kolhoz,* where you will work with machinery in a modern organized way, with the best seeds obtainable and under the direction of experts. You accuse us of making false promises. Let us see. And please do not interrupt and do not giggle — Hear me, all."

He stepped forward, unbuttoned the collar of his blouse, and wiped the sweat from his face and neck. "What did you say five years ago when the Soviets offered you a landlord's home for a schoolhouse if you would only move it to the village? You called mass meeting after mass meeting and you voted down the proposition. I do not belong to your village, but I know your condition. I worked on the school board. You said, 'Let the Soviets move the building at their own expense.' Well, you lost that building, and only last year you got a schoolhouse; and have you forgot-

ten how we of the Party and of the Soviet had to work
to squeeze out of you through the voluntary tax your
share of the cost of the schoolhouse? And now? Aren't
you glad your children can attend school? Haven't you
yourselves said that the schoolhouse is a blessing because in winter children can develop their minds and
acquire real culture, instead of loafing around in the
streets and becoming little savages? Tell me, were we
wrong when we urged this schoolhouse on you — yes,
and insulted and denounced you because you wouldn't
meet us halfway on the project of building it? Were we
wrong when we urged you to build a fire station? Were
we wrong when we urged you to lay decent bridges
across your stream in the swamp? Were we wrong
when we threatened to fine you if you didn't take home
two loads of peat to mix with the bedding for your
stock so as to have good fertilizer for your fields?
Were we wrong when we urged you to subscribe to
newspapers? Were we wrong when we urged you to
join the coöperative where you can get goods — "

" There isn't any," someone interrupted.

" *Nu*," retorted the agitator, " don't be silly. You
mean there is not everything you want? "

" There is not even tobacco paper any more," someone shouted.

" If there is none now, there will be some in a day
or two," continued the agitator, " don't expect everything at once. Yesterday there was cigarette paper, I
myself got a package. Tomorrow there may be some
more. But everything you get at the coöperative costs
you one-half or one-third of what it would in the open
market. Isn't that something? Everything we proposed
you opposed. You always knew so much more than we

did. You thought yourselves so all-wise, you ignorant creatures. You swore and cursed and threatened vengeance, but yet the bridge is laid across the river, the roads are mended so they are passable after a rain in the spring, the schoolhouse is built, the coöperative is supplying you with necessaries — some promises we have fulfilled."

"The *kolhoz* is different," shouted the old man.

"So you said about everything we proposed," the agitator shot back impatiently. "Different? Of course it is different. If we didn't believe in making things different, we never would have overthrown the Czar and the capitalists and the *pomieshtchiks*,[12] and we wouldn't have worked ourselves to exhaustion arguing and quarreling and fighting with you. Different? Of course; but better. Don't you see? Isn't it about time you stopped thinking each one for himself, for his own piggish hide? You *koolacks* of course will never become reconciled to a new order. You love to fatten on other people's blood. But we know how to deal with you. We'll wipe you off the face of the earth, even as we have the capitalists in the city. Make no mistake about our intentions and our powers. We shan't allow you to profit from the weakness of the *bedniak*. And we shan't allow you to poison his mind, either! Enough. But the others here — you *bedniaks* and you *seredniaks* — what have you gained from this stiff-necked individualism of yours? What? Look at yourselves, at your homes — mud, squalor, fleas, bedbugs, cockroaches, *lapti*. Are you sorry to let these go? Oh, we know you *muzhiks* — too well — we who are ourselves *muzhiks*. You can make strangers believe that we are

12 Landlords.

cutting you to pieces with axes. You can whine eloquently and pitifully. Yes, you are past masters in the
art of shedding tears; you have done it for so many
hundreds of years. You may fool a visitor like this
countryman of yours from America. But we know
you — you cannot fool us. We have grown hardened
to your wails. Remember that. Cry all you want to,
curse all you want to. You won't hurt us, and I warn
you that we shan't desist. We shall continue our campaign for the *kolhozy* until we have won our goal and
made you free citizens in a free land."

Late in the evening we dispersed. I went home with
an old friend, to sleep in his haybarn. There in the
darkness I saw before me again the excited faces in
Yekim's house and heard those vehement voices. What
doubt, what indignation, what forlornness! I recalled
the peasant meetings in the village five years previous.
Then the *muzhiks* had complained of a shortage of
salt, kerosene, dry goods, leather, soap. Women were
heartbroken at the collapse of religion, and bewailed the
self-assertiveness of children, especially of their sons.
The mere mention of taxes brought forth howls of
wrath. Now, in 1929, salt was plentiful and cheap; soap
also was available, and kerosene. Dry goods and
leather were scarce; cigarette paper was lacking — but
they had evidently become used to that. As for taxes;
one-third of them paid none at all, and the others —
with the exception of Sergey and about five men like
him who were considered well-to-do — were not overburdened with them. The women no longer seemed
worried over the collapse of religion. Not one of them
had mentioned it throughout the entire evening.

Of course they wanted a better life; but what assurance, other than the word of this young and implacably determined agitator, had they that the *kolhoz* would offer it to them? These peasants never believed in anybody's words; they had always mistrusted the whole world. None of them had ever bought even a *bulka* in the bazaar without first picking up the white roll and feeling of it to make sure that it was not hollow inside; they never bought a scythe or a sickle without eyeing it carefully from every angle, feeling of it with their hard hands, striking it against their boots, snapping their fingers on it and listening to the resulting sound, or even biting upon it with their teeth in order to make sure that they were not being fooled by the metal. And now they were to give up their individual land, their horses, their cows, their farm buildings — the things that had given them bread, protection against starvation, the very security they needed to hold body and soul together — all on the mere promise of a youthful agitator that this would enrich their lives! True, they could remain on their own pieces of land; as yet there was no effort to push them into the *kolhoz* against their will. But they realized that they would not be favored. They saw what had happened to Sergey and to others like him who had worked their way to a semblance of material comfort.

They were overwhelmed with perplexity, and at the time little did they or I realize that this agitator and his speeches were but the first light breezes heralding the advance of a mighty storm.

III

THE SPIRIT OF SUNDAY

LIKE farmers the world over, Russian peasants rise later on Sunday than they do on weekdays. On that day even the *nochlezhniki,* the boys and girls who ride their horses to pasture, return not before but after sunrise. The only exceptions are the women who milk the cows and the shepherds who drive them out for the day. Cows must begin feeding early, before sun and flies ruin their appetites.

On Sunday all life in a Russian village, like water in a river after the spring thaw, spills into the open, with ripples and roars of excitement. Nowhere is there a trace of the tranquillity that broods over the Protestant Sabbath. Mass meetings, debates, lectures, games, dances, songfests, quarrels, drinking bouts, fist-fights, enliven the day. At all affairs the stranger is welcome as an onlooker and even more as a participant. Doors are never and nowhere shut, for nothing is private in a Russian village, neither sorrow, nor joy, neither shame nor glory. Life inside and outside unfolds before the onlookers like petals before sunlight.

The sun was already high in the sky when my host came into the barn and roused me out of the fresh hay in which I had been sleeping. He apologized for waking me, but I knew that he and his wife had long finished their chores and were too hungry to wait longer for breakfast. A distinctive couple they were, detached from the surrounding turmoil, absorbed more in their individual selves than in the social tempest that was blowing about them. Some years ago they had been converted to the Baptist faith, and piously they fulfilled the tenets of this faith as propagated in Russia. They never smoked and never allowed anyone to draw a breath of tobacco in their house. No liquor ever passed their lips or their threshold. They eschewed all violence, never even quarreled with their neighbors. They never sat down to a meal without pronouncing a benediction, and their speech was free from the scurrility that spices peasant talk. Their house was the cleanest in the village — the floor always scrubbed, the walls whitewashed, the windows wiped. No chickens strutted around their living room and no pigs ever tumbled in for a feeding, as in other peasant homes. It was the only house in the village where one could sit down to a meal without being obliged to engage in a perpetual duel with flies. "When flies gather inside," explained my hostess, "we carry our food out, darken the room, open the doors, and they fly out" — an effective method of attack, but one needing continuous repetition.

Breakfast was on the table when I entered the house — boiled millet, griddle cakes, bacon, milk in a huge earthen jar, butter in a red earthen plate, and the inevitable cucumbers. As we were eating, neighbors began to dribble in, some with gifts for me — eggs, apples and honey. One old man asked if I had newspapers to give away — not to read but to use for cigarette paper. Young women inquired whether I had seen their husbands in America. They had been there a long time and had stopped writing letters or sending money. When I replied that I had never seen them they burst into tirades. " All plagues in the world on them," cried one. " If only someone in America would cut them to pieces with an axe," fumed another. " Or bring them back to us in chains, so we could lash them good and proper with stout leather whips," still another shouted. A delegation of young people came to invite me to give a report at a meeting on conditions in America. They told me that everyone was eager to hear about the latest developments in American rural life, the new machinery in use, new crops grown, programs of social welfare and, of course, collective farming. They were obviously puzzled when I told them that collective farming in the Russian manner was unknown in America.

While we were talking we heard the shouting of children in the street. We peered out of the window and beheld a spectacle that was in itself an eloquent commentary on the transforming powers of the Revolution. A group of boys and girls of school age were at play in a neighboring yard. One boy had stuffed quantities of straw inside his clothes in order to look like a *bourzhui,* whom Russian caricatures and posters always portray as rolling in fat. This boy stationed himself near a tree at the head of a squad of his followers all armed with long sticks of birch wood. Opposite them another group of boys and girls, also armed with sticks, formed another party. Each party represented an army, one in the service of the bourgeoisie, the other in the service of the proletariat. The birch sticks were their guns. Each " army," led by its commander, marched around and around, until finally both armies halted and both commanders exclaimed, *"Pali!* (Shoot!)" " The " soldiers " lurched forward as if in attack. Thereupon the *bourzhui* commander toppled over with loud groans, and all his soldiers fell " dead " on top of him.

I could not help thinking of the change in the form and spirit of children's play in this village since my boyhood days. We, too, had used birch sticks, not for guns but for horses. The stouter and smoother the stick, the more finely mottled its bark, the more valuable a horse it was. We ran races, held fairs and " bought and sold horses," wrangling furiously like Gipsies. We played games involving sheep, cows and wolves, games which derived from the everyday experiences of our elders and from the folklore of our people. No element of social conflict, of political partisanship colored anything we did, said, or thought. But now even the children in this far away village were so filled with the spirit of the class struggle that they joyously infused it into their everyday diversions; even in their play they divided mankind into two classes, *bourzhuis* and proletarians, the one a symbol of evil, the other a symbol of good. And in their games, as in a fairy tale, the good always triumphed over the evil.

After breakfast I strolled out into the street, and soon half the village had gathered around me. Astir with curiosity as never before in their history, these *muzhiks* would not miss an opportunity to hear news of the outside world. This time I led in the questioning, and, it being Sunday, I inquired if any of those present were going to church. They replied with shakes of the head, mutterings of " nay, nay," and half-smothered snickers. " They don't even wear crosses any more,

these countrymen of yours," volunteered old hunchbacked Adarya, who had once enjoyed the reputation
of being the champion scold of the village.

"Ask her if she is wearing one herself," someone
exclaimed.

I looked at Adarya with accusing eyes.

"Is this true?" I asked.

She shrugged her shoulders. "True and not true,
that's how it is."

"But, Adarya," I continued in amazement, "you?
Do you remember how, five years ago when I was in
your house on a Sunday, you picked up a stout
piece of firewood and threatened to hit your husband
on the head if he didn't stop making fun of the ikons?
What has happened, Adarya?"

The crowd roared with amusement, but Adarya,
quite unembarrassed, explained:

"You see it is a new world now; nothing is as it was.
We have all been changing. But I am not like others.
I don't say there is no God. Maybe the atheists are
right, and there is none. But maybe they are wrong, and
there is, and He will punish sinners for their lack of
faith. Do you see?"

"Ekh, you shrewd hag," sneered a bearded *muzhik*
who was standing beside me, "you don't want to take
any chances with your future, so you're trying to stand
in well with both God and the devil. A sharp *baba!*
Fie!" He spat violently in the direction of Adarya and
walked off muttering curses on all *babas* and atheists.

Once on the subject of religion, I pressed for further
information. Extraordinary were the changes that had
come about during the last five years. Infidelity was

sweeping the land like a fierce gale, uprooting all obstructions. The two little chapels that had once graced the gateway at either end of the village were now gone. On my previous visit they were already collapsing, for the *muzhiks* would not bother to repair them. Now they were no more. Boastfully the boys explained that one evening they got together and carried them off. " They were only an eyesore anyway," remarked a chubby lad with a flushed face and a squeaky voice.

An eyesore! Imagine an ordinary *muzhik* boy speaking with such contempt of a chapel! Gone from him was all sense of blasphemy, all feeling of reverence for the old faith.

Even the women, the boys informed me, were now being shaken by doubt. For a time they had prophesied calamity after calamity — plague, drouth, famine — if the unbelievers would not again turn their faces to God. But in the end they got tired of prophesying, for crops were good in spite of infidelity, aye, better than ever, this year's rye promising the best crop they had had since the Revolution. The younger women and girls, too, had made a complete face-about. Five years before, even when they failed to attend church services regularly, they still clung to established church ceremonial. They would not marry a man unless he agreed to a church wedding. But during the last Trinity, only two months previous, out of the fourteen weddings in the village, only two were performed in church. The others were secular celebrations with food, drink, songs, speeches, but without a priest, without ikons, without the kissing of crosses. Two couples did not even register their marriage, but lived together in free love. At first people talked about it, but now nobody bothered. At the coming wedding season, in October, it was doubtful whether any couple would be married in church, the youths avowed. And as for funerals, the priests were steadily losing out there, too. More and more of the dead were being buried without a priest. It was cheaper, anyway.

Set against the overflowing piety of the *muzhik* in the old days, this new condition strained one's credulity. Yet among the crowds that had gathered round me and listened to these instances of waning faith there rose no voice of dissent, nor any manifestation of grief, at the collapse of the ancient religion.

I broke away from the crowd and started for the parish church several versts away. Were other villages succumbing as easily as this to the blandishments of infidelity? I wanted to know. It was a bright day, with glowing sun and cool breeze; the roads were dry and smooth. Peasant after peasant in straw-loaded cart was driving up and down, but not to church. I found it almost deserted. Only nine people were in attendance — five men, three women and a child; not a single young man or woman, though in pre-war days — and how well I remembered it! — there was never a Sunday, rain or shine, but the church and the vestibule and the yard were packed with worshipers. A group of young people who had been standing on the porch of the clubhouse opposite the church followed me inside, evidently out of curiosity to see what a visiting American would do in a *muzhik* church. That it was only curiosity which impelled them to enter was clear from their manner. They did not make the sign of the cross, as does a believing person on passing the threshold of a house of worship. They walked in, stood about near the door and looked on with silent amusement.

A sorry spectacle the church presented. It had obviously had no repairs for years. The ceiling was flecked with dry rain-spots; plaster was crumbling from the walls; the floor was in places rotted through in great holes like evil eyes gaping out of the dark ground below; panes in two of the windows were broken, and the frame of one was falling apart. In the midst of this desolation the officiating priest in his gorgeous raiment glowed like a bright star on a dark night. He was a new man in the parish. The old priest, whom I had known as a boy, famed for his kindness and humility, had died two years before. I did not know where the new man had come from, but he was an impressive personage, tall, broad-breasted, with red hair and a red beard growing only about the chin, and radiant with energy. In a gown of shimmering silver striped with gold, with a gilded crown on his head, a gilded cross in one hand and a smoking incense container in the other, he paced majestically up and down the inner pulpit, chanting prayers with lusty and heroic fervor. That the house of worship was all but empty seemed not to disturb him. He was bent on his devotion, with heart full of ardor. The deacon's reverberating response, " *Hospodi pomilui,*" [1] seemed to be inspiration enough for him. Oblivious he seemed to the blasts of enmity in the turbulent world outside. A lonely and a brave man!

When I walked out of the church, the young people who had followed me in came out and bombarded me with questions. They wondered why I visited the church — surely I was an unbeliever like themselves,

[1] " Lord have mercy."

wasn't I? Weren't all men of culture unbelievers? Were
Americans different? Really? Wasn't I jesting? And
America such a land of *technic* — machines — with her
Ford, her Edison, her skyscrapers, her scientific magic,
her modern miracles! No, Americans couldn't possibly
take religion seriously, and an awakening would come
some day!

I didn't argue with these zealous crusaders for a god-
less world. I never do argue with Russian revolutionaries when the fundamental dogmas of their creed are
in question. It is of no use. Yet the presence of such
dogmatically minded atheists in a peasant village was
a historic event which the wise and earnest believer
will not dismiss with a mere gesture of contempt or
levity. Irrefutable proof it is that the Orthodox Church,
which only fifteen years ago held within its hand the
spiritual ministration of more than one hundred million souls, is now a crumbling edifice, its foundations
caving in so fast that one can almost see and hear the
process of collapse. Will a miracle intervene and save
it from annihilation? Miracles do happen — though
not very often. . . .

I went back to the village and arrived in time to witness an episode which could not have happened in any
other land in the world, and which revealed a fresh
facet of this ever flashing and ever swelling Russian
drama. As a means of furthering the political awakening of the women in the villages, visiting agitators
sometimes called special mass meetings for women
only. Such a meeting was now in progress. It was held
outdoors, directly in front of the coöperative store. Not
only women, but men also, had gathered, the latter
lingering on the fringe of the crowd and watching the

proceedings with sly amusement. A visiting lecturer was explaining the advantages which women would reap from a *kolhoz*. They would have to bother hardly at all with their babies, he declared, for these would be cared for in well-equipped nurseries. They would not have to roast over ovens, for community kitchens would do all the cooking. They would no longer need to use their smoky kerosene lamps, for there would be electric lights. They would not have to bury themselves evenings in their little homes, for there would be clubhouses and parks with all manner of diversions for their entertainment. In short, the *kolhoz* would, according to his words, usher in a new redemption for the weary overworked *muzhik* woman.

When he had finished his lecture, the presiding woman, directed by another visitor, a Party man,[2] called for questions and discussion. Not a word came in reply. Nobody seemed to have anything to say. Again the Party man prompted the chairman into calling for expressions of opinion; again no response. He was baffled. What did it mean? Did they all agree with the lecturer? It they did not, why wouldn't they state their objections? At last one woman summoned courage to speak, and there followed of a sudden an explosion of voices, a babel of shouts. The Party man called for order. He insisted that only one person at a time should speak. Again he prompted the tragically inexperienced chairman to call for expressions of opinion; again there was silence. Then once more someone spoke up, only to be instantly overwhelmed by a fresh burst of shouts. The Party man became wroth. With a violent flourish of his arms he restored silence, and with stern earnest-

[2] Member of the Communist Party.

ness he pleaded for orderly behavior. But to no avail. Try as hard as they might, those impassioned women could not speak one at a time. No sooner would one of them begin saying something than all the others would follow suit until the air shook with their booming voices. After a few minutes of this disorder a humped old woman with a dusty kerchief on her head spat violently at the whole gathering in the manner of *muzhiks* when they are displeased with something, and exclaimed: "Only pigs have come here; I might as well go home."

The remark might have passed off without an aftermath had it not been for the new orator of the village who was an old playmate of mine, a man with coalblack hair and gleaming eyes. He leaped forward, pushed through the crowd, mounted the bench on which sat the helpless chairman, and loudly calling on the assemblage to quiet down, he began:

"Citizens, dear; dear citizens, women! Hear me, all of you! You have gathered here for a worthy purpose. New trials and new problems are facing you; a new life is beginning for you, for all of us. Never had we need to be so serious and so thoughtful. Yet what do we see? What do we hear? One of our citizens, a poor woman, but one with a decided *koolack* quirk in her mind, has just called us pigs! Think of it — pigs! I ask you, citizens dear, to consider it: Are we pigs, or are we not? A serious matter this is. It made my heart bleed to hear such an expression coming from one of our own kind, and you cannot, you must not, continue this discussion until you answer my question — Are we pigs, or are we not? Answer! You who say we are pigs, raise your hands. Nobody? You who say we are not

pigs? — Raise your hands! Good! It is well to be clear
about such important matters. Now we know that we
are serious-minded citizens of a free land, which all the
capitalists of the world are seeking to smash; and they
will smash us if we are so small-minded, so *koolatzky-*
inclined, as to think of ourselves or of our neighbors as
pigs or to tolerate anyone who says we are pigs. Remember that."

He jumped down from the bench. Nobody laughed.
Nobody protested. Nobody appeared offended. It
seemed as proper a speech as a lecture on the *kolhoz.*
Only the Party man glanced at me from the corner of
his eyes and winked as though to say, "This may seem
barbarous to you, but *nichevo,* we'll learn better and
at any rate here is something to amuse you."

The meeting continued, not without confusion, and
as I stood there watching the proceedings I felt someone nudging my arm. "Father wants to know," said a
clean-looking well-dressed youth, "if you will come up
to the house and have a drink of milk." I followed the
youth to his home. His father, an old acquaintance of
mine, was one of the few so-called "well-to-do" peasants in the village, though by no stretch of imagination
could he have been called that in America, Germany,
England or any other western land. He lived in a small
house with a thatched roof, like any other *muzhik.*
Though there were two rooms in his house he lived
only in one; the other he rented to visiting surveyors.
The only visible mark of well-being was the samovar
standing on the ground in a corner, and so crusted with
fly specks, soot and dust that it had lost not only its
original luster but even its yellow color. The furniture
was no better than that in any other peasant hut — a

polati,[3] benches, a table, a crib suspended on ropes from the ceiling. Under the *polati,* beside the long trough in which the hogs were fed, lay a little pig stretched out at full length, heavily snoring. Chickens strutted in and out of the room through the open doors. Flies in swarms, in dark clouds, hovered about the oven, the samovar, the table, the dishes and the windows. But this man held eighteen dessiatins of land; occasionally he employed hired labor to help with the harvesting; and therefore he fell into the category of *zozhitschny,* and was treated with neither ceremony nor mercy by the Soviets.

He was no more than forty years of age, square-shouldered, with a face that was still unlined. He placed an earthen jug of milk before me, and a plate of cheese cakes fresh from the oven. He had sent for me, he said, because he wanted advice on a most serious subject. His son had graduated from the four-year school. He was a bright lad and wished to continue studying. But the Soviets would not admit him to a higher school. They were growing terribly strict about keeping children of *muzhiks* like himself out of the high schools and universities. In the market place he had heard of a man who had sent his older son to the university. The boy was studying to be an engineer. He was a brilliant student, and his teachers prophesied a great future for him. One day when he came to class he was told to pack up and go home — there was no place in the university for him, the son of a *koolack!* The boy begged, pleaded, assured the authorities that he had no notion of being a *koolack,* that his ambition was to serve the new society. But it was useless. They dis-

[3] A platform which serves the purpose of a bed.

missed him for all his pleas. He was at home now, a wreck of a youth. Nobody would intercede in his behalf, neither the local Soviet, nor the Party, nor influential friends. It was always so with the son of a well-to-do man. Nobody cared for him. What could he, my old acquaintance, do about his Nikolai? Of course there was a way out. If he were to join the *kolhoz* he would regain all his rights and Nikolai would not be dis-criminated against. But he loathed the thought of sub-merging himself in the *kolhoz*, and his wife was dead set against it. The very word *kolhoz* inflamed her to fury. She shuddered at the idea of mixing with other folk in her everyday work and of being told by others what she should and what she should not do. What was he to do? What would I advise him to do?

Even as he was speaking his wife entered, a shriveled woman with bright eyes and an animated face. She greeted me affably and laid before me the armful of ripe heads of poppy seeds that she had brought with her. Her husband informed her of the subject of our conversation, and immediately she grew livid with rage. She would rather starve to death than live in a *kolhoz*, she announced vehemently.

" You silly *baba*," chided her husband, " how much worse could our life be in a *kolhoz* than it now is? Our black bread we'll always have — surely that much even the worst *kolhoz* will offer its members; and at least we won't be constantly hounded by officials, delegates, lecturers, investigators, agents, Party men and what not who come and tax and confiscate and don't let us hold what we have."

" So, now you're going over to the *kolhoz*," raged the woman at the top of her voice. " Well, go — go now,

if you want to! But I shan't follow you. You can't drag
me there with a pair of oxen. I'll dig myself into the
earth right here with my hands, my feet, my head,
and I'll die before I rise up to go to the *kolhoz*."

The doors and windows of the house were open, and
the loud talking attracted outsiders who, in the informal manner of Russian peasants, flocked inside.
The mass meeting of the women, which was just across
the way, was breaking up, and some of the people
from there were also coming in. Even the Party man
turned up, serene, amused, well-satisfied.

" See," he addressed me, " what a powerful thing
this *kolhoz* is, how assiduously it is breaking up the
old world."

" Yes, it is breaking up everything," shouted the
woman with disgust.

" Only to put it all together again," calmly responded the Party man.

" You cannot put together a broken heart as you can
a broken wagon," protested the woman, " and all you
are doing is breaking people's hearts. Fathers, mothers,
husbands, wives, children — all are breaking away from
each other, becoming enemies of one another, that's
what they are doing."

" Only to become friends again," continued the
Party man, with his wonted calm and self-assurance.
" *Nichevo*, when there is no more exploitation in the
world, there will be no more fights, no more feuds."

" But meanwhile," someone burst out, " you are sap-
ping the very blood out of our veins."

" Only of those who themselves feed on the blood
of others — of exploiters. Bloodsuckers must be
destroyed."

" But listen, Fedya," began a stranger, a visitor evidently from some other village. " Where is your conscience? What did your crowd do to N—— in the village of K——? You treated him worse than a dog."

" We did," responded the Party man, " and rightly so."

The stranger drew close to me, seized my arm as if intent on holding me in my place, and began: " Listen to what has happened to N——. He has twenty dessiatins of land, and he is as hard-working a *muzhik* as ever lived. No Party man will deny that. During the recent bread collections he hid away ten sacks of rye. When the grain collector learned of it, he pounced on him like a wild beast. N—— didn't really mean to cheat the government, but like all of us he was afraid that perhaps the amount left him by the agent wouldn't be enough, or that there might be a poor crop the following year and he would need some reserves, so he hid ten sacks of rye in the back of his barn. A member of the committee of the poor had seen him do it and denounced him to the agent. Well, the agent confiscated the hidden rye, the man's best horse, his best cow, his best calf, a mowing machine, ten sheep, seventeen geese, and even the fiddle which the poor fellow had inherited from his grandfather. Not only that, but he was expelled from the village coöperative — not an ounce of salt, not a drop of kerosene, not an inch of dry goods can he buy there. Everything he needs he must obtain in open market, where the prices are from two to four times as much as in the coöperative. Even the forty roubles that he had paid down as a membership fee were forfeited. To complete his disgrace they put his name on the public blackboard. Tell me, what shall the rest of us do in the face of such cruelty? "

I waited for the Party man to say something, but he only smiled. He seemed unperturbed by the recital of this story. Clearly, he was a man beyond pity and forgiveness, and beyond repentance.

Late in the afternoon the young people were gathering for their weekly dance. Headed by the village orchestra, in which a drum now took the place of a tambourine, and an accordion, they marched to the farther end of the village where the ground was smoothest. I went along. Since the sun was still hot and the dust thick, some of the boys fetched pails of water and sprinkled the ground. As I watched the others waiting for the dance to begin I was impressed by the vast improvement in the dress of these peasant youths since my previous visit five years before. Not one, boy or girl, any longer wore *lapti,* the age-old bast sandals of the *muzhik.* Not one was barefooted. The boys wore finely made boots of soft leather, the girls' feet were neat in factory-made shoes, their coarse hand-knit stockings replaced by machine-woven ones. Gone were the babyish caps which the girls used to wear. Now they sported kerchiefs — white, red, green, blue, yellow — wrapped around their heads or resting on their shoulders. Finger rings, too — mostly of tin and brass — gleamed in the sun as hands moved one way or another, and handkerchiefs, previously unknown, were as common as boots and shoes. Some of the girls carried them wrapped around their hands; others pinned them inside their waists for safekeeping. Scarcely any wore dresses of homespun fabrics, now considered inferior; cottons, satins, city fashion, replaced them. Older folk might wail over high prices, high taxes, shortage of goods, but youth was moving onward in spite of economic distress. It had discovered city styles, city tastes, city smartness — even perfumes and face powder, which the girls of my boyhood days had never known. What next, I wondered?

The dance started. Couple after couple circled away to the tune of the sprightly music. They hopped and jigged, and whirled and swayed. They executed their steps with zest and gusto, like artists responding to the mood of creativeness. They radiated gladness. They surcharged the very air with animation. Seeing them giving themselves over with beautiful unconsciousness to the rapture of melody and motion, one forgot the wrath and the chaos of the Revolution. One remembered sorrow as a flitting phantom that vanished with its flight. One was conscious of something indestructibly lovable and noble, a freshness, an innocence, a gayety, a health, a purity that is the very epitome of grandeur — man at his best in tune with the sun and the wind and the trees and all else that surrounds him. All afternoon they danced, these hardy, unspoiled boys and girls. Again and again the ground had to be sprinkled, so quickly did the sun dry up the moisture. But save for brief pauses they kept on and on, changing partners, changing poses, flitting gayly along on a wave of ever heightening rapture.

Darkness was coming down and the gatherings in the village broke up. Older people went home and retired, but youth had the night still ahead, with *nochleg*, the pasturing of the horses, as a fitting climax to a day of revelry. *Nochleg* always was a part of the adventure of living to the village youth in this part of Russia. There, more than at dances, more even than at the spinning socials in winter, youth, in its irrepressible urge for romance and gayety, claimed the world for itself. There nothing and nobody ever interfered with the flow of fun and play and good fellowship. In my years of sojourn in America my mind often went back to the adventures of youth, and always the thought of *nochleg* roused a swell of emotion.

I went along. One of the boys furnished me a horse with a hemp cloth for a saddle and my host offered me his immense sheepskin coat. I rode on with an army of boys and girls all on horseback. The night was dark and windless, with a heavy dew falling in a drizzle, but that did not dampen the mood of the riders. They burst into song. The melodies were old, but the words and the themes of some of the songs were new in thought and sentiment, songs of battle, of triumph, of a world in which no priest, no god, no *koolack*, no capitalist, would rule or have a place.

When we reached the pasture, some versts away, we tethered our horses and let them graze. Two other villages were using the same pasture for *nochleg*, and their boys and girls were already on hand, running races, singing, wrestling, making love, turning these boggy lowlands in spite of darkness and drizzle into a scene of unalloyed hilarity. Our boys and girls joined them and their screams and shouts and giggles only heightened the gayety of the night.

Then, breaking up into groups, we marched to a rise of ground on the bank of the river which flowed through the marshes. The grass was damp, but that did not matter; our sheepskin coats held back the moisture and we felt comfortable enough sprawled on the ground. The first excitement was now over; laughter and chatter had subsided. Cautiously I broached the subject of the revolutionary innovations that were coming to the villages, to find the response of these youths in strong contrast to that of their elders. They showed no rancor, nor even disappointment; they prophesied no doom. They were amazingly good-humored, and bantered back and forth about dowries, free love and the independence of women. Even the *kolhoz* did not appall them. They were not sure what it would do to them: it might improve life — organizers were promising them clubhouses, parks, motion pictures, radios, even automobiles — but if these promises did not materialize, people could go back to individual landholdings, and therefore they saw no reason for worry. They looked toward it expectantly.

The night advanced. The dew grew heavier and heavier and chilled our faces. All around horses with tinkling bells were grazing on the coarse grass of the marshes. Now and then a colt, frightened by some sound or sight or merely in a spurt of exuberance, would break into shrill whinnying and bound wildly away. One by one the boys and girls wrapped themselves snugly in their sheepskin coats and went to sleep, with lovers in each other's embrace. The night was still, with nowhere a sign of travail, of doubt, of conflict, of sorrow.

Five years ago and now — What a stupendous revolution! A schoolhouse, a nursery, a fire station, handkerchiefs, boots, perfumes, powder and this oncoming *kolhoz,* with its roaring machines and its momentous changes in the relationships between man and man, man and woman, man and society, man and nature and, above all, man and God! Yet the lowlands were the same as then, the brushwood as unchanged, the sky as immense. What, I wondered, would things be like five years hence. Would these boys and girls, now so pleased with themselves and so elated with the prospect of fresh adventures, find their hopes and their fervor justified? Or would they, like their elders, grow disenchanted and heartsick, seeing only doom ahead? Five years hence — a brief span of time, but an age, an epoch, in Russia.

However, I did not have to wait five years for events to move to a climax.

IV

THE COMING OF THE STORM

REVOLUTIONS, like unruly winds, have whims of their own and shift their courses with scarcely any warnings. I had hardly crossed the Russian frontier when information began to dribble through of a heightened socialist offensive in city and village. The Soviet newspapers which were reaching me bristled with news of it. Then on January 5, 1930, the Politbureau, the highest functioning body in the Communist Party, drafted an epochal declaration. Stalin has spoken of 1930 as the "year of the Great Break." If there was nothing else but this declaration, the year would merit Stalin's dramatic designation. The events that followed shook Russia as nothing else since the cessation of the civil war and the abrogation of military communism. So intimately does this declaration concern the story of this book that I feel it necessary in this chapter to lay before the reader the circumstances which had brought it into being.

Russian agriculture under the Soviet had reached an impasse. The chief causes of this impasse were parcelization of the land, attacks on the prosperous peasant, and the prevailing financial and manufacturing difficulties. Each of these merits close scrutiny.

With the increase of population and with the cultural awakening of the younger generation in the villages, especially of the women, who, upon marriage, often objected to living with their husband's family, as had been the custom in Russia, there began a continuous division and subdivision of land. Between 1917 and 1927 the number of individual farms had leaped from seventeen million to twenty-seven million. This automatically removed from cultivation millions of acres which were taken up by the buildings and the yards of the new households, and by the ridges and the dead furrows which in Russia, in the absence of fences, have since days immemorial divided one strip of land from another. Nothing so impresses the visitor to rural Russia as these ridges and furrows which stretch snake-like in every direction to the very horizon, and which, like a scourge, contaminate nearby fields with noxious weeds. One scientist estimates that these Russian " fences " take up 7 percent of the land, and another reckons that their aggregate acreage, if properly tilled, would raise enough bread to supply the yearly need of half the total population of all Russian cities. A relic of feudalism, these wasted areas constituted a barrier to the advance of Russian agriculture.

A further by-product of the incessant division and subdivision of the land was its diminishing productivity. Under Russian conditions of individual farming the owner of a small acreage could not afford to have a horse of his own, a good plow, or any other modern machine; yet without these he could not hope to whip out of the land all that it had to offer. In 1928 there were eight million Russian farmers who found themselves in the toils of this inescapable dilemma — they could not raise the productivity of their lands unless they possessed themselves of horses and modern ma-

chinery, and their individual acreages were so small
that they could not make the investments necessary
to obtain these without a serious and perhaps a fatal
drain on their capital funds. Besides, the more individual owners there were on the land, especially when
they cherished a deep dread of innovations, as do all
Russian peasants, the more difficult it was to win them
to new methods of tillage.

The evils incident to these conditions could be overcome through a system that would promote increasing
instead of decreasing acreages. Large farms would
eliminate the parasitic boundary ridges and dead furrows, and would make possible the purchase of machinery and other equipment necessary to the introduction of modern methods of tillage. But under a
system of individualistic control of the land the Soviets
could not contemplate such a policy without scrapping
the law forbidding the sale and penalizing the renting
of land; and such a move would of course strike a death
blow at the basic tenets of the Revolution, which demand the annihilation of private property.

The war on the prosperous peasant only intensi-
fied the existing difficulties. It led to continuous and
disastrous conflicts with the so-called *koolack*. Literally the word means a fist, and applies to a man who
is supposed to gather material possessions into his own
hands and hold them tight. Legally, a *koolack* is a man
who indulges in some form of exploitation, employs
hired help or derives an income from rent or interest or
the operation of an agricultural or industrial machine.
Actually, however, a *koolack* is a successful farmer
as success is measured in Russia. He is a man who
has lifted his household to a plane conspicuously above

that of the average peasant. He has built up what Communists call a *moshtshnoye khoziaistvo,* a well-to-do
household. In America the average Russian *koolack*
would be a poor man, and even in Russia there is no
permanent class of *koolacks.* They shift with their
fortunes, which depend as much on themselves as on
external conditions. All over the country there are
koolacks who never had had any land until the Revolution gave it to them, and there are also *bedniaks,* poor
men, who were once *koolacks* but who have been the
victims of some catastrophe — a fire, a drouth or an
epidemic which killed off all or most of their stock.
Usually the *koolack* is not the fat lazy barbarian that
he is pictured in Soviet motion pictures. A thrifty
energetic man, sometimes miserly, he is no idler like
the landlord of the old days who had all his work done
by outside help. He is one of the hardest-toiling people
in Russia, and so are his wife and children.

But under existing conditions, with the basic aims
of the Revolution always in the foreground of their
thoughts, the revolutionary leaders could not consistently assume an attitude of leniency toward him. Regarding material accumulation as the chief menace to
the Revolution, they could not fail to see in the prospering individual farmer the chief menace to their
plans. When therefore a man came into possession of
two or three horses, as many or a few more cows,
about half a dozen pigs, and when he raised three or
four hundred poods of rye or wheat, he fell into the
category of *koolack,* and it was always easy to find
a legal excuse to brand him as such. For the least
infraction on existing laws he was dealt with severely,
and since 1928, as a further means of keeping down

his material accumulations, he had been forced to pay a so-called "individualistic" tax.

In retaliation, the well-to-do peasant embarked on a passive strike. He limited artificially his productivity and withheld much of his surplus produce from the market. I do not wish to clutter these pages with statistics, but a few figures on the decrease of cattle in Siberia, for example, will bear testimony to the devastating results of the policy of penalizing the prosperous peasant. In pre-war days Siberia was a famed dairy land. More than 57 percent of its peasants were owners of four cows, while peasants having only one cow made up a little over 7 percent of the farming population. In 1928, peasants having four cows totaled slightly more than 13 percent, and those with one cow 33 percent, of this population. The civil war had done serious damage to the dairy industry of Siberia, but the chief devastation resulted from the treatment of the so-called *koolack*.

The financial and manufacturing straits of the Soviet government added to the agrarian crisis. Gold had ceased to circulate, and paper money did not tempt the peasant. He saw value chiefly in goods, and whenever he sold grain, a calf, a pig, he wanted to buy something. But the Soviets were unable to supply him with the amounts of goods demanded; the capacity of their factories was limited, and from foreign lands they were importing negligible quantities of so-called " consumption goods." In consequence, the poor and the middle peasant, as well as the *koolack,* sold less and less of his surplus. He consumed more himself, and the remainder he kept for future advantage.

The cumulative effect of these conditions — the

parcelization of the land, the attacks on the prosperous farmer, the financial and manufacturing straits of
the government — were pushing the country toward
disaster, actually threatening the city and the army
with famine. To avert a possible catastrophe, the
Soviets compelled the peasant, through so-called
" grain collections," to sell to them his surplus grain
at prices which they fixed. The peasant stormed in
protest, and in the summer of 1928, after enough grain
had been collected to meet the needs of the city for
the ensuing year, the Soviets issued an announcement
promising that they would not again resort to grain collections. Since the basic conditions remained unchanged,
this promise was broken the following year when they
once more embarked on grain collections in an even
firmer and more organized manner.

The poorest peasants, who raised no surplus grain,
were exempted from collections, as they were from all
taxes. But the others were obliged to sell the government all their surplus, the amount of which was determined not by them but by Soviet agents. Though
intended originally as an emergency measure to end a
severe shortage of bread, grain collections had become
an indispensable fixture of Soviet internal administration.

This is not the place to examine the vehement con-
troversies that raged within the ranks of the Communist Party as to the proper solution of the agrarian
crisis. I am concerned here, not with Rykov's or Buk-
harin's or Kondratye's proposals, but with Stalin's
actions. He, after all, held control of the Party policy,
and he, through the operation of *sovhozy*[1] and

[1] State farms.

through the *kolhozy*, opened the road to the much needed large-scale farming without invalidating the basic Bolshevik aims of the Revolution. Here I am concerned, of course, only with *kolhozy*. As early as 1927 the Fifteenth Congress of the Communist Party had passed a resolution making collectivization a definite part of the Party's program. But the resolution had remained essentially a paper document. Only in the spring of 1929 was it accorded energetic action, and in the autumn of the same year the collectivization movement had gathered conspicuous momentum. Encouraged by the initial results, and desirous of making them more sure and more permanent, the Politbureau under Stalin's influence drafted its famous declaration of January 5, 1930. This declaration embodied two vital decisions: to liquidate the *koolacks* and to achieve complete collectivization of the land within a specified time. The *koolacks* were to be economically exterminated. Their properties were to be confiscated and they exiled to Siberia, to the far north in Europe, or to a remote strip of poor land away from their former homes, where, with limited animal power, few implements, and with no aid from the state or the coöperatives, they were to make their way in the world as best they could. Since *koolacks* constituted between 4 and 5 percent of the population, this decision doomed more than one million families to loss of their property and to banishment from their lands.

It is easy enough to see the reasons for the imposition of such a cruel fate on the *koolacks*. Being the more prosperous men in the community, they naturally would be most energetic in opposition to collectivization. Not only would they themselves refuse to join, even

were they given the chance — which they were not —
but as men of standing in the community they would
influence others to follow their example. Besides, their
presence would sustain the innate urge of every peasant to come some day into individual prosperity.
" Every peasant," confessed to me a high official in the
Commissary of Agriculture, "has his own five-year
plan, at the end of which he wants to attain to the position of a *koolack*." But with the *koolack* out of the way
and the example of his fate fresh before the population,
the averag*e muzhik* would not be so eager for advancement through an individual household. Then of course
the *koolack* had the best cows, the best horses, the best
pigs, the best tools, the best buildings, the best seed,
and these the government sorely needed to equip the
multitude of newly formed *kolhozy*.

Simultaneously with this movement against the *koolacks,* the country was divided into three dictricts, one of
which was to achieve complete collectivization in the
spring of 1931, the second in the spring of 1932, the third
at the end of the five-year plan, in 1933. I must add that
the declaration of the Politbureau made clear that not
coercive but persuasive methods were to be employed by
field organizers to win the peasant over to collectivization, and that the type of *kolhoz* to be favored at this
stage of the country's development was the artel, in
which only land, work animals, portions of other domestic stock and implements are held in common.

The months of January and February were tempes-
tuous months in the Russian villages. Collectivization
was sweeping the land, and the newspapers screamed
with joy at the success of the movement. Like mercury
in a thermometer that is being artificially heated, their

figures for collectivization rose higher every day, and the reader was led to imagine that peasants were of their own accord flocking to *kolhozy* as to a place of deliverance. Complete collectivization seemed not a question of the two or three years which the Politbureau had set for it, but of months only. I was in New York at the time, and the news which the Soviet papers and the dispatches from Moscow carried seemed incredible. I could not imagine the Russian peasant making such a complete turn-about overnight in his attitude toward collectivization.

Then came the crash, and the very newspapers that had been featuring the success of collectivization now began even more loudly to announce its failures. The movement had developed into one of force, not in all instances, of course, but in many throughout the country. Organizers in their impassioned desire to outdo one another and to bring about complete collectivization in a lesser period than that prescribed by the Politbureau, discarded persuasion in favor of coercion. Under threat of confiscation of property, exile, deprivation of citizenship, they drove the peasant in masses into the *kolhozy*. They did not even bother to assure him that whatever property he might turn over to the *kolhoz* would yield him an extra return.

The peasant, sullen and desperate, struck back in his own manner. If he was to be forced into the *kolhoz* he would go in empty handed, and let the government find its own means of running the affair. He began to dispose of his personal property, sell what was saleable and kill what was killable. In village after village it was the same, and the slaughter of stock was appalling. At least one-half of all the pigs in the country went under the knife, in addition to a full fourth of the cattle and an even larger share of the sheep and goats.

Stalin and the Central Committee have since avowed that the men in the field, in using forcible measures against the peasant, were acting without the knowledge and authority of the Party and in violation of its will and instructions. In the statement of the Central Committee of March 15, 1930, in which it condemns and forbids coercive methods of collectivization, it admits that "in a series of districts compulsion was substituted for voluntariness and men were made to join under threat of dekoolackization and deprivation of citizenship rights . . . there are instances of a decidedly vulgar, nasty and criminal treatment of the population on the part of certain workers in the field — compulsory socialization of homes, of small stock, of domestic birds (which should not have been touched) . . . perfectly intolerable perversion of Party line in the realm of the fight on religious prejudices and on trade between city and village. We have in mind the closing of churches by administrative order without the consent of an overwhelming majority of the population of the community . . . the closing of a number of market places, thus aggravating the food conditions in the towns. . . ."

Stalin himself, in his famous letter on "dizziness from success," in which he likewise takes the organizers to task for violating the principle of voluntariness, which was to be the basis of the organization of collectives, says: "In certain parts of Turkestan attempts were made to catch up with and surpass [in collectivization] the advanced regions of the Soviet Union by means of military force and the threat of deprivation of water for irrigating the fields and the refusal to sell manufactured articles to peasants who were not ready to join the *kolhoz.*" In his " Answer to the Comrade *Kolhozniks,*" in which a month later he goes at greater length into the subject of coerciveness, he cites devastating evidence of the frequency with which it was practiced.

The question arises, why did Stalin and the Central Committee, which he dominated powerfully at the time, wait until March, a period of about two months, before putting an end to the "perversion of the Party line" in the villages? It is absurd for them to plead ignorance of the situation. No government in the world has at its disposal the multitude of highly sensitized agencies of information that the Central Committee of the Russian Communist Party has. There is the GPU [2] with its far-seeing eyes and far-hearing ears. There are the half million village newspaper correspondents who are always leaping into print with full reports of any untoward events in their communities. There is the Red Army, with its mass of peasant soldiers to whom parents and relatives rush with their grievances against the government. There are the numerous secretaries of the Party and a host of social workers who are always out in the field — teachers, nurses, agronomos, lecturers and others — whose heads had not turned dizzy and who realized the danger of the methods which multitudes of organizers pursued, and surely reported their observations and complaints to their superiors or to the GPU. The Central Committee and Stalin could not help knowing what was transpiring in the villages.

One is forced to the conclusion that they had a pur-

[2] State political police.

pose in delaying action. They were gambling for big stakes, and one is aided in understanding the nature of these stakes when one examines the gains which, in spite of abuses and barbarities, the campaign had yielded. It put into the hands of the government, according to Stalin's own words, two hundred million poods of seed, enough to ensure the necessary sowing of the spring crops. It turned over to the *kolhozy*, again according to Stalin's own words, *koolack* property, implements, grain, stock and buildings to the value of four hundred million gold roubles. It left more than one-fourth of the peasantry settled on the *kolhozy*, with thirty-six million hectares of the best tillable land under their control. Thus thousands of large farms, so indispensable to the productivity of the nation, had actually been formed out of the puny peasant holdings. Moreover, for the time being it put these farms within easy reach and control of the government, thus assuring the latter of easy access to about half of all the marketable grain of the land and promising as easy access in the future to vast supplies of vegetables, fruit, meats, and milk foods. It was owing to these collective farms, and to a much lesser extent to the state farms, that in 1930 Russia became once more a power in the grain market of the world. For the first time since their existence the Soviets had become largely independent of the individual peasant for the needed supply of bread.

From a Party viewpoint these gains were stupendous. But the cost was equally stupendous.

V

MOSCOW MARCHES ON

I HAD no more than come off the train at the Alexandrovsky railroad station in Moscow early in June, 1930, when I sensed the effects of the revolutionary blast that had swept over the country in the preceding winter. I asked an *izvoshtchik*[1] how much he would charge to drive me to the Grand Hotel.

" Six roubles," he replied firmly.

I gasped. The year previous he would have been glad to do it for two or at most three.

" Jesting? " I twitted him.

" Jesting nothing," he flung back with irritation, " I, too, have to live."

" Well, what of it? " I demanded rather heartlessly.

" This," he replied, " bread is fifty copecks a pound, meat two and three roubles and hard to get, oats twelve roubles a pood, boots seventy to a hundred roubles a pair."

Passersby attracted by the *izvoshtchik's* loud plaint paused to listen, and one of them, a middle-aged man with drooping moustaches who was bent beneath a massive wooden box he was carrying, deemed it his duty to proclaim the *izvoshtchik* a liar. The latter, unperturbed, urged his disputant to visit the market places in Moscow, check up on prices and then hurl insults at people!

[1] Cab driver.

The man instantly edged back and asked the *izvosht-chik* if he were a *lishenetz*.[2]

" What do you suppose? " the *izvoshtchik* replied.

" That is different," the man admitted gently, almost apologetically, and proceeded to explain to me that a *lishenetz* was barred from the coöperative stores, where the government maintained low and stable prices, and had to do his trading in the open market where prices were under no control.

The dispute at an end, the straggling onlookers dispersed and I resumed my bargaining with the *izvosht-chik*. I offered him three roubles. He refused to budge. I left him, and he did not follow me. I approached another driver, and he too demanded six roubles. I left him also, and he likewise did not bother to pursue me. That was unheard of — an *izvoshtchik* not running for blocks after a prospective customer and haggling at the top of his voice over every copeck! Was this *izvoshtchik*, benighted relic of a vanished age, who fits no more into the new regime than does his *droshky* into the five-year plan, at last beginning to acquire a semblance of self-respect? That would be a miracle!

I settled down in my room and began to call up Russian friends, almost every one of whom inquired if I had extra soap or cigarettes. It seemed unbelievable that Moscow would run short of these common commodities. The year previous, cigarette vendors in the streets had been as multitudinous as officials with brief-cases, and soap could be obtained in unlimited quantities in drug stores and the coöperatives. Now soap was being rationed out at the rate of one piece a month, and superior brands of cigarettes had completely disap-

[2] One who has lost his citizenship rights.

peared. Only the atrocious *deli*[3] were available, and these had to be waited and stormed for at the *kiosks*.[4] In the open market a package of twenty-five sold at a rouble.

I learned soon that everything was being rationed out, with the exception, oddly enough, of cosmetics. There was no shortage of these, even though the demand had increased beyond all expectations. Bread, meat, fish, gruel, sugar, tea, cheese, eggs — everything was obtainable only by card and in prescribed amounts. The population was divided into two general groups, proletarians and non-proletarians, of whom the former were allotted more substantial rations than the latter.

The proletarian was allowed 2 pounds of bread and ½ pound of meat daily in addition to his monthly rations: 2,500 grams of cereal, 750 grams of sugar, 25 grams of tea, 10 eggs, ¾ liter of vegetable oil, 250 grams of butter, 1,000 grams of fish, 600 grams of herring. The non-proletarian was allowed 1 pound of bread a day and ¼ pound of meat. Of the foods which were rationed out by the month, he was allotted 1,200 grams of cereal, 100 grams of butter, ¼ liter of vegetable oil, 500 grams of fish, 400 grams of herring, 25 grams of tea. Children were allowed special rations of rice and other light cereals as well as eggs, milk and butter. These rations, though stripped of luxuries, were ample to sustain life, provided they were always available. But they were not. Bread, sugar, cereals and certain vegetables could always be purchased in the prescribed amounts, but there was a chronic shortage of meat, eggs, butter, cheese, and other vegetable and animal fats.

[3] A brand of cheap cigarettes.   [4] Booths.

Nor could one just walk into a coöperative store, as do purchasers in the private shops of the outside world, and be waited on with little or no delay and with a show of appreciation and courtesy on the part of the attendants. The endless queues on every street in every part of the town testified to the annoyance and torment of shopping in Soviet stores. Never since the coming of the nep had these queues been so long and so crowded. They had become as much a part of the Moscow scenery as the very Kremlin. In the clothing sections of the largest department store the crowds were so immense that I could make my way through them only by insidious pushing. Clerks were so overwhelmed that they had no time for discussion of style, taste, or fittings, and indeed, there seemed to be no need of it — customers bought eagerly whatever was offered.*

Only in the bazaars, the independent market-places were there no waiting lines. But here prices were fabulous. The *izvoshtchik* had not exaggerated; here cheese cost 3 roubles a pound; meat, 2 to 3 roubles; butter, 7 and 8 roubles; eggs, 2½ to 3 roubles for ten; a wilted winter radish, 50 copecks; beets and carrots, also 50 copecks each. Some peddlers spurned money altogether. They would exchange eggs, cream and cheese for cereals, textiles or other things which they could use, but not for money.

I made the rounds of the restaurants. The socialist offensive of the previous winter had swept the private ones out of existence. All were now under Soviet coöperative control. On the much-abbreviated menus which I scanned, I found that everything smacking of luxury had been removed. The soup plates were still

* Of late, however, the queues in Moscow have been growing shorter and more rare.

as large as in former times, and the portions of soup as substantial, but gone was the lump of meat which had always been so inseparable a part of the soup. In its place floated a few drops of some vegetable or animal oil. There were days when no meat at all appeared on the menus, when only salt fish, or mashed potatoes, or gruel was served as a second course or as the main dish. Gone were milk, butter and desserts, except for an occasional piece of pastry or a compote made of dried fruits and sparsely sprinkled with sugar. Bread, though, was everywhere abundant and of good quality, and restaurant prices on the whole remained astonishingly low — from sixty-five to eighty-five copecks for a meal consisting of two courses. But the service, with rare and notable exceptions, was unbelievably slow and sloppy. Only in the few good hotels in which foreigners stopped had the food suffered no perceptible deterioration; and here, during the months of the summer tourist season, Russians were barred from the dining rooms in order that visitors might be accommodated.

The economic changes had worked their greatest havoc upon the vegetarian restaurants, which had been among the best in Moscow and which had gained an immense and deserved popularity. In these the food, service and cleanliness were immeasurably superior to those in the coöperative eating places. The soups, the salads, the cereals, the boiled cauliflower soaked in melted butter, the meat substitutes, the puddings, the incomparable *bliny* [5] with luscious sour cream and fresh butter, the compotes, the other desserts, the rich milk, the well-prepared cocoa — all these would have pleased

[5] Griddle cakes.

the most exacting palate. The prices were nominal and the courtesy of the attendants beyond reproach.

Now a shadow of neglect and desolation had settled over them. They were like a house without a mistress — unkempt, sloppy, with littered floors, unwashed windows and swarms of flies. In both quality and variety the food had deteriorated beyond recognition. Seldom was there any cauliflower on the menu, no more *bliny*, no more milk, no more butter — only soups with a dash of oil, meat substitutes made largely of potatoes, salads with unpalatable dressings, cereals so dry that the particles did not cohere. As in the other eating places, bread here was in abundance and the prices had remained low. Otherwise these restaurants were now only a pathetic memory of their former opulence.

Gone also were the food peddlers, chiefly older women, who would trudge the streets of the city carrying baskets loaded with white rolls, pastry, candies, hard-boiled eggs and all manner of sandwiches — caviar, cheese, ham, sausage, beef, chicken. Late at night on one's way home from a party, or sitting in one's room over a book or gossiping with visitors, if hunger arose, one had only to run down into one of the main streets and he would be sure to stumble into one of these dispensers of food. Like the police and the *izvoshtchiks*, they never deserted the streets. Now, save for an occasional man or woman offering questionable sausage, stale bread or dried fish, these food vendors have vanished.

The socialist offensive of the past winter, with its death-dealing blows to private enterprise, had struck hard not only at the available food supplies but likewise at all the agencies of distribution. Only bread and the commonest vegetables, such as beets, potatoes and cabbage, were available in sufficient amounts. The Soviet's continuous export of eggs, butter, caviar, cheese and canned fish, in a desperate effort to gather enough *valuta* [6] to meet the obligations incurred in the purchase of machinery in foreign lands, did not of course lighten the existing distress.

Hardly an aspect of life had remained untouched by the socialist offensive. Church bells, for example, were now silenced. Moscow, from whose church towers bells had been incessantly clanging by day and by night for hundreds of years, now heard these bells no longer. On main avenue and remote side street, on week-days, on Sundays, even on such a high holiday as Easter, no bells tolled forth their wonted message to the populace. They were declared a public nuisance, disturbing to the population, and the churches were ordered to ring them no more.

Moscow no longer knew even its Sunday. The five-day non-stop working week, whereby people work four days and rest on the fifth, had stripped Sunday of all solemnity and reduced it to the commonplaceness of any other day. Stores, factories, theaters, schools operated as actively on that day as on any other. Nor had Sunday been supplanted by another universal rest-day. Such a day was gone from the life and the calendar of the nation — except of course in the villages, and even there the spread of collectivization threatens in time to achieve a similar change. Every day four-fifths of the population works and the other fifth rests. Thus with a bold stroke of her revolutionary hand Russia had wiped out a sanctified practice of centuries. A new

[6] Foreign money.

generation is growing up without the slightest appreciation of the meaning of Sunday in the history of mankind.

In consequence, festivities in Moscow are limited to the five days of the year which have been designated as revolutionary holidays, and a wave of puritanism, Soviet bred, has spread over the city. Though possessed of incomparable theaters, numerous motion picture houses and workers' clubs, Moscow has no night life in the European sense of the word. There are no public dance halls, cafés, night clubs, cabarets. In deference to visiting foreigners, the Grand Hotel and the Savoy are making half-hearted attempts to preserve a semblance of night life in their restaurants, but the atmosphere there is always strained. The somberness of the outside world seeps into the brilliantly lighted dining rooms, and one is always conscious of the incongruity between the indulgences here and the crusade against such indulgences on the outside. A few beerrooms and restaurants had been affording a retreat for that portion of the populace which would not or could not merge its hedonistic destinies with workers' clubs. The best of these featured Gipsy choirs, which always drew crowds, for the Russian is music-loving and responds with especial verve to Gipsy melodies. Now that Gipsy music has been banned in Moscow, all the Gipsy choirs except the ethnographic one had been dissolved, and the singers variously absorbed into proletarian pursuits. Gipsy music, like the balalaika orchestra and the fox trot, had been declared, by those powers which control the artistic life of the city, to be void of any virtues which the proletarian might emulate or respect.

Yet despite its outward glumness, I found that Moscow had yielded to no spirit of resignation. With its loins girded for the severest battle in its history, it fairly roared with effort and determination. Streets were torn up; old buildings were being wrecked and new ones erected; fleets of trucks and automobiles clattered and honked along the avenues; piles of brick and stone cluttered the highways; dust from the building processes rose in clouds; tumult and excitement reigned everywhere, and people moved about with unwonted briskness. Perhaps the most astonishing change in the city was the comparative absence of beggars in its streets. For ages they had been an integral part of the very landscape of Moscow, and now with numbers of them absorbed in industry or picked off the streets, their ranks had thinned so perceptibly that one almost missed them.

Moscow spurted with a new energy that was almost desperation. It had clutched time by the throat, so to speak, in the hope of disciplining it to its own far-flung uses and missions. Work, construction, the machine — these were its new deities, and fiercely it exacted unswerving allegiance to them. It had no use for anyone who would not bring them his best gifts. It never before had been so brutally intolerant of the doubter, the intruder, the laggard, of everyone who would not forget the rest of the world and himself, even his very soul, and push on with this work, this construction, this machine — the biddings of these new gods. The five-year plan in four — this was the new slogan and the new ambition, and from hundreds of posters and banners floating from buildings, plastered on corner posts, staring from street cars, stuck onto automobiles, the words flashed their imperious message. Anybody who questioned the wisdom or the possibility of packing a generation of industrial development into four years, an enterprise so gigantic that the mere thought of it made one's head swim with wonder and dismay, was an opportunist, a defeatist, a deviator, a traitor, a blackguard, a counter-revolutionary — anything but a true soldier of the Revolution and of the one and only cause. Whoever he was, whatever his past, however long and faithfully he may have worked for this cause and for the proletarian advance, if he doubted now he was only an obstructionist, of no account, to be ruthlessly struck down and brushed out of the way.

The newspapers made one think of war. They were speaking the language of war — of an industrial front, an agricultural front, of battles for grain, for vegetables, for meat, for coal, for oil, for steel, for cotton, for tractors; of shock brigades, of light cavalry attacks, of militant discipline, of campaigns, of Red offensives. They flared with resolution. They thundered for conquest. They cried down the least hint of relaxation. They fumed at explanations of mistakes or failures. They raved against objective conditions and uncontrollable causes. They clamored for results, for advances, for conquests along the whole socialist front.

News and discussions of purely human import they cast out of their columns. Even the section dealing with court trials, which often reflected poignantly the great drama which Russia in these days of social transformation is enacting, disappeared. Foreign news, unless of immediate relation to Soviet politics or to the revolutionary movement or bearing on the big battle at hand, was either ignored or tucked into a remote column on an inside page. The *Komosomolskaya Pravda,* the daily journal of the Communist Youth, the one public organ that would occasionally skip away from Communist piety, break into a laugh or make a wry face at its over-sedate elders, now had no place for laughter and fun. Discussions of the personal problems of youth in these days of violent social change, which had always been a priceless feature of its columns, had been abandoned. It had no time for the drama and the problems of the individual man. It had time for nothing but the pro-gram of construction, the building of the big machine, the relentless socialist drive. Even more lustily than the *Pravda* or the *Izvestia,* it clamored for conformity to the Party line, for one hundred percent allegiance to the Party program and for the five-year plan in four.

All organs and institutions of culture were sum-moned to join in this crusade for an industrialized and socialized world. The theater, the ballet, the novel, the short story, the opera, the motion picture — all were commandeered for the great cause.

"Do you know why we outlawed Gipsy music?" asked the youthful and engaging director of the work-ers' club, "Kauchuk." "Because it has no relation to our five-year plan and to our construction program," he informed me earnestly. The *Rabochaya Gazeta,* in an account of the new plays of the Moscow Art Thea-ter for the ensuing year, pointed out with indignation that none of them took cognizance of the Party's build-ing program. In the dramatization of Uspensky's novel, *Rassteryaeva Ulitsa,* written at a time when the Rus-sian proletarian in the small town did not know whether Karl Marx was a new brand of herring or a rare chil-dren's disease, a proletarian character is made to stalk about the stage shouting revolutionary phrases in the manner of a Soviet-bred worker. The Moscow ballet, too, hurried along with its special offering, " The Football Player," in which the inevitable tractor, a coal shaft and a derrick were parts of the stage setting, and which featured in its program a harvest dance, a coal dance and an oil dance, together with endless marching and physical-culture formations which in verve and brilliance fell far short of the amateur exhibitions of young physical culturists to be seen in any of the large city parks.

The Literary Gazette, official mouthpiece not so much of as for the literary world, preached incessantly of the duty of writers in these days of trial and battle. Writers were to devote all their talents to the Socialist offensive. They were to glorify the nobility of the proletarian and the grandeur of his cause. They were to indulge in no portrayal or analysis of human character which was not calculated to advance the success of this cause. The *koolack* and the private *entrepreneur* they were to depict solely as political foes deserving and meeting utter defeat. They were not to bother with the purely human vicissitudes and the personal tragedies of such outcasts unless these happened to fit into the scheme of proletarian supremacy. Writers were not to endow enemies of the proletarian with personalities which might win the reader's sympathy, but were to portray them as lacking any redeeming virtues. In every respect literary creations were to be rigorously utilitarian, rigorously partisan, rigorously schematic, and, like so many American motion pictures, all were to end in the glorified triumph of the hero, the one and only hero in the world — the proletarian!

Everything and everyone were to be drafted into the service of the proletarian Leviathan. There were to be no exceptions. There was to be no leave. As in war, there was to be fierce discipline of man's thoughts and acts, with no mercy for the noncomformist, the doubter, the objector, the deserter.

The men in command of this historic battle were as hard as the steel and the coal that they worshiped. Queues and food rations failed to dismay them. They spoke a grandiose language. The peasant, they confessed, had, through his ruthless slaughter of stock, struck a fierce blow at them and their plans; but in two or three years, when the stock-raising program on the socialized land, in the *kolhozy* and *solhozy*, had been achieved, the shortage of meat and fats would be overcome for all time. Russia, they assured themselves and their followers, was on her way to becoming the leading food mart in the world. Already the *kolhozy* alone had under cultivation as vast an area of land as had both France and Italy. With the aid of the tractor they would speed up socialization and would break into use millions of fresh acres, for wheat, for cotton, for tea, for flax, and for other much-needed crops. Their tractors, these leaders pointed out, were continually increasing in number. Now they had sixty thousand in operation; next year they proposed to increase the number to one hundred thousand, and the year after to a quarter of a million. To ensure realization of their spectacular program they would even make Russia independent of other nations for her great agricultural machines. With the Stalingrad tractor factory almost finished, with the one in Kharkov begun, and another in Cheliabinsk, Siberia, risen to its foundation, Russia would in time attain an annual output of one hundred fifty thousand tractors in these three factories alone, a record which no other nation could rival. Nor would any other nation be able to match Russia in the manufacture of agricultural combines when the factories in Rostov and in Novo-Sibirsk, the capital of Siberia, were finished and could fling out yearly the fifty thousand machines they were scheduled to produce.

On the industrial front, these commanders affirmed, equally great triumphs had been achieved. The Turksib railroad, already laid out, was opening for exploitation a vast new world of fertile lands and mineral riches in Central Asia. Dnyeprstroy, the largest electric dam in the world, was pushing on to completion. The Ford plant in Nizhny-Novgorod was rising higher and higher above ground, and the socialist city which was to surround it had also attained to an impressive stature. Magnitostroy, in the wilderness of the Urals, a steel city planned to outstrip Gary, Indiana, was likewise begun, and so were other projects of lesser size though of equally momentous significance. With these ambitious schemes of industrial and agricultural development launched and others in prospect, with universal education in view, with hundreds of new schools and colleges linked directly to the factory and to the farm, and with socialized dining halls, nurseries, club-houses in the very forefront of the Party's program, the Revolution, these commanders boasted, was pushing onward into gigantic strides to its ultimate destiny. And Stalin allowed himself the luxury of the following peroration:

" We are marching full steam ahead on the road to

industrialization, to socialism, leaving behind our age-old Russian backwardness. We are becoming a nation of metal, of motors, of tractors, and when we have placed the Soviet Union in an automobile and the peasant on a tractor, then let the esteemed capitalists of the world who so proudly vaunt their civilization attempt to catch up with us. We shall yet see which lands will merit the designations ' backward ' and ' advanced.' "

When one sees in Moscow's streets the multitudes waiting in queues for food, the spell cast by Revolutionary rhetoric fades, and one faces the sinister force behind it — the brutal intolerance of differing opinion that has banished hundreds of honest doubters and non-conformists to far-away parts of the land, or to fates even worse. Then the bright promise of tomorrow fails to lighten the gloom of today, and one asks himself again and again, Why this haste? Why the five-year plan in four? Why not in six, in seven, in ten? What nation ever had sought to achieve so ambitious a program under such crucial circumstances in so short a time? Why this relentless drive of a people who never had known speed, who are only now discovering the machine, and who need time to familiarize themselves with it and to attain mastery over its intricate workings? Why not a more leisurely pace, instead of this breath-taking forced march to the socialist land of promise?

I turned for enlightenment to persons of importance. I shall relate my conversation with one of them, who voiced the sentiments of the group that is at present in power.

" Every animal," he began, " has its sense of smell

which warns it of dangers ahead. We have our sense of smell, our class-consciousness, which warns us of dangers ahead."

" Just what dangers? " I demanded.

" First, boycott. The attempt to stop our exports tells its own story. There can be no double meaning to this attempt. If we cannot sell, we cannot buy, can we? That is the simplest law of economics, and the time may come when we shall be barred not only from selling but from buying in the outside world. Yes, even America may not want to sell us anything — not an engine, not a bolt, not a nail! That's why we must hurry, buy while the buying is good and build as fast as we can, no matter what the sacrifice! Do you suppose we are ascetics? Of course not. We believe in ample living. We'd like to keep for ourselves the caviar, the butter, the eggs, the cheese, the jams, the canned fish that we have been exporting. But we dare not. Everything that can fetch a price abroad must be sent out, if we can scrape along without it — everything. Every scrap of iron that we import from a foreign land is so much gain, so much triumph. Tomorrow the bars may be up and no more goods offered us on the international market; instead, the thunder of guns may be crashing down upon us."

Hearing words like these, one is at first amused, then dismayed and terror-struck as he realizes with an overwhelming shock how earnestly Moscow believes them. It is well enough to reason that, in view of the economic slump the world over, the deliberate repudiation of Russian trade is unthinkable, and the possibility of an armed crusade against the Soviets even more remote. But Moscow, with its hypertrophied class-consciousness, cannot and will not read any other meaning into the efforts to stop imports of Russian coal and lumber to America, and into the world-wide cry of alarm over Russian dumping. Deep down in their hearts perhaps the Moscow Communists do not regret this outbreak of ill will against the Soviet Union, for it confirms them in their pet obsession that the capitalist world wants to draw Russia into combat — that it is only awaiting a favorable hour to strike the first blow. Expecting this blow, Moscow is determined to fight back with telling effectiveness, and is seeking to set her agricultural and industrial house in order, so as to make herself independent of outside markets as rapidly as the best engineering talent in the world and the regimented effort and sacrifice of the nation can achieve the result.

I do not mean to imply that other considerations do not count in Moscow's feverish haste to achieve industrial self-sufficiency. The sheer momentum of the Revolution with its call to battle, the conflict within the Communist Party over the tempo of industrialization, the determination of the ruling group to justify its policies, the very character of the leaders of this group, who, like Peter the Great, are not concerned with human values in the struggle to attain their ends — all these factors must be considered for a proper comprehension of Moscow's state of mind. But it is the boycott that she fears most; it is this specter which goads her leaders into a determination to speed their plans to fruition, regardless of costs.

VI

BEYOND THE PALE

A PART from the official world with its tumult about the five-year plan, international boycott, outside attack, inter-Party strife, are the thousands and thousands of houses in Moscow, crowded one- and two-room apartments in which life flows on and on like deep water in a stream that is constantly whipped up by storms. In this undercurrent of the city, life is quickened by conflicts of a different kind — personal and temperamental. Heart-searchings, such as people in other lands hardly ever face, constantly beset the dwellers in these houses and make Moscow, more than any city in the world, a stage of never-ending dramas.

In one of these apartment houses on a side street lived Natasha, student in an engineering *technicum,* whom I had known for several years. Soon after my arrival in Moscow I went to call on her. I mounted the three flights of dilapidated stairs to her door and rang the bell four times — Natasha's ring. The door opened, but instead of Natasha there appeared a smiling freckled-faced girl with bobbed hair. She wore an apron, and soap suds dripped from her hands. She told me that Natasha's health was bad and that she had gone to a sanatorium in the Caucasus. Brimming, Russian-like, with hospitality, she invited me to come in, and ushered me into Natasha's room, which she was now occupying. It was a small room, clean and freshly papered, with a bed, a couch and two hard chairs. Several of the wooden boxes which Russians use for suitcases were piled on top of one another in a corner; the walls were hung with rows of photographs and with pictures of Lenine, Stalin, Gorki and Tolstoy.

After a moment the girl excused herself and dashed out, to return presently without the apron, her hair combed, her freshly powdered face flushed with excitement. She had been doing her washing in the communal kitchen, she explained, but she was glad of an excuse for a respite. With the disarming frankness which is so innately Russian she narrated to me bit by bit the story of her life. Her name was Tanya, and she would soon be nineteen years of age. She had come from a small town in the interior; she was the daughter of a school teacher who had been a revolutionary in the old days and had suffered exile. On graduation from high school she had come to Moscow, where she was now working in a candy factory. Her ambition was to enter a medical institute, specialize in children's diseases and practice somewhere in an industrial section or in a *kolhoz*. Natasha she had met at a regional *Komsomol* conference, had entertained her in her home, and regarded her now as one of her best friends. She expected Natasha back in about a month.

As we were talking, neighbors who lived in the same flat came into the room, and Tanya introduced me to them. We conversed for some time, and as I was leaving a certain Maria Lvovna, a woman in the thirties with big brown eyes and a wealth of black hair combed straight back, invited me to call at her home some evening. Her husband, she told me, was an official in a

Soviet trust. She was a physician. Both she and her husband, she assured me, would be pleased to have me spend an evening with them. Shut off from the outside world, seldom even reading foreign journals, they would be so happy to hear from someone who actually lived in this world — what life and people and conditions there were like. I made a half-hearted promise to come, and in the rush of affairs in the days that followed hardly gave it a thought.

One evening I received a note from Tanya. Maria Lvovna, she wrote, invited me to come to her home the following Saturday evening. Her husband was to be there, as well as several friends — all people of interest whom she thought I would enjoy knowing. Tanya urged me to do my best to come.

On the appointed evening, therefore, I went to Maria Lvovna's. She lived in the same flat, almost next door to Tanya, in a large room that was tastefully furnished with two tables, a bed, several soft chairs and a sofa. The walls were hung with pictures, including two small oil paintings; decorative curtains were at the windows, and the floor was covered by a huge rug. A samovar sizzled pleasantly on its brass tray, and the table was set with jam, bread, butter, sardines, cheese — foods which, in spite of the acute shortage, some Russians manage to obtain. Her husband was visiting a neighbor and she immediately called him. He was a short man, of about the same age as his wife, with a thin face and thick gray hair, alert and cheery. Tanya came in, and one by one neighbors and some people from the outside dropped in, many of them without knocking. Among the visitors was a stubby man with a pock-marked face and earnest eyes. Nikolai Borisovitch was his name. He was of proletarian origin, I learned, and the only Party man living in this flat, which was occupied chiefly by members of the intelligentsia. He was director of a factory and seemed on intimate terms with his neighbors, joining eagerly in the conversation, especially in the barrage of questions on life in America. Were there abundant supplies of meat, sugar, butter, candy and white bread in American stores, they wanted to know. Were there ever any waiting lines? How expensive were clothes, shoes, silks, satins, woolens? How much did I pay for my shirt, my shoes, my suit of clothes? Were American women really taking to long hair and long skirts? And how expensive were automobiles — Fords, for example? When I told them the prices in Russian money at the official rate of exchange, they were beside themselves with surprise. The Communist and the others instantly agreed that if automobiles were as cheap in Russia as in America, most factory workers would buy them.

" *Nu, nichevo* "[1] the Communist remarked, " *dognat ee peregnat*[2] — that is our motto and our goal. When we reach it, then we too shall have everything."

" And when will that be? " someone queried.

" When? At the end of the five-year plan."

" Which five-year plan? " broke in Maria Lvovna.

" Which? There is only one."

" You mean there is only the first one," she suggested. " After the tenth or the fifteenth five-year plan, things may be glorious, but by that time we shall all have passed into dust."

" Then others will enjoy it. Must *we* have every-

---

[1] " No matter," or " Never mind."
[2] We shall yet catch up with and outdistance the capitalist world.

thing? Your grandfather never sat before an electric
light, as you do now. What does it matter? "

" Oh, nothing, nothing at all," said the hostess with
gentle irony, " especially as we shall be dead anyway."

Tanya now broke in with a volley of questions as to
the height of American houses, the speed of house
elevators, the prevalence of steam heat, the presence
of schools in factory districts, and a host of other
queries pertaining to the everyday life of the American
people.

" Don't be so impressed with America," the Communist warned her. " Don't forget the crisis there:
eight million people out of work, stocks in Wall Street
crashing, factories closing, world markets collapsing.
Moreover, colonial peoples throughout the world have
grown aggressive, and with guns in hand are driving
the imperialist exploiters, including the Americans,
from their countries. Don't you see," he pursued, ex-
pounding Communist dogma with increasing zest,
" America has reached the crest of her development, and
cannot rise higher under capitalist control. Henceforth
she must begin to disintegrate, and some day our valiant
tovarishtshui there will leap into power and make
America Soviet. All capitalist countries must eventually
break up and become Soviet."

" Nikolai Borisovitch," an unmistakably well-bred
middle-aged woman interceded, " for God's sake, don't
you ever tire of your phrases? "

" What do you mean, phrases? " he challenged. " It
is the truth. You all get so envious when you see a
comfortable looking foreigner. Supposing this man has
nice clothes and has bought them at a low price; can
the American proletarian buy such clothes? Ask him.

Sometimes perhaps he can. But what of the eight millions out of work? The *Pravda* had a long article on the American crisis, and it told a lot about the strikes and conflicts that are spreading there. *Nichevo,* the revolutionary wave is rising higher and higher even in America."

"Rising and rising," commented the middle-aged woman deprecatingly, "and never spilling over. What's holding it back? Did the *Pravda* say anything about that?"

"The social patriots, of course," the Communist flashed back, "they are holding it up, the renegades. But *nichevo,*" he went on cheerfully, "things will happen even in America. Capitalism is in its last stage of development; it must break down and die."

"All we know," interrupted Maria Lvovna, "is that up to the present things have been happening only here. I am a physician, and even I cannot obtain all the soap I need."

"Perfume you can get," someone blurted out.

"And why not perfume?" said the Communist. "In the old days the proletarian did not know what perfume was. Now a good many proletarians buy it. Some of the girls who work in our factory smell of perfume when they come to work, and it is not bad. That is progress."

"Now, *tovarishtsh* American," Tanya turned to me, "what do you think of a revolution in America? Would you say there is really no prospect of it?" Before I had time to say a word the Communist burst in with a question of his own.

"You are not a Party man?"

"No."

" And of what political shading are the journals in which you print your articles? "

" None," I replied. " They are literary and non-political."

" What do you mean, non-political? " he contested with impatience. " There is no such thing as non-political; everything anybody says and writes is political, is derived from a definite class consciousness or class orientation. These journals are not Communist? "

" No."

" Well, then it is clear; they are capitalist, and express the capitalist viewpoint; and you writing for them need to harmonize your ideas with this viewpoint, or in other words support the viewpoint of the master class. Don't you see, *tovarishtsh* Tatyana," he turned to the girl, " that he would deny that there is a revolutionary wave in America? "

" But you have not been there, and this man has just come from there," someone remarked.

" I have not been in India either, but is there not a revolution in India — a bourgeois revolution, but a revolution just the same? "

" India is different."

" Of course it is. India has a Gandhi and America has a Ford. A big difference."

The woman laughed.

" *Akh,* Nikolai Borisovitch, how glib of tongue you have become! " It was evident that she and the Communist were in perpetual disagreement.

" What do you mean, glib of tongue? " he replied with indignation. " Think for yourself. Ford is a builder of factories, helps swell the ranks of the proletariat and is therefore bringing the world closer and closer to the day when the proletariat will bring humanity the redemption it needs. But Gandhi is only an idler. He would destroy all factories, keep a proletariat from developing, and hold the world in perpetual darkness. There now."

" You surely have crammed up on your catechism," complimented Maria Lvovna's husband, " I congratulate you on your studiousness."

The Communist was visibly pleased, but said nothing.

" And you really don't believe that a Revolution in America must come? " Tanya persisted.

" You silly girl," said Maria Lvovna, " can you imagine a revolution in a country where there are no waiting lines in shops and where meat and bread and cheese and butter and sugar and candy and dry goods can be obtained in abundance everywhere? "

" Don't forget the eight million unemployed, Maria Lvovna," the Communist exclaimed.

" Have you lemons and oranges in America, too? "

" Yes."

" And here there is not a lemon or an orange to be had," the middle-aged woman broke in bitterly.

" There will be, there will be," the Communist assured her, " and all of us will be able to buy them. In America they have these things, but only the rich can enjoy them. The proletarian does not know what oranges and lemons are, excepting perhaps when he is sick."

" How do you know all this? " the woman questioned impatiently.

" Well, read Upton Sinclair and see what he says about the life of the American proletarian. You will get another side of the picture. It cannot be otherwise in a land where there is exploitation, can it? The other day I read in the *Pravda* that the American government is asking the farmer to reduce his wheat acreage by 25 percent. That means less income, and therefore greater distress for the farming population. And when they have a surplus in America, what do they do? Dump it into the ocean so as to stabilize prices. Imagine dumping fruits, and other things which people might use, to the fish! And they burn corn for fuel, too, so as to get rid of it. It is clear that under capitalism there is always economic anarchy, and under socialism, economic integration and rationalization. That is why under capitalism you have on the one hand storehouses packed with goods and produce, and on the other, millions of people unable to make use of it because they are poor. . . ."

"And under socialism," someone added, " we have nothing anyway."

"No storehouses and no goods," someone else remarked.

"Wait, wait. Have patience! " the Communist insisted.

"Until the end of the five-year plan," said Maria Lvovna. Everybody, including the Communist, chuckled.

Thus, with much drinking of tea and eating of excellent sandwiches, the conversation flowed on and on, touching subject after subject, livened up now and then by a merry exchange of banter between the Communist and the others.

Later in the evening we were joined by two other people who lived in this flat, Grigory Mikhailovitch, and his wife, Sofya Fyodorovna. He was tall and slender, with a stooping back, thin lips, and a receding chin. He appeared crestfallen. His wife was a small vivacious-looking woman. They had just come from the street, and their clothes were glistening with particles of rain. Both, I learned, were literary people, he a writer and she on the editorial staff of a coöperative publishing house.

"Let us start this conversation about America all over again," Sofya Fyodorovna suggested, when I told her that earlier in the evening the questions she was putting to me had already been answered in considerable detail, with objections and amplifications and corrections on the part of Nikolai Borisovitch.

"You must at least give me an American cigarette," she said gayly.

I told her that the supply I had brought with me had already been used up.

"*Nu,* Nikolai Borisovitch," she joshed the Communist, "if your American proletarian would do something about that revolutionary uprising that is supposed to be spreading in the world, we could at least get some decent cigarettes."

"*Nichevo,* Sofya Fyodorovna, don't despair."

"But cigarettes — that is such a small thing. It's really a disgrace," she continued with good-humored irony. "All these capitalist nations have cigarettes to burn, and their revolutionary proletarians are not making the least effort to lay their hands on them and send them to us. Isn't that disgraceful, Nikolai Borisovitch?"

"Wait, Sofya Fyodorovna; it won't be long now. We'll have cigarettes and everything else," the Communist solaced her.

" After the five-year plan," someone volunteered, and everybody chuckled.

The conversation went on in a gay, friendly fashion, with Sofya Fyodorovna, bright and pleasant and brimming with humor, turning arguments into jests and parodies that amused even the Communist. Only Grigory Mikhailovitch was silent. He was not even drinking his tea. The conversation passed by him without stirring any perceptible response. He did not seem to hear the quibs and laughter. He sat huddled over the table as though he were cold, sunk in reflection. Once his wife turned to him and said:

"Cheer up, my dear, tomorrow is meat day, and what is more, at my office we have been promised cigarettes — a good brand, too."

" I hope they keep their promise; that will be something," he replied glumly, and lapsed into silence again. The others, however, carried on the conversation with unabated zest. They had touched on the subject of the past winter's crusade against private property, and the methods resorted to by Party men and officials — sordid stories most of them were.

There was a famous physician's widow who was so frightened when the brigade of searchers invaded her apartment that she jumped out of the window. There was a girl whose father could not pay the tax that had been levied on him. All her possessions were confiscated, including her bed, which, according to the law, was not supposed to be taken. There was a well-known merchant's son whose wife was on the point of giving birth to a child. The husband went to the chairman of the house committee, a former janitor of his, with the request that they be allowed to remain in the apartment long enough for their baby to be born. Whereupon the former janitor replied: " Citizen L —— , all these years you have been drinking our blood; now it is about time we drink a little of yours." There was the wife of an employee, a non-Party man, who had all her dresses, all her bedding, all valuables, including her wedding ring, seized and confiscated. There was the regulation ordering non-citizens to bring gold with them if they wished to have gold fillings made for them by dentists. Story after story, all emphasizing the mercilessness of the Russian revolutionaries in their attacks on their enemies. The Communist listened without perceptible annoyance. He neither denied nor affirmed the stories. He seemed not especially interested. Now and then he said " Yes, there might have been abuses, with the searching brigadiers exceeding their powers. They were not supposed to do these things."

" Why, then, weren't they stopped at once? "

" The authorities didn't know of it." His answer evoked general laughter.

" You have the courage to tell us that," chided the middle-aged woman, " when all these depredations took place right under the nose of the Kremlin! "

" Have it your way," said the Communist calmly. " I say the Kremlin did not know the details; when it learned of them it brought the guilty men to account."

" Ah, the things those brigands did! " someone else exclaimed. " Bozhe moy," [3] what a nightmare! People were put out into the street with no place to go to for shelter — and their children too — No pity, no human feeling. And the dekoolackization in the villages —

3 " My Lord! "

what a horror that was! The whole thing was like a
nation-wide pogrom, that's what it was."

"Now, please don't use such strong language," the
Communist for once spoke with resentment. "We
didn't kill anybody except when we were attacked."

"Yes, it is true, you did not dash babies' heads
against brick walls like the Old Black Hundreds,[4] and
you did not rip people's bellies open with butcher
knives. No, you did not do these things. But think of
the men and women and children whom your con-
fiscations and banishments have left without bread,
at the mercy of the winter and hunger?"

"Of course, it is revolution," Tanya interceded,
"and, sad as it may be, in a revolution opposing classes
do battle against one another."

"Of course!" the Communist interjected. "A revolution is no football game. It is fight to the death!"

"But is it not time to bring this fight to an end?
How long must it continue?"

"Yes — how long?"

"As long as we have enemies."

"So you'll keep on until your enemies are exterminated?"

"Why exterminated? Let them stop wrecking our
plans."

"Oh *tovarishtsh* Communist," the middle-aged
woman cried, "if only there is a God in heaven who
some day will give you Communists a dose of your own
medicine. How I'd like to be present and hear what
you'd have to say."

"Let God rest in his eternal peace," said the Communist.

---

[4] Reactionary Czarist organization.

Then something happened, so suddenly, so violently, that it left us all speechless. Grigory Mikhailovitch, who had said scarcely a word all evening, jumped to his feet, trembling, and shouted at the top of his voice:

"What are you all whining about? Why are you wailing like cats? What is the matter with you?"

We stared at him in astonishment; not even his wife was able to say a word.

"Get rid of your silly pretensions and your silly claims," he shouted again.

"What on earth do you mean?" Maria Lvovna at last found her voice.

"You all ought to know what I mean. You are not children. Tanya is right. This is revolution, class war, and it cannot stop."

"But all people have a right to live?"

"Not always, do you hear?" He pounded the table with his fists. His face went white and twitched convulsively. "All people, you say," he hurried on with a tremor in his voice as though he were on the verge of breaking into tears, "but you and I are not people. We are only worms. Once for all remember that."

"Oh, your crazy fantasy again," his wife chided him.

"Supposing we are worms," continued Maria Lvovna, "we have the breath of life in us and we are entitled to consideration."

"You are getting all the consideration you are entitled to," he snapped.

"Ask him," said his wife, "how he feels when I come home and tell him there is no meat to be had at the coöperative."

His wife's words seemed to enrage him. He raised his fists in the air and shook them above his head as he shouted once more so loudly that his voice snapped into a squeak.

" Damn your meat! Damn your soap! Damn your sugar! What right have you to demand anything, you or I? Worms have no rights."

His wife tried to calm him, but he brushed her aside. The Communist, in an evident desire to restore equanimity, also begged Grigory Mikhailovitch to control himself. Finally he sat down and relaxed.

Then one after another took him to task for letting his temper run away with him and for giving vent to such horrible thoughts.

" What a philosopher you have become all of a sudden," his wife chided him, " a new Nietzsche — Hear, hear! "

" Once we are born," said Maria Lvovna, "and have the breath of life in us, we have a right to our share of happiness."

Indeed we have," agreed her husband.

" Indeed, indeed! " several voices chimed in.

Suddenly Grigory Mikhailovitch was on his feet again.

" Who gave you that right — who? " he shouted, striking the table with his fist. " How much happiness did the *muzhik* or the proletarian have in the old days? Who ever thought of their rights? Who ever gave a hang about them? The proletarian was weak and he submitted, and exploiters rode on his back as on a camel. Now that he has power, of course he cares only for himself. All you moaners and grumblers make me ill! "

This time laughter greeted his words — rather forced

laughter, I thought, impelled by a desire to suppress an unpleasant situation and bring back an atmosphere of repose and cheer. But Grigory Mikhailovitch would not be muffled.

"How censorious he has become," said his wife. "Hearing him, you would think he never misses anything. If you are so disgusted with us, darling, what about yourself?"

"Do you suppose I am pleased with myself?" he answered. "All you empty-minded dreamers, you good-for-nothing phantoms — make up your minds that you do not count. You are good for nothing. You have no muscle, no blood, and no nerve. You are no good. None of us is. We are a cursed lot — worms, worms! Only in the way! Be glad that you have not been stood up against a wall and shot — "

"Hear him, hear him!" his wife interrupted in an effort to turn aside his intenseness. Her face looked troubled.

But he raced on, heedless of the interruption.

"If you are not satisfied, do away with yourself, blow your brains out. But for God's sake, don't weep, don't whine. It will do you no good and it only makes you contemptible. Let those who have strength live and rule and speak of rights. But you," he pointed at Maria Lvovna, at her husband at his own wife and at several others in the room, "you are dead. You are dead! You walk and eat and sleep, but you are dead. I am dead. We are all dead."

"I will not hear such language from you!" his wife protested, in tears.

"You had better hear it, all of you," he shot back

vehemently. "Hear it, and then for God's sake shut up! " He dashed out of the room. His wife, brushing the tears from her eyes, followed him, and Maria Lvovna, saying he might need medical attention, left also. A buzz of whispering stirred the room as everybody worried about Grigory Mikhailovitch and wondered what could have come over him. Never, his neighbors declared, had they seen him so wrought up, though he never had been of a cheerful nature, like his wife. In a few minutes Maria Lvovna returned. It was only a case of shattered nerves and over excitement, she said. Soon Sofya Fyodorovna also joined us, smiling reassurance. Grigory Mikhailovitch, she said, had gone to bed; in the morning, after a good night's sleep, he would be himself again.

We talked in little groups, and Maria Lvovna, fetching a freshly boiling samovar, poured more tea. I sat near Sofya Fyodorovna, and as she was passing tea and sandwiches to me she said she felt like apologizing for her husband. He was, she assured me, a delightful fellow, brilliant, kindly and genial. Only he had been having endless troubles with Soviet editors because of his apparent inability to infuse into his characters the kind of ideology that fitted the revolutionary spirit of the times. That very morning he had two stories returned, though the editor was lavish in his praise of the style and the plots. "He is a sensitive person," continued Sofya Fyodorovna. " These tilts with the editors disturb him greatly; he feels discouraged and regards himself as a failure. Otherwise he is such a charming man. You must visit us some evening; I am sure you'll find Grigory Mikhailovitch delightful."

Late at night I went home. As I walked along the deserted streets I caught sight now and then of posters and banners bearing the inscription " the Five-Year Plan in Four." The words now held for me a meaning which they did not have before.

VII

THE DAILY ORDEAL

MY chief objective, of course, was not Moscow but the old village where I was born, and its surrounding countryside. It was the effect of the socialist offensive on the peasantry that I wished to ascertain, and a few days later I was on my way to my ultimate destination. I reached the city of M—— early one morning, and learned that the train for the final lap of my railroad journey was not leaving until evening. Here I was, then, in this provincial town with a full day at my disposal.

But in Russia, if one has an interest in the passing scene, time never drags. In the midst of friends in a bustling metropolis, or among utter strangers in a mud-sunk hut out on the steppes, the physical surroundings may be oppressive, but the social panorama never is, for Russian humanity is always of absorbing interest, and never more so than in these days of stress and excitement over the collectivization of land and the five-year plan. Wherever you go, people are in a communicative mood. GPU or no GPU, they will talk, and with an intimacy and an eloquence that move and often overwhelm and charm no less. I was quite content, therefore, with the delay. I knew that there would be much to see and even more to hear.

I had spent some hours in this town seven years

before, on my first visit to Russia after the Revolution. Of its railway station at that time I wrote that it was " a wreck with only the front part held together, none too securely, by stalwart logs and manifold scaffoldings." Now it was completely rebuilt, and its immense waiting rooms with their huge windows, their cement floors and whitewashed walls were a joy to the eye. They were clean, too, with no paper, no remnants of food, or débris of any kind scattered about — and, miracle of miracles, there were but few flies! As always, masses of people were waiting for trains, most of them peasants, with teakettles, sacks of provender, and bundles of bedding piled around them. They sprawled on the benches, the floor, the doorsteps, the sidewalks outside, singly and in groups, some awake, some asleep, and, whatever their inner feelings, their faces showed no signs of disturbance. Well-booted, decently clothed, amply fed, they seemed comfortable and contented. Some of them were eating, food they had brought along, of course — raw salt pork, hard-boiled eggs, cheese, butter, home-made sausage, delicacies which could not be obtained in town, except in the open market and at atrocious prices. Some of them were smoking funnel-like cigarettes which they rolled deftly, using scraps of newspaper. Others gazed listlessly at the passing scene, read newspapers and pamphlets, or conversed with their neighbors. A group of them had gathered around a youth with a shaven head and were listening to his loud and animated reading of the program of the Commissary of Agriculture for the ensuing year. In a corner, squeezed in between a long table and the walls, another group surrounded a beggar with one blind eye and a wooden leg, who was playing an accordion and singing humorous limericks. Bursts of laughter and applause greeted his neatly phrased thrusts at the new rulers and their ways. Several soldiers and a GPU officer who were among the listeners, laughed with the rest at his parodies, perhaps not as boisterously as the others, but with evident enjoyment none the less. Outwardly at least, these crowds in the waiting room were in a holiday mood, without a care in the world, intent solely on having a good time.

Only when I turned to the buffet was I made aware of the desolation which the socialist offensive of the past winter had brought in its train. Except for a few pieces of herring, a plate of fly-specked cheese, a bowl of paper-wrapped candies and stacks of black bread cut in huge slices, its counters were bare. Only the enormous samovar, sizzling audibly, reminded one of the plenty of former times. Gone were the platters of cheese, the strings of sausage, the heaps of boiled beef and fried chicken, the white rolls, the pastries, the mounds of chocolate bars that only a year before crowded the buffet counters in every fair-sized railway station. Yet crowds of people were waiting in long lines to purchase what food there was. " Any biscuits? " I asked the attendant when my turn came. " Not one," he barked. Then, without waiting for an order, he handed me two slices of black bread on a plate, gave me a ticket for tea, and immediately turned to the next man.

I partook of the bread and the tea and went off to the post office behind the station to send a telegram to a friend telling him I would arrive the next morning. Here, as everywhere else, a long queue was waiting.

I obtained a blank, wrote out my message, and took my place at the end of the line. It moved with incredible slowness, for there was only one clerk on duty, and he was the whole post office. He sold the stamps, registered the letters, sent off the parcels, received and paid out postal saving deposits, accepted money orders, dispatched telegrams and sold stationery. Through the glass cage that separated him from the public, I could see him hard at work writing, blotting, figuring on the ever present abacus, clipping receipts with the scissors, counting and recounting change, pausing now and then to argue with a customer over the writing of an address or the wrapping of a parcel. The numerous official details required to complete each transaction did not of course speed up the service, and the many persons waiting to post parcels, the mailing of which in Russia is always a ceremonious affair, slowed things up still more.

A woman carrying a basket loaded with produce took her place directly behind me. She was large and heavy, with a moist red face and an open mouth through which she breathed audibly. She was restless, and kept straining her head from side to side impatiently, as if in the hope that this would somehow quicken the movements of the queue. Several times she asked me to hold her place for her as she stepped out to see if anything in particular was holding up the line. She talked continuously. She could not understand why so many people had come with parcels just at a time when she was in such a desperate hurry. That was her luck! She had left a three-months-old baby at home in charge of a six-year-old girl who was no more dependable than a kitten. For the past three hours she had been standing in line at the coöperatives and looking through the bazaars; in the meantime heaven only knew what had happened to the baby! Several of her neighbors in the queue commiserated with her and proceeded to tell of their own troubles. One had a husband whose heart was bad and who could eat only milk soup and rice. But the local coöperatives had been out of rice for weeks, so she was now sending money in a registered letter to a friend in Moscow, a Party man, in the hope that he could obtain rice there and send it on to her. A young woman with a flushed face and tragic eyes said that she was waiting there to send money to her father, a former merchant who had been exiled to a village in Vologda early that spring. As she spoke her eyes grew moist. The fat woman, catching my eye, shook her head dolefully and sighed. Soon these women were chattering with one another like old friends, though it was evident that they had never before met. I know of no place in the world, not even the hard coaches on Russian trains, where people get so intimately acquainted with each other in a short time, as in these endless Russian queues.

A loud voice at the head of the line suddenly silenced the babble of conversation and everyone listened to an argument which had flared up between the clerk and a customer. The customer, a broad-shouldered youth whose sun-baked face and workman's suit were equally besprinkled with lime, demanded everything necessary for a letter. The clerk gave him an envelope and a stamp, but no paper, explaining that he had none left.

"How can I write a letter to my mother if I have

no paper? " queried the youth earnestly. The clerk refused to answer. "Why are you sold out? " the youth demanded indignantly.

"How should I know? " said the clerk. "Ask my superiors." Meanwhile the line was held up and everyone in it bawled at the young fellow to move on. Slowly he turned around, shouted *Vreditel!* [1] at the clerk so loudly that everybody could hear, and walked away. The clerk, not disposed to tolerate such an insinuation, jumped to his feet, thrust his head out of the window and called after the youth.

"What sort of a *vreditel* am I? Shame on you for flinging such an insult at me." He turned to the waiting crowd as if for vindication, and continued, "I am forty-three years old. I sweat every day in this stuffy post office for forty-two roubles a month, and he says I am a *vreditel!* "

"Shame, shame," exclaimed several voices, and the youth, recovering his good humor, explained that he meant no harm, and had blurted out the word because he had lost his temper. The clerk, satisfied with the explanation, returned to his work, while the youth, smiling and blushing and as if in apology to the people who had heard him, admitted that he had used the epithet unjustly. I pulled out several sheets of paper from my brief-case and offered them to him. Instantly the eyes of everybody were on me and my brief-case, and I could hear the remarks: " Evidently a foreigner," " Sure, a foreigner," " What a beauty! " (meaning the brief-case). The girl whose father was in exile informed me that, being a foreigner, I did not have to wait in line, and several others, with that respect and

[1] Literally " damager."

generosity which Russians never fail to show to a foreigner, suggested that I go right up to the window; the clerk would attend to my wishes immediately, they assured me. That, of course, I knew. By showing his passport or his credentials, a foreigner in Russia can usually obtain instant service. But this time I refused to avail myself of my privilege. Since I had plenty of time it seemed to me that I might as well stay here and wait for further incidents.

Quiet ensued. The clerk continued to write and blot and compute on the abacus. Engrossed in his work, he often read the addresses on parcels, and even messages in telegrams, aloud to himself, which of course he was not supposed to do. But nobody resented this betrayal of privacy. What is privacy to people who, with little or even with no encouragement, turn their very souls inside out to a chance acquaintance?

In my preoccupation with watching and listening I failed to notice that my turn had come at the window. But my companions lost no time in reminding me of it. I disposed of my telegram, but I did not go out. The queue was now growing longer and longer and two of the latest arrivals, both women, were arguing heatedly over their places. I stationed myself in a corner and began to write letters. The proletarian youth approached me again and asked apologetically if I would oblige him with another piece of paper. When I offered it to him he did not depart. Instead he began to talk, or rather to ask questions, in the manner of Russians when they meet a foreigner. Where had I come from? What was I doing in town? How did I like the Soviet regime and the new building program? How was the revolutionary movement progressing in foreign lands? What was the foreign proletarian saying about the Bolsheviks? And how much did I pay for my brief-case; would I sell it if he paid me cash at once? Ah, what a brief-case! What leather, what workmanship! He had never seen one like it. But then, at the end of the five-year plan they too would have brief-cases like mine; perhaps even better ones; they would have everything in abundance and there would be no more waiting in line, for everybody would have his orders delivered at home — *Nichevo!* Only, people must have patience and forbearance and not complain too much.

As he was speaking, a basket-laden woman marched up to the clerk's window and took her place at the head of the line. In answer to the chorus of protests at her action, she explained calmly that she did not have to stand in line.

" What do you mean, you don't have to? " someone challenged angrily.

" Yes, what do you mean? " several others repeated.

" I am drawing out money from the savings department, and that I can do out of my turn," she retorted.

The clerk put his head out of the window and confirmed her words.

That ended the protests, but not the dissatisfaction. A woman near the end of the line raised a fresh complaint. She did not understand, she declared, why anyone should come to this particular post office to withdraw money, when there were scattered all over the city so many other places that paid out savings deposits. Several persons in the line agreed with her, and their comments did not escape the ears of the accused woman.

"What else could I do?" she said pleadingly. "I am on my way to Moscow with my sick daughter. I leave an order with the porter to buy two tickets for the hard coach, and he informs me that sleeping places in the hard coaches are all sold out; he can get us sleeping places only in the soft coaches he says, but that costs a good deal more. I have to get the money in a hurry. At the savings window in the waiting room there is a long line of people, so I come here." The explanation was unanswerable, and now, instead of censure, people had only words of sympathy for her.

Hardly had she gone when a little man, a hunchback with a wiry black beard and a protruding nose which imparted to his face a rabbit-like appearance, hurried into the room and dashed up to the service window in front of the queue. A volley of angry voices shouted at him to get into line, but he did not budge.

"I have brought money to deposit," he announced, "so why shouldn't I be waited on ahead of you?"

That seemed to be a satisfactory answer, for nobody made any further objection, though one man, speaking as if to himself, remarked that he did not see why any exceptions should be made for people with money to draw out or to deposit. Someone else felt called upon to explain that if such a ruling had not been made, people would not readily bring their money to the savings department; they would keep it at home, and that would be bad for the government, would deprive it of the use of all these sums.

"All these sums," muttered the original complainant, "these miserable pennies!"

"But," protested the other with feeling, "these

miserable pennies buy machines and tractors, and that is helping the five-year plan, isn't it? "

The man muttered something inaudible and dropped the discussion.

The queue now began to move more quickly, and it looked as if the interruptions might be at an end. This was reckoning without Russian realities, however, for soon the clerk's stentorian voice boomed out again.

" You haven't written a return address on your letter." He was speaking to a youth who wished to have a letter registered.

" Write it, then," said the youth, " village P——, district T——, section O——."

" Write it yourself," said the clerk. " Don't you see all these people waiting for me to attend to them? "

" But, *tovarishtsh*," the youth protested meekly, " I cannot write; I have never learned."

" You? " burst out the hunchback, " So young, too! What are you, a proletarian or a peasant? "

" I am a peasant."

" And you never went to school? "

" Never."

" Aren't you ashamed of yourself, when our government does so much to teach people, especially the young, to read and write? "

" But I'm not to blame? " the youth protested, his face red with embarrassment. " My father always wandered about from place to place, and when he finally settled down, it was in a village where there was no school."

" And where do you come from? "

" North, away up in Murmansk. There the Soviets

have not built as many schools as here in the city. The proletarian always gets the best of everything."

This was an unfortunate remark for a peasant youth to make in the presence of city people. It caused an instant commotion.

"You peasants," a woman burst out hotly, "you don't have to get the best of everything, you have it already — pork, butter, cheese, eggs, milk!"

"And you scrape the hides off us city people, proletarians or no proletarians," added another woman bitterly.

Others joined in, and excitement rose so high that even the clerk, who put his head out of the window and begged for order, could not quiet the crowd. Seeing this, the clerk did not insist; instead he lighted a cigarette and listened.

"Seven and eight roubles for a pound of butter, that's what the peasants are asking."

"Three roubles for ten eggs."

"Twenty-five roubles my neighbor paid for a little pig, and when she brought it home it died."

"And they cheat on the weights."

"And water their milk."

"The dirty cheats!"

"The militia ought to do something about it, arrest the rascals."

"The militia! They are too busy admiring themselves in their new boots."

The young man, speechless with perplexity and dismay, looked like a hunted animal. Only when the excitement had abated did he find his tongue.

"But you don't understand," he stammered out to the throng, "up north where I come from it is different. We haven't even enough bread. Things don't grow there like they do in these parts. We have only the fish that we catch."

Another youth, evidently city-bred, for he was smoking a factory-made cigarette, tried to reassure his countryman:

"*Nu,* when the land is collectivized, then there will be everything for everybody everywhere, even in Murmansk, and at low prices, too."

A loud guffaw from a tall man who was leaning on a cane greeted these words. So loud was this guffaw and so obstreperous that people turned their eyes on the man, and he, suddenly aware of the attention he had attracted, drew back as though conscious of guilt and fearful of punishment. That he was or had been a man of means — a merchant, a lawyer, a contractor, a man of repute in the town, was evident from his appearance, from the trim of his beard, the cut of his clothes, and the collar and tie he was wearing. The youth with the cigarette eyed him with stiff contempt and muttered something under his breath. But the man never even turned to look at the speaker.

"Well," said the hunchback to the boy, "give me your letter. I'll write the address for you; but you go to school. It is a shame for a young man like you in these days to be illiterate. If you live in this town, come to the *likbez* [2] of my union, we'll take care of you."

I left the post office and strolled into the street. The sun was high and warm and masses of people with their cumbrous bundles were streaming in and out of the station. Whence had they come? Where were they go-

[2] Illiteracy Committee.

ing? Why were people travelling so much in Russia these days? It was not autumn, when students start for school. It was not spring, the season when peasants from this region stream homeward from the city. It was the beginning of summer. Of course the constant call for new hands from the hundreds of factories under construction all over the country, accounted in part for this rush to the trains, but only in part. Something else was drawing people somewhere, everywhere; and whatever it was, the spectacle of them surging in masses to all parts of the country made one stirringly aware of the fresh waves of feverishness that had come over Russia.

I sauntered around the public square which spread apron-like in front of the railway station. On one side, within the shadow of a tumbling fence that was overhung by the tops of little trees, a long row of *izvoshtchiks* had stationed themselves. Their *drozhkys* were the most battered I had seen, with tops, bodies, and wheels patched and repatched until they looked as ancient and scrappy as the drivers themselves with their unshaven faces, their frayed and massive coats and their tattered boots. Several of them hailed me and offered to drive me into town, but I waved them aside, and stood facing them.

One of them asked for a cigarette, and when I gave it to him, the others — all of them, it seemed to me — hastily swarmed round begging for cigarettes. Luckily I had enough to go round, and as they smoked they launched into eager, heated talk. Times were bad for the *izvoshtchiks*, and they were much upset. The peasant, the proletarian, the office man, were living in security and knew one day where their bread would come from the next, but not the *izvoshtchik*. And why not? Because he had no friends — everybody hated him. The very Soviets who had come to succor the poor were snatching the last slice of bread from the *izvoshtchik*. For ages and ages he had handled all passenger traffic in that town, to the satisfaction of everyone; and now the Soviets had built a trolley, so that folk could ride all over the town for ten copecks — ten dirty copecks! As though there were not enough other things that the Soviets could build — bath-houses, children's homes, workers' clubs. Why did they have to start a trolley? And above all, why did they import buses that ran all the way to the suburbs and carried folk fifteen versts for twenty copecks? And now there was talk of a flock of taxis to be brought in the following year. What for? Did not *izvoshtchiks* have to eat? And every day prices were jumping higher and higher. If only bread had not been put on rations. The year previous they could buy enough for themselves and their horses, and it was so much cheaper than oats. But now one was allowed only enough bread for one's own needs, and the *izvoshtchiks* had to buy oats for their horses, at eight and ten roubles a pood. Where were they to get the money? People did not want to pay decent prices any more; they called the *izvoshtchik* "robber," "koolack," "damager," "counter-revolutionary." No respect, no tolerance, no sympathy — what a life and what a fate for an *izvoshtchik* under the Soviets! Of course the authorities proposed a way out — the one they were proposing to everybody they were ruining — the *kolhoz*. A new heaven it was, this *kolhoz*, for all sinners and all saints and everybody else. But an *izvoshtchik* was no *muzhik* and no shop-keeper and no loafer. He knew only his horse, his *drozhky*, the streets of the city and nothing else! What would he do in a *kolhoz?* This summer he might be able somehow to struggle along; but when autumn and winter came, what would he do?

I rambled on from street to street until I strayed into the big market place. Here life roared. Row on row of peasant carts with all manner of produce — butter, cheese, eggs, meats, vegetables, live chickens, live pigs — stretched from one end of the square to the other. City people, chiefly women with their omnipresent straw baskets, marched in an endless procession from cart to cart, feeling the produce with their hands, sniffing the meat and the cheese and the butter, dipping their fingers into things and sampling them. They asked for prices and tried to bargain with the peasants, but usually in vain. The latter stuck to their demands, and the city people snapped up the food eagerly, buying everything that was offered, from scabby old radishes to squealing pigs.

"Why are you asking eight roubles for a pound of butter?" I heard a pretty young woman ask a heavily moustached *muzhik* who was leisurely chewing away at his black bread and raw salt pork. "Over there is a man who is selling his for seven."

"Then buy from him," calmly replied the peasant.

"He has no more left," the woman remarked.

"Am I to blame for that?" chuckled the *muzhik*. "Do I control other people's lives? Do I tell you what to do and where to go? You are your own master, and I am mine. Do you understand, lady? I cannot sell butter for less than eight roubles a pound. Maybe the other man puts sawdust into his; how do I know?"

Without further protest the woman paid him his

price. " Children," she muttered to herself as if in apology, " must have butter."

" People are queer," pursued the peasant, addressing no one in particular and everyone who cared to listen. " If they'd bring soap, tobacco, kerchiefs, leather — for such things we could barter our goods. But no, they want to buy only for money, and they think that money nowadays is the same as it used to be, when you could buy a pair of soles for twenty-five copecks. Now you go to the shoemaker, ask him to put on a pair of soles on your boots, and he wants twelve roubles. In the old days, for twelve roubles you could buy two new pairs of boots. . . ." He turned to wait on freshly arrived customers.

Everywhere there was the same swell of excitement, the same exchange of pithy banter, interspersed with words of acrimony and contempt. The peasants of course were impervious to sharp language. They would have their price or they would not sell.

Above the tumult a voice boomed angrily: " Swine! You swine! Get away from here, get away." The speaker, an elderly, bearded peasant in heavy boots, was standing on his wagon, pushing back a throng of buyers with his hands. They protested vehemently, but he would not listen to them. " Get out! " he shouted. " I have nothing more to sell, nothing. I'll take every-thing back home and dump it into the pig pen. Get out, I tell you! " He seized a hand that was exploring the straw of his cart and thrust it out. Then he spread out his arms and forbade anyone to touch anything in his wagon.

" Come, grandfather, don't be foolish," a passerby chided him.

" Foolish, foolish," he grunted in anger. " Two

cheeses they have already ruined with their mauling, and the other day they broke half a dozen eggs. Who is the loser? I am. They must dig their dirty hands into everything and break it — the swine! Get out! " he roared afresh. " I'll sell nothing, nothing more! I'm going home."

Some of the women evidently knew him and sought to flatter and coax him out of his ill-humor. They praised his cheese, his butter, his eggs, above all, his fair-mindedness. Gradually the flattery and entreaties mollified him and he told the women that if they would line up as they did in a coöperative store and promise not to push and thrust one another aside, he would resume trade. They agreed, but he would not rise from his seat until they had actually carried out his wishes.

To me it was an amazing spectacle. A mere *muzhik,* perhaps illiterate, enforcing his own discipline on city women in full view of crowds of people. In the old days he would have been so obliging and apologetic that he hardly would have dared to speak above a whisper to women out shopping in the bazaars. And now . . . how desperately times had changed!

In another part of the bazaar a crowd was storming at a peasant who had brought several live geese to market, and still further on another crowd had lost its self-control and with harangues and shouts was pushing against a cart in which a middle-aged peasant woman sat. She had just arrived with three live pigs and everybody wanted to buy them, each offering the price she demanded. Everybody, in fact, was thrusting money toward her, and she did not know whose money to take. Frantic with distraction, she pleaded with them to control themselves, and wait until she could attend to them. But they clamored for the pigs, flourishing their money before her eyes, pigs to supply the fat that everybody wanted for seasoning potatoes and *kasha* and soups. Frightened and overcome with perplexity, the woman did not know what to do. Her voice trembled and her hands seemed paralyzed. Presently a man came to her aid. Forcing money into her hands, he helped himself to one of the pigs. Two women did likewise, and the crowd dispersed as quickly as it had gathered.

I felt someone nudging me. It was a tall peasant with a swarthy face, enormous moustaches and good-humored heavy-lidded eyes. He excused himself for intruding, but explained that he thought I was a foreigner and just wanted to make my acquaintance. I followed him to his cart, where, with a flow of exuberance he proceeded to tell me of the respect that he had always had for foreigners. He knew something of them, for during the War he was a prisoner in Germany for three years, one in a military camp and two on a farm in Westphalia. He used to go to market in Westphalia. People were so different there; they didn't push, they didn't shout, they didn't grab; they were cultured, not like dark-minded Russians.

He stuck his hand into a linen sack and brought out a handful of dried pears which he offered to me with an apology for not having a more worthy gift for " a foreign guest." Or perhaps I was hungry? He had bread, pork, pickles, and would gladly share them with me. Then, growing more intimate, he confided that he was through with the bazaar. Never again would he take his produce to any bazaar. The devil was in the bazaars. Everybody was cheating everybody else there.

Was it not insane for peasants to demand, and for city folk to pay, eight roubles for a pound of butter? But the peasant was not to blame. The other day he wanted to buy a raincoat for his wife, and how much did I suppose they asked for one in the open market? Seventy-five roubles, and in the coöperative the same coat was selling for sixteen. The manager of the coöperative had told him that if he would bring eggs, butter and meat, he could get goods in return for the full amount of his produce, and he would not have to wait in line. He had a pig at home weighing ten poods, and he would take it straight to the coöperative. Why, in the open market a kilo of sugar was eight roubles, and at the coöperative, only eighty-three copecks; a pair of boots in the open market cost seventy-five roubles or more, and in the coöperative, only twenty or twenty-five. He was through with the open market, where people were just skinning each other.

Several women approached, and without even asking whether he had anything for sale, thrust their hands into the straw of the cart in search for possible produce. When they moved on he laughed and shook his head in disapproval. " They don't behave like that in Westphalia. *Akh,* people are so polite there! "

Continuing his confidences, he informed me that he was a *primak,*[3] had married a woman with a home of her own and gone to live with her. They had five children and were a happy family, though only two of the children were his. Ah, if I would only pay them a visit! Would I? They would all be so happy to entertain me for a week, a month — as long as I cared to

---

[3] A man who, at marriage, goes to live in his wife's house and assumes charge of her household.

stay. Of course their home was no palace. They were not landlords. But his wife was an excellent house-keeper; he had taught her a few things that he had learned in Westphalia, and they kept their house clean. They had their walls papered and hung with pictures, and no pig or chicken ever crossed their doorstep. Never. Animals were kept in their proper place, out-side, just as in Westphalia.

"You would like our home," he raced on with in-creasing eagerness, "you would enjoy my family, my wife and my children, and I want to tell you that we have things — meat, milk, eggs, pickles, dried fruit, even white flour, all our own. Please come."

I assured him that much as I should like to avail myself of his invitation, it was impossible, as I was scheduled to leave that very evening for a different part of the country. He was visibly disappointed.

"Well," he suggested after a lengthy pause, and with that friendliness and humility which makes the Russian peasant as touching and lovable a person as there is in the world, " if you cannot come now, maybe you can some other time. We'll have so much fun to-gether, and it will be interesting for you to see our village and make the acquaintance of the people there. Come on a Sunday if you can, and see how our folk dress. Oh, peasants protest and whine and say they have nothing, but you should see the way our girls dress up on Sunday. You would never think they were peasants — soft-leather shoes and rubbers, satins even, and silks."

Then he shifted to a more serious subject.

"There is a *kolhoz* in our village," he went on gravely, "but I haven't joined it, and I am bothered

a lot as to what I should do. Of course I am very
happy as I am. We have seven dessiatins of land, two
cows, this horse, twenty-five hens, six sheep and three
pigs, and we work our land not like other *muzhiks*
but with sense and system, just as a *Bauer* in Westphalia would do. I earn something on the side, too,
playing the accordion. I play quite well. Once I hear
a tune I can play it right off. I am besieged with invitations to play at weddings. But I have to be cautious,
or the Soviet might say that I was making too much
money, that I was a *koolack,* and, citizen, I'd rather
be dead than be branded as a *koolack* and run the risk
of being banished with the family to some God-forsaken
forest in the north. But I won't be caught. I won't
give them a chance to call me a *koolack.* I'd never hire
an outside person to work for me even if all my crops
were to rot in the field. I am a literate man. I read the
papers and pamphlets. I know what is going on in this
country, and I have learned to keep just within proper
limits. Do you suppose that I couldn't keep four cows?
Of course I could. But I only have two, and in the
fall I'll sell one. I am safer with one. But this *kolhoz* —
the devil knows what is going to come of it. The local
Soviet people give me no rest. They say they must
have me in the *kolhoz.* I could establish order and discipline, and make it go. But I hate to give up my independence. I am so happy with my family now. *Akh,*
if you would only come, so that we could all get together and talk it over at length! Please do try to
come sometime this summer. We shall be so pleased,
so honored! "

Sauntering about the town late that afternoon, I
entered a coöperative restaurant. I thought of eating

dinner there, but the crowds at the table and the closely packed queue at the door were not encouraging. I tried several other restaurants, but the same condition obtained everywhere, so I went back to the railway station. Being a transit passenger I was entitled to special consideration in the buffet, but I had not reflected that there were hundreds of others who deemed themselves entitled to the same consideration. However, I took my place in the far-stretching line to obtain my dinner checks from the cashier. Meals here were simple, they consisted of two courses, a vegetable or milk soup and either fish or *kasha*.[4] There was no meat and no dessert, but the price was modest enough, only eighty copecks. Tea could also be had, with plenty of sugar, at five copecks a glass.

The ordeal of obtaining the checks over, I hunted for a vacant seat. At last I found one at a table near a window. Two young men and a girl were occupying the other three chairs. The men kept their hats on, as did most of the people in the dining room, and they had brief-cases with them; evidently they were officials from the provinces. The girl, bareheaded and barelegged, was holding a parcel and an open book.

The three must have been trying for some time to attract the attention of a waitress, for one of them, as much in fun as in disgust, began to clang his pocket knife against the glass. Waitresses with red and sweaty faces, dressed in white gowns that were badly spotted with grease, scurried up and down between the tables, replying to impatient customers with the universal *ceichas, ceichas,* a word with an elastic or rather a variable meaning. Ordinarily it signifies " right away." Lit-

---

4 Gruel.

erally it means " this hour," and actually it means, " this or any hour today, tomorrow or some other day." At last a waitress favored us with her attention. She picked up the dishes left by the previous diners, brushed the spillings on the floor, took our checks and departed. Soon she returned with our soup, and then once more forgot us. We hailed her several times as she flitted by, but she dismissed us with her ever ready *ceichas*. Someone nearby then started beating with his spoon on a plate; other impatient would-be diners joined in, and presently the room was a bedlam of noises. One gray-haired man sitting at a neighboring table kept muttering to himself, but quite loud enough for us to overhear, " *bezobrasie, bezobrasie!* " [5] As a waitress was passing by, he seized her arm and shouted: " Why do you torture us like this? Why are you workers in social dining halls such callous bureaucrats? "

This particular waitress had evidently not yet learned to feel the sting of the word " bureaucrat," or else she had grown hardened. Quickly she wrenched herself loose, and dashed off to wait on people in the lower part of the room. Thereupon the man jumped to his feet, shoved his chair back violently, and muttering " Scandalous, scandalous! " flung out of the room with such a show of annoyance that half of the restaurant turned to stare at him. Two men rushed for his chair, a youth with a shaved head and a middle-aged man with a red face and a fluffy beard. The youth got there first, and the middle-aged man, after a searching survey of the room with his big, naïve eyes, took a place at the window immediately behind our

[5] " Shame! Shame! "

table and waited for another vacancy. Irrepress-
ibly loquacious, he turned to us and began straight-
away:

"There is no use getting impatient nowadays. A
man with no self-control, like the citizen who just
walked out in a huff, may in a moment of excitement
kill somebody or drop dead with a burst heart." There
being no reply, he drew away. Presently the two men
at my table could no longer restrain their indignation.
This lassitude, this disorder, this disregard for human
patience and human needs! It was a shame — and they
in such a hurry, too, to catch their train! They shouted
at a passing waitress, but she paid no heed. Then one
of them decided to go and give the manager a piece
of his mind. He soon came back, and shortly afterwards the manager himself, a little man with a bald
head sunk between his shoulders, brought two portions
of fish for the officials. "I told my *nachalstvo*,"[6] he
said, as if to justify himself, "that we needed more
help, but they pay no attention to me, so what can
I do?"

The officials hurriedly bolted down their food and
left, and the bearded man instantly jumped into one
of their seats. A woman with a huge shawl over her
head occupied the other. The man seemed to be in an
expansive, yet pleasantly informal, mood.

"If people only knew," he said as if pursuing the
vein of thought in which he had started earlier, "how
important it is always to be in full control of one's
impulses, they would be much happier than they now
are." He paused and looked at the woman and the
girl and me as if to ascertain whether we were com-

---

[6] Chiefs or superior officials.

panionable, and then continued: "Here I am, fifty-three years old. All my life I have been rushing about in search of happiness, always collecting things, more and more of them. Then came the Revolution and smashed everything, my belongings, my plans, my future. But one thing it left untouched — my disposition." He leaned over toward the girl as if to see what she was reading, but she never raised her eyes.

At last our waitress brought the orders for the girl and me. She set them down, picked up the checks of the newcomers, and was gone again. The man looked about the room which was now so packed that the gangways were all blocked and the waitresses had to shout to make their way through. Then his eyes rested on me and I could feel his fixed stare. Presently he asked me where I came from. When I told him he exclaimed:

"Such a long way from home, ah!"

Now of course I knew I was in for a volley of questions, and they came one after the other. Then as if out of a feeling that he owed me information in return for that which I had given him, he proceeded to narrate the story of his own life. He had once been an architect, a *samouchka*, self-educated. His father was a well-to-do peasant and lived in a village some fifty miles away. He had put up many a building of note on the estates of various landlords, but now his career was at an end. Day after day he sat at a desk, going over drawings and columns of figures and getting one hundred and thirty-five roubles a month. Once he had planned to go abroad and perhaps to travel in America and see something of the skyscrapers there. But all the travelling he now did was an occasional trip to his native village to buy flour, eggs, butter, meat. He did not even go to Moscow any more.

The waitress came up again at this point with his and the woman's soup, and both began eating with that rhythmic audibility which in Russia accompanies the consumption of all fluids. Suddenly he sat up as if struck by a startling idea. "*Da!*"[7] he exclaimed, pointing at me with his forefinger, "you are just the man to tell me something. The other evening some friends came to visit us, and we were talking about America. One of them said that he had read somewhere that Americans do not marry until late on thirty, thirty-five and even older. Is that true? "

" Quite often it is," I replied.

" Really? And I thought that it couldn't be true and argued that it wasn't. It seemed so impossible! Why do such people marry at all? " He stared at me as though expecting an answer, but I offered none. " Now here I am," he resumed, " I married at nineteen and now I have three children, all sons. Two of them are no longer at home — no use hanging around a father who cannot help them under a proletarian regime. One of them has almost disowned me; he is ashamed of having a father with a bourgeois past. He is a mechanic in the tractor factory in Stalingrad. He has not been home for three years and has even stopped writing letters, much to the distress of his mother. But he is still our son, and we have his picture on the wall! Do you understand? He still means a lot to us and he always will, whether he comes to see us or not. The other is away studying agriculture and he does keep up a more or less desultory relationship with us. He

7 " Yes! "

comes to see us once or twice a year, and we have his picture, too, on the wall. Then there is the youngest, about seventeen. He is still with us. Now supposing my wife and I had not married or had married late — she is fifty-two now and I am fifty-three — well, we should have each other, but that would be all, and at our age people might die from some unforeseen cause. Suppose then that one of us did die, can you not see how dismal life would be for the other? Children, citizen, good or bad, are the greatest boon in life. Have you a wife? "

" No."

" Ah! You know there is a Russian saying, ' Not married at thirty and rich at forty, your life is lost! ' "

" What rubbish," murmured the girl, looking up from her book.

The man eyed her resentfully.

" Rubbish! " he snorted. " ' Bourgeois ideology,' little girl, would have been a more becoming expression." Turning to me again he continued:

" And now the slogan is, ' If you are not ruined at thirty and dead at forty, you are no good anyway! ' "

The girl squirmed with indignation.

" Why are you spewing out this nonsense? " she cried reproachfully.

" Nonsense? Is that what it is? " he shot back with irritation.

" Yes, nonsense, revolting nonsense. You just admitted that you were fifty-three, much older therefore than forty, yet you do not look in the least ruined and you certainly are not dead. You can talk more nonsense than anybody I've ever seen."

" Haw, haw, what a girl! " and he laughed heartily.

"How old are you? " he asked her.

"Eighteen."

"A *Komsomolka?* "[8]

"No."

"A plain citizeness? "

"A plain citizeness."

"And a militant one! Well, well! "

The girl tired of the wrangle and returned to her book.

"Eighteen," repeated the man solemnly, "eighteen and she knows so much. She could surely tell us how many stars there are in the sky. They are all like that, these young people. Take my son, Vassily, my youngest. He is not yet seventeen, and the other evening as we were sitting down to tea he confessed to his mother that he was in love with the daughter of a neighbor, a railway engineer, and what do you suppose he told us he wanted to do? "

"Marry the girl? " ventured the woman.

"Nothing of the sort," replied the man with a grimace of exasperation. "Marry the girl! — Hm — If it was only that he wanted! But no, he asked us if he could bring her to the house and live with her. Imagine that! "

"Well, well, not so bad," remarked the woman with amused astonishment.

"We told him that it was impossible," he continued. "The boy is so young, with his whole future ahead of him — study, work, a secure position somewhere in this chaotic Soviet world. And our two rooms are so small, with such a tiny kitchen that when a sack of flour or potatoes is set down or an armful of wood

[8] Young Communist girl.

brought in my wife can hardly turn around. We argued long and earnestly with him and heaped reproaches on him, and what do you suppose he said? If we didn't agree to let the girl come, he would leave us, go off to Stalingrad, where his oldest brother is, take the girl with him, find work for both and live with her there. That's what he said."

"And what did his mother say?"

"Ah, his mother, she is on the verge of collapse. Of course she pleaded with him, put her arms round him, telling him in tears that if he ran away, she would die or go mad with loneliness. And she would, too; believe me, my dears, she would. Her whole life is wrapped up in the children, especially now that everything else we ever had, every hope and every ambition, has gone smash. Vassily is her idol — her youngest — and contact with him makes her, and me too, feel our other sons near again. When we see him or hear him speak, we seem to hear and see them too. And do you suppose he was much upset? Not at all! He was just indignant. It was only after his mother had cried her eyes out that he at last promised to go on living with us as he had been and never again to bring up the subject of the girl. But he may change his mind and carry out his threat and run away with her. Who knows? But certainly we won't let him bring the girl home. *Akh,* these children!"

He sighed and covered his eyes, as though to hide the surge of emotion that was shaking him. The woman and I exchanged glances but neither said a word, and the girl was so absorbed in her book that she seemed oblivious to the world.

The waitress reappeared with fish for the woman

and *kasha* for the man. The woman at once began to eat, but the man only looked at his food.

"Of course parents don't count any more," he resumed, "but thank God children do. Here they do," he said, striking his breast hard. He took a mouthful of food, then pushed his plate aside.

A priest who happened to be passing fixed hungry eyes on the uneaten food. He was humped and uncouth, his robe soiled and tattered, and his boots spattered with mud. In one hand he grasped a bent staff and with the other he held a sack slung over his back. He was muttering something which I could not hear, but the man did, and, indicating the *kasha* with a glance, he said, "*Poshaluista.*" [9] With a pathetic smile of self-abasement the priest hurriedly picked up the *kasha,* the bread, and the scraps of fish on the plates, rolled them all up in a piece of paper and tucked them into his sack. Then, crossing himself and bowing profusely, he slouched off.

Dusk was now setting in, but soon a flood of electric light splashed over the dining room. The time was drawing near for my train, and I parted from my companions. The crowds at the station were growing larger and more and more tumultuous. The ticket office had not yet opened — they never do in Russia until just before the trains arrive — but masses of people had already fallen into closely packed lines. They were orderly, for they were chiefly composed of peasants with an age-long tradition of patience and forbearance, and with no idea of the meaning of time. Pushing through all these people with their bulging boxes and bundles and baskets and the heavy smells of sweat,

[9] Help yourself.

sausage and leather, a porter led me out to the platform. My train was, he said, due at any moment. Since in Russia " at any moment " may mean anything from ten seconds to a full hour, I strolled down the platform to pass the time. On a side track among a row of freight cars were two bearing the label:

Perishable goods — *eggs*.
Destination, *Königsberg*.

VIII

"THE RETURN OF THE NATIVE"

AFTER a sleepless night on a train that chugged along at the speed of a trotting horse and shook like an ocean liner in a storm, I reached the town of S——, the last railroad stop on the way to my old village. There I lingered only long enough to exchange greetings with old friends and to make ready for the journey on foot to my final destination.

It was early afternoon when I started out and I had no more than struck the road, when I was conscious of being in a world that presented a joyous contrast to Moscow and the other cities I had visited. Here were no cobbled streets, no dispiriting lines of people, no dismal horizons. Here were quiet and brightness, cheer and promise and at every turn horizons alluring in their blueness. The sun was high and warm, the sky swept clean of the least clot of cloud. The larks had never seemed so numerous or so lively. Visible and invisible they were pouring out a rich flow of melody. The fields had assumed a festive appearance. Winter crops and spring crops had pushed high above the ground and spilled over into a sea of magnificence. All around were miles and miles of lowland sinking away into a blue void, nowhere was there a suggestion of neglect or desolation, everywhere there was only peace and cheer and promise of bountifulness.

I walked on revelling in the scene about me until, some miles out of town, I caught up with a barefooted boy who was carrying his shoes peasant-fashion on a stick slung over his shoulders. He wore no hat, and his hair was freshly clipped to the very skin. Under his arm in a ragged satchel he carried books. He was about twelve. He, too, had been in the town of S——, he told me, to receive a fresh supply of books for the library of the *kolhoz* on which he lived. We chatted of his village and of the *kolhoz* there, which his father had joined the previous spring, and then I asked him what he had planned to make of himself.

" An engineer," he replied.

" And why an engineer? " I questioned.

" So that I can build bridges, barns, factories and everything."

" And would you like to be rich? "

He laughed and did not reply.

" Why do you laugh? "

" Because it is foolish to be rich." He laughed again. Then, sobering, added, " Rich people exploit the poor."

" Wouldn't you like to have things of your own — a lot of real things? "

" No," he said, staring at me with curiosity and some suspicion.

" Supposing someone gave you an automobile, a lot of land, horses, cows. Wouldn't you be glad? "

" I'd turn them over to my father's *kolhoz*," he answered.

" You would? "

" Of course." After a reflective pause he added, " In our Soviet Union, citizen, we have deposited the word riches in the archives."

I glanced at him — a peasant lad, so small, so young, and seemingly unconscious of the significance of his words. He had learned his catechism well, and believed it, too; there was no questioning that. Yet somehow his words sounded unreal. Perhaps it was because I had only recently come from the outside world, where children had never even heard of the ideas he had just expressed. But there were challenge and fire in his words. And I wondered, as the whole world is wondering, whether the spirit of contempt for personal riches that characterized this boy and his generation would stay with them as they grew up. If it should, then the Russian Revolution, in spite of its barbarities, will put to shame all the other movements, including religion, that have been striving for ages to draw out of man his lust for individual accumulation.

At a turn of the road we parted, and I fell to looking at the countryside again. It was the time of year when peasants have little work in the field, and the few people working were chiefly women and girls weeding millet, their hands tearing greedily at the grasses like the mouths of hungry animals. I was passing fields and pastures and swamps that were all familiar to me. At last I reached the boundaries of the village. Here the road broadened out and coursed down in a straight line to the swamp that lay carpet-like at the very edge of the village.

A mere glimpse of the fields brought home to me the reality — in this part of the world — of the "Great Break" which Stalin had spoken of so eloquently. The face of the land on one side of the road was now transfigured. Gone were the long strips with their grassy furrows and ridges stretching out to the horizon. Now, like a river flowing into a sea, there lay before me an immense field that lost itself somewhere in the ancient swamp that had once been a forest. Clearly it was the land of the *kolhoz*.

So what the peasants had worried and fumed over the previous summer had actually come. It was here, this awesome *kolhoz*. It had pushed upon them like a natural phenomenon which they were too feeble to hold back. They had not all joined it — that was evident from the small fields on the opposite side of the road. Yet a group had risen above inertia, habit, tradition and had ventured into this unexplored Canaan, where they had been assured that material want would never again torment them. Whatever the future of the village, it would never again be what it had been in the hundreds of years of its history. An end had come to its isolation and to its idyllic calm. If the machine had not yet arrived it would soon roar into the village's midst, shaking it into sophistication and a fresh orientation. Clearly a new destiny awaited the village.

So absorbed was I in my meditations that I did not notice, until I was almost upon her, a little girl sitting at the roadside humming a tune and weaving a wreath of freshly plucked daisies, buttercups and the incomparable corn-flowers. I paused and watched, and my thoughts flashed back to the time when I had gathered the same flowers in the same fields and woven the same wreaths. It seemed so recent, and yet nearly a quarter of a century had gone by. Only, in my days, children seldom ventured singly into the rye fields, where corn-flowers grew in such abundance. They were afraid of the *rusalkas,* the water-nymphs who were supposed to be the lost souls of drowned girls and whose favorite haunts were the woods and grain fields. With the very milk of our mothers we imbibed the notion that there was no resisting the *rusalkas*. With their eyes, we were told, they could mesmerize a person, especially a child, and then tickle him so powerfully that he would laugh himself to death. I could not imagine myself or any of my playmates sitting out alone on this lonely road at this time of year, when rye had already eared out and was so tall that a grown person could lose himself in it. Yet here was this little girl about two versts from the village, right on the edge of a far-spreading rye field, without a soul in sight and with apparent unconsciousness of danger.

I spoke to her. With a start she turned and, noting that I was a stranger, hastily picked up her flowers as though afraid I would lay my hands on them. I assured her that she need not fear me, and to win her confidence I offered her some candy. She smiled a little, but hesitated to accept the candy. Bending down I put it into her hands and drew her fingers together. Then I asked her if she was from my village, and who her father was, but she would not speak. And suddenly, as if seized by panic, she gathered up her flowers, jumped to her feet and dashed away, calling at the top of her voice: " Marusia, Marusia, O Marusia! " Several times she turned and looked back, still shouting for Marusia; and somewhere from another part of the field there floated back the long-drawn-out melodious response: " Here, here, O Annushka." Then the child disappeared in the rye.

I pursued my journey as far as a path that made a short-cut to the far end of the village. There, as if shot out of the earth, a group of boys and girls bobbed up before me. They were all about the same age, eight or ten, all bareheaded and barefooted and all loaded with flowers. The little girl who had run away from me was among them, with her arms around the hips of an older girl. I passed around candy. Laughingly they accepted it and held it in their hands or thrust it peasant fashion into their bosoms. They explained that they were from a nearby *sovhoz,* and had come here for flowers because they were more plentiful than in their own fields.

" Aren't you afraid of *rusalkas?* " I asked.

" *Rusalkas?* " wonderingly repeated a freckled-faced boy with smiling gray eyes.

" Yes, *rusalkas.*"

They glanced at each other, puzzled, and laughed.

" Don't you know what a *rusalka* is? Have you never heard or seen one? " I asked, remembering how in my day children of their age constantly told one another that they had seen and heard *rusalkas* in the woods or in the grain fields.

They shook their heads and again laughed heartily.

" What is it, tell us? " asked a little girl.

Incredible it seemed that in this part of the world peasant boys and girls should not even know what a *rusalka* was! The Revolution had evidently drained the very word out of the vocabulary of the people.

But whatever might have happened in the village, whatever the feelings of the people, the lands that stretched before me were rich in promise. The rye on the land of the *kolhoz* was gorgeous, tall, clean, heavily eared and in even rows, sowed evidently not by the irregular human hand but by the mathematically controlled grain drill. Only slightly less gorgeous were the spring crops on the other side of the road — potatoes, barley, oats, and large patches of flax, all so high that they hid the earth with their sweep of green.

I walked on, and soon reached the cemetery with its area now freshly enlarged and marked off from the fields not by a fence but by deep-dug ditches. On previous visits I had accorded it passing notice, but now, because it lay in the midst of the *kolhoz* and because of the extension of its boundaries, it aroused a fresh interest. I stopped to look at it, pathetic in the neglect that had overtaken it. The fence that marked its old boundaries had fallen into ruins. The trees were growing lopsided with some of the white birch drying up at the top and their trunks infested with scumlike rings. Only the wild brush was flourishing. Like an army in aggression it was spreading in all directions and encroaching on fresh territories, even on the graves. Not a single grave was marked with a cross, not even the two fresh ones over which the dirt had not yet settled. But then, peasants had good memories and remembered the burial places of their kin.

Abandoned completely to its own fate was the little shrine that nestled in the very bosom of the cemetery. In my boyhood days I thought of it as of a house of death, something to be avoided. But in it were stored the banners and crosses and other paraphernalia that were used in funeral processions, and by virtue of these it became a sanctuary to be cared for and reverenced by the peasants. Now all that remained of it was a battered framework. Most of the shingles had fallen from the roof and the walls were tottering. The two little windows were gone, and the door, cracked and unhinged, leaned against the sagging posts. Inside the floor was rotted and weeds had pushed their way through it. All that was left of the banners and crosses, the ikons and the linens in which they were swathed, were damp strips of canvas half-buried in sand, and a few rotting frames that had once held the figures of famous saints. Obviously these *muzhiks* were no longer giving heed to matters which in the old days commanded their awe and reverence.

I passed on to the village. The sun was setting, but it was still daylight, and as I viewed the street and the double rows of houses that lined it I was impressed with a fresh slovenliness that had come over the people. Houses, yards, fences, were in sad need of repair. The gay festival of Trinity was in the offing, yet nowhere was there a sign of paint on windows or shutters or a roof with a fresh coating of thatch. Was this neglect a mere accident? That I could not believe. The uncertainties that the *kolhoz* had spread abroad were no doubt holding people back from improving their households.

The village boomed with life. From all directions people were returning from work, with sickles and hoes on their shoulders, with sacks of weeds, food for the pigs, and with loads of stumpwood on their backs. Mothers were carting home their crying babies. Young people were leading or driving cows from pasture. *Kolhoz* teams with groups of workers were clattering along the street. Children shouting with glee dashed up and down, running races, chasing after squealing pigs and, as in ancient times, pulling bristles from their backs; and dogs, as ever, were barking furiously. Everywhere there was noise and bustle, chatter and laughter. From the round black chimneys that towered ghostlike over the thatched roofs smoke was crawling out, now in a blue vapor and now in dark coils illumined with shooting sparks. Again through window after window I could see hearths blazing with freshly made fires. At almost every step I was stopped by friends who showered me with greetings and invitations to drop in for a chat and for a drink of milk.

I made my way to the home of the boyhood friend with whom, since the departure of my cousin, I had been stopping. My host and his wife hurried through their chores and we sat down to supper — a really sumptuous meal compared with the limited rations that obtained in Moscow and other cities. Here were potatoes, eggs, cheese, and the ever-present *kasha* with freshly boiled milk and all the melted butter one might wish to pour over it. As we were eating, my friend and his wife regaled me with a detailed account of the happenings in the village since my last visit. The biggest thing, of course, was the coming of the *kolhoz*, but of that, they assured me, I would hear a lot — more than of anything else, for people were heated up about the subject — quite heated up. Other things had also been happening. The daughter of an old neighbor of theirs had borne a child out of wedlock, and there was a bit of a scandal about it. The man she accused of being the child's father refused to marry her. She sued him for support, but for some reason the court dismissed the case. Now she was living at home with her parents and all seemed well again. . . . Many people, older ones especially, were dying. Saddest of all was the death of Michael, the son of Tikhon the Rabbit. Griefstricken over the neglect of his two sons in America who had not written him since pre-war days, Michael had fallen ill with a bad heart. He was taken to the hospital and seemed to be improving, but one day he broke into a rage at his son and the doctor because they refused to give him sugar. In his fit of temper he fell out of bed and died from a heart attack. And had I heard what had happened to Michael's son, Havrillo? Poor fellow! He had been dekoolackized, and his own and his father's life-long accumulations, including the house, had been seized. Banished to a plot of swamp outside of the village, with no horse and hardly any implements, he and his wife were toiling away in the bogs, seeking somehow to raise enough grain to maintain life. Yet at one time Havrillo had lived so well — Ah, how well! Such were the times now — it was beastly to be well-to-do!

There was silence for a moment, and then my hostess asked if I remembered Lohvin? The mention of the name brought to my memory the most exciting romance in the village. Handsome, talented as a singer and dancer, and always jovial, Lohvin, a close friend of my older brother, was the idol of the girls, and especially of Anna, the daughter of Yevdokim, a dignified and ambitious personage. The son of a poor man with a puny allotment of land, working during his spare time as a *batrak* for a nearby landlord, Lohvin had no prospect of becoming rich. Therefore Anna's parents disapproved of him. They wished to marry their daughter to a man of standing. Indeed, from far and near such men flocked to pay court to Anna — young men, widowers, older men, with large holdings of land, many horses, cows, pigs — and gold, too. Anna was in love only with Lohvin, and whenever a suitor came to her home she would run off to some neighbor and sob out her heart. In the end she married a hunchback, the son of one of the wealthiest men in the countryside, and went to live with him in his village some twenty versts away. People talked much and excitedly about her ill luck and some there were who prophesied a life of misfortune for her and for Lohvin. When, therefore, my hostess with a show of concern brought up the name of Lohvin I wondered what she meant.

"You tell him," she turned to her husband.

They exchanged grave looks as though wondering if it would be proper to relate the incident to a newly arrived guest. I urged them to proceed, and my host finally said:

"Well, poor Lohvin hanged himself. His was the first suicide that has ever been known in this village."

"Think of that!" remarked the hostess shaking her head in sorrow.

"A Red soldier was visiting the village and he and I found the body suspended on a rope in the hay-barn and we took it down," the speaker added.

Nobody knew what had driven Lohvin to suicide. They were sure it was not Anna, for he had been married over twenty years and seemed happy with his wife and children.

"And Anna?" I asked, "what has happened to her?"

"Everything," replied my hostess, "since her marriage she has had nothing but misfortune. A few years after her marriage, her hunchbacked husband went to a fair with a load of pears. After selling the pears he got drunk, and on his way home, not knowing what he was doing, he drove over a condemned bridge. The bridge collapsed and he fell into the water and drowned."

"Just think of that for bad luck," interposed the host.

"That was only a beginning of misfortunes," the hostess resumed. "Shortly afterwards she married again, a rich widower this time, and moved to another village. Then the Revolution came and bandits killed her husband. The bandits were caught and shot, but that brought no relief to Anna. Her second husband's oldest son did not like her and threw things at her in an attempt to drive her from the house. One night she jumped out of the window and fled. But the Soviets took a hand in the affair and now she is living with her stepson, but is very unhappy."

"And she is still beautiful," added my host, "though she is getting on in years."

"I heard her brother speak about her the other day," the hostess continued with a fresh show of zest, "and he said that if it was now that she was in love with Lohvin, she would have married him and both might have been happy. O, how he swore at his father — it was pitiful to hear him, because the old man has been dead more than ten years."

"And do you doubt his words?" asked the host. "Of course Anna would have married Lohvin and been proud of his poverty too. It is a new age now. In the old days if you called a man *holish*[1] even if he was that he would smart with rage and want to spit into your face. It was such an insult to be called *holish*. Nowadays call a man *holish*, and even if he is well-to-do, he will be so flattered that he'll remove his hat, bow and thank you for the compliment. It is such an honor to be a *holish*."

[1] Pauper.

Presently my host and hostess followed with another tale even more touching than that of Lohvin and Anna. They asked if I remembered Avdotya, the daughter of Klim, the son of Korney. I did remember her quite vividly, for only the summer before, at a dance, I had photographed her with a group of her friends. I told them that I did, and they again exchanged grave looks and proceeded to narrate the story of her tragic end. When only eighteen, she fell in love with a certain Styopa who was thirty. It soon developed that he had tuberculosis and the physicians despaired of his life. But he did not. He followed the physician's advice and took his medicines and soon began to recover. Finally he got so well that he could work again.

Throughout his illness Avdotya remained steadfast in her devotion to him, and when he recovered they never separated. At spinning socials, dances, festivals, they always were together. On returning home from a party they would linger long at the gateway, just talk and profess love for one another. Neither rain nor snow deterred them from their nightly love-tryst, much to the irritation of Avdotya's mother, who warned the girl of the dangers of exposure. Surely enough, Avdotya caught a severe cold and began to cough and spit blood. Her mother and Styopa took her to town to be examined by the doctor, and he said that she had tuberculosis. He gave her medicines, but she failed to improve. Then she had a bad hemorrhage. Styopa was upset, but remained faithful to his troth. He visited her every day, cheered her and even gave her the medicines that had helped him. He assured her that as soon as she improved he would marry her.

Then something happened to him. He ceased visiting

Avdotya. She sent for him, and when he came, he was not the Styopa she had known; he was aloof and uncommunicative. In the presence of her mother she asked him if he had ceased to love her, and he said nothing. On his departure he promised to come again, yet he never did. Finally she sent for him, but he did not come. Desperate with longing she would sit at the window and look outside in the hope of seeing him pass, and when he did she would scream and shrink away from the window and beg her mother to draw a cloth over it so that she could not see the street. And all the time her lungs were growing worse, and only a short time ago she died.

" You should have been at the funeral," continued my hostess. " To my dying day I shan't forget it. Her girl friends came with wreaths of freshly gathered flowers, and when they laid her out in the coffin in her best clothes and put the flowers around her, she looked so beautiful and so lifelike, only so yellow. Her mother prostrated herself before the coffin, embraced the dead body and wept. ' Darling mine,' she cried, ' sit up my precious, all your girl friends have come not to your funeral but to your wedding. Look at the flowers they have brought you! Arise, my beautiful Avdotya, my lovely little girl, my pretty bride.' It broke our hearts to hear the mother's despair, and we all wept as we never had wept at a funeral. We blubbered like children. The mother, poor thing, has gone mad with grief, and even now whenever she passes the cemetery she stops at her daughter's grave, prostrates herself on it, and cries for her to come to life."

After supper I went out into the street, and soon a crowd gathered about me. old and young, *kolhozniks* and non-*kolhozniks* and two of the dekoolackized peasants. All were bursting with eagerness to talk. Why, asked person after person, had I not come in the winter, when the village, aye the whole countryside, boiled with excitement? *Akh,* what things had happened — meetings, debates, quarrels, fights, denunciations, and everybody wondering what would come of the effort to make people join the *kolhoz* whether they wanted to or not.

Even Red soldiers came and made the rounds of houses seeking to persuade people into joining, and some folk imagined that they were an advance guard of an army that was soon to arrive with guns and bayonets and everything, as in war, and drive people into the *kolhoz* like cattle to pasture. Dark people that they were, they could not make headway through all the turmoil over dekoolackization and the *kolhoz,* and they were so overcome with fright that they were ready to believe anything anybody said. Things were not as bad in this village as in others, for the organizers here were more decent, though they too did all they could to make people believe that they had to join the *kolhoz.*

Then news came of a letter which Stalin had written,[2] ordering organizers to stop driving people into the *kolhoz.* At once people braced up. They rushed to the post offices and to the town to buy the newspapers that printed Stalin's letter. They paid three, four, five roubles for a copy of such a paper, that was how eager they were to see the letter with their own eyes. In the market places peasants gathered in groups and read it aloud and discussed it long and violently, and some of them were so overjoyed that they bought all the vodka they could pay for and got drunk. Others stuck

[2] The letter of March 2, 1930, on " Dizziness from Success."

the paper inside their bosom and rushed home to show it to their neighbors and went to the Soviet offices and, flashing it before the officials and the organizers, gave them a piece of their mind. In some places officials and organizers hid themselves, and it was well that they did, for they had told people that they had to join the *kolhoz* and give up all their property for nothing, or else suffer exile to Siberia or Kotlas, and now that people learned from Stalin himself that this was not what the *tsentr*[3] favored, they were so exasperated that they might have done something desperate to these *svoyevolniks*.[4]

Ah, what a winter it had been, what a time they had had! If only it was over! If only Stalin would keep his promise and make entrance into the *kolhoz* voluntary and clap into jail every scalawag who sought to make it compulsory. But they had heard that by the end of the Five-Year Plan everybody would be in the *kolhoz*, and what did that mean? Supposing people did not want to join, would they be made to? Then it would not be voluntary, would it? And Stalin had said in that letter that it must not be compulsory. What did I make of it? Perhaps I had seen Stalin and the other big men in Moscow or heard them say what they meant. If only Stalin would not change his mind, if only he would keep those brigadiers in their place and stop them from tormenting innocent and hardworking *muzhiks!*

I went late to the hay-barn to sleep. It was a chilly night and I wrapped myself snugly in a sheepskin coat and dug deep into the hay. But I could not go to sleep. Excitement kept me wide awake. I had been in the

[3] Central government.
[4] Arbitrary autocrats.

village only one evening and what a deluge of news had poured over me! The figures of Lohvin, Anna, Avdotya, Styopa flashed alternately before my mind and it seemed impossible that experiences so mighty and so shattering had happened to such simple and trusting souls.

I heard footsteps outside, and presently someone was prying open the door.

"Who is it?" I inquired.

"Open, open, please — it is I, Sergey. I want to talk to you."

I jumped out of the hay, lifted the huge wooden fork which I had propped against the door, and Sergey entered. It was so dark that I could hardly make out his face; his beard seemed blacker and heavier than ever. He lay down on the hay beside me and at once plunged into talk. He had been away at work in the *sovhoz* and had come home late, but on learning that I had arrived he felt that he had to see me at once and tell me everything. It was so good to have a chance to talk one's self out. It was the only solace left to him in these days of trial and uncertainty. Had I heard that in the winter he had been dekoolackized? Yes, all his property had been confiscated, and he and the family driven from their house. But thank God he had been reinstated and his property, including his house, had been returned to him. Yet he was not happy — life was so uncertain and he was so perplexed. He was no idler. He knew something about land and fruit and stock and bees. If he worked he would produce and would gather good harvests, and that would again only rouse suspicion and trouble. . . . God, what a life!

"Last year when you were here," he went on, "they

demanded of me one thousand roubles for allowing me to remain in my own house and on my own land. Finally I compromised with them on a smaller amount. I had planned to sell one of my cows, a pig, and some other things and get the money, and of a sudden they changed their policy. They wouldn't let me remain on my land at any price. I was a *koolack,* and all that I had was to be liquidated. I argued with them. I asked them what sort of a *koolack* was I, when my hands were so black and blistered from toil? But I did myself no good. In their eyes I was a *koolack* and I had to be destroyed. You know what a good *khoziain* [5] I am. In barn and house I love to keep things in their proper place. I had little shelves, for example, on the walls of the living room for dishes and other things including the few books that I have had all my life. Well, one evening when I came home Soviet men had arrived to take possession of the house and had begun to pull down the shelves. My heart was bleeding when I saw them wrecking the things that I had fashioned with such care with my own hands, so I said to them ' *tovar-ishtshui,* you are driving me out of the house, but why are you tearing down these shelves? You might make use of them, if only for books.' They paid no heed to me. Oh, brother, you have no idea how I felt. I couldn't hold back the tears, but I said nothing. There was no use.

" I arranged with my brother-in-law to move into his house. There were five of them and there were six of us, and we all had to live in a little hovel. Well, my wife came to take out of the oven the pots of gruel and

[5] Householder.

potatoes that she had cooked for supper. Meanwhile several Red soldiers had arrived with musical instruments — they were to give a concert in the new clubhouse —my house — that very evening. My wife wrapped her cooking pots in towels, and as she was going out she turned to the soldiers and said, 'Now, brothers, farewell. May all of you who are going to stay in this place have a happier end than we are having, and now strike up a march so that we can go out with music in our ears.' As soon as she was out of the house she broke down and cried — How she cried! I lingered a few minutes longer, and I saw one of the soldiers wiping tears from his eyes. Of course the musicians played no march, but there was music inside of us, dear friend — sad music! " An emotional man, he broke down and sobbed, and there in this dark barn, so late in the night, in the midst of the awesome stillness of the Russian countryside, his sobbing seemed pathetic beyond words.

"Well," I said, seeking to cheer him, "but now you are back in your own home. It was only a *peregib*, an abuse of the local authorities, and surely you have no reason to feel distressed."

"You are right, you are right, my friend," he answered, regaining control of himself, "I have gotten everything back, everything. It was a *peregib*, and of course in a Revolution things do get mixed up very badly. I am not blaming anybody, but it is so painful, all this uncertainty. It is so hard to know one day what the next will bring. Take this *kolhoz* here. When they started everybody was told to turn his cows in, so that the good ones could be kept and the bad ones sold off for money to buy other good ones. Now there is a new order, a *kolhoz* member may keep one cow for his own use, and do you see what's happened? The men who joined the *kolhoz* in the autumn have no cows and have to buy their milk, but the men who joined later and who are joining now can have a cow of their own and don't need to spend hard-earned money on milk. If that were the only blunder they made, one could dismiss it, but take the matter of gardens. At first no individualist could have a garden of his own — all our garden land was to go to the *kolhoz,* and what is a *muzhik* without a garden? Folks howled so loudly that they changed their minds and now, thank God, we are allowed to keep our individual gardens. But we haven't been so lucky with pastures. The *kolhoz* got the best and nearest ones, and we individualists now lose no end of time in leading our cows and horses to and from far-away and poor pastures. Is that a good thing — I mean, good for the Soviets, for the whole country? People get so discouraged, so exasperated, that they lose interest in their work, in their stock, in everything. And then take my case and see what I have gone through — and for the sake of what, or whom? I was told at first that if I paid one thousand roubles I might remain on my own premises, and then I was told that under no circumstances would I be allowed to continue on my own land and in my own home. I was dekoolackized, and suffered misery and heartache — I and my wife and my children. Now I am reinstated. Thank God! Don't you see all this lack of purpose and order and understanding? So how can I join the *kolhoz?* What guarantee have I that they won't continue to blunder and mismanage and ruin things? And besides, supposing something happens — a war, for example. I read the papers, and every day they tell us that the capitalist nations are preparing to attack us. Supposing they do, what then? What is a man to do? What shall I make out of it all? What do you make out of it?"

IX

THE VOICE OF THE MASS

ON Sunday I rose early and went to a village some ten versts away. I had been invited to come by the young folk, who had arranged a party for the evening, and by some of the older people, who insisted that they, too, were deserving of the notice of their American countryman. I knew this village almost as well as my own, for it was perched on the bank of a fine river, where, as a boy, I had often gone fishing and swimming. Besides, I had many friends there. It was one of the largest villages in the whole countryside, though as primitive and desolate as my own, or, indeed, as any of the others, with its thatched roofs and barns, its unpaved street, and its quota of surly dogs. Also, it had a *kolhoz*.

I called on several members of the *kolhoz* whom I happened to know, and then I went on to see some old friends of my family. Finally, I finished up at the house of Palahya — a little woman with puffy cheeks and large gray eyes, noted for her kindliness — who had several times asked me to come and look at the embroideries of her eldest daughter, Malanya. The living-room was swept and clean, and unencumbered by the innumerable objects which clutter up Russian peasant homes in these parts. Even the *polati* — the platform which serves as a bed — was free from straw ticks, hemp cloth and cast-off garments.

When I reached the house, the husband, a man of about forty, with a wavy moustache, was just starting off for town with some sacks of old potatoes and several live chickens. Townspeople, he said, were giving good prices for food, and sometimes you could get dishes, clocks, clothes and even wine in exchange. One winter a man gave him a bottle of red wine for ten eggs; it was the first time that he or his family had ever tasted wine. They liked it, too, even his wife did, though she loathed vodka, and would not let him touch it. Perhaps there would be a chance of finding another bottle in the market. With the feast of Trinity coming on, wine would be welcome, and so on, and so on.

He drove off, and Palahya showed me into the little, dark room at the back of the house where peasants store their possessions, especially their best clothes. She undid a huge, home-made trunk, and, with the door open to let in the daylight, she unfolded a mass of towels, sheets, tablecloths and blankets, all gorgeously embroidered, and all, she proudly boasted, the work of Malanya. " It is her dowry," she remarked almost in a whisper. " Not a girl in the village has as fine a one as my daughter, and she is adding to it all the time." With lingering fondness, she folded up the things and packed them neatly back into the trunk. As she did so she kept up a flow of chatter. " The Lord only knows," she murmured confidingly, " why the girl won't marry. I have argued and quarreled and fought with her, and so has her father, but she won't budge. She says that there is plenty of time. Suitors have been coming from all round, but she won't even look at them —

nice well-to-do men, too — and she no longer so young as she once was. She was twenty, three weeks before last Easter."

"Come, that's young enough," I ventured to suggest. "She can quite well wait another five years."

Had I pronounced a curse I could not have shocked the mother more profoundly. "God forbid," she hastily replied. "Why, my dear, I'd rather die than see my daughter remain unmarried for another five years. Peasants have to marry young to have children and get on in the world."

We went back to the living-room, and soon Malanya herself and two friends came in. In their soft-leather shoes and their Sunday dresses, these village girls were hardly distinguishable from town girls. Malanya herself, full-breasted, ruddy-faced, with a wealth of soft brown hair and large blue eyes, and an authoritative air with her, easily deserved her reputation of being an uncommonly pretty lass.

"Well, will you take her with you to America?" said the mother in fun.

"Would she come?" I asked, catching Malanya's eye and watching the blush steal over her cheeks.

"Certainly we would," cried one of the friends. "We'd all come if we had the chance, either to work or to get married, or to do anything," and the three put their heads together to hide their embarrassment and giggled with delight.

"Do they go for the *koolacks* in America?" asked Malanya.

"No," I replied.

"All the better," said one of the other girls, and they again started giggling.

" If you marry a rich man in this country," continued Malanya with that assured manner which
lent her such distinction without in the least detract-
ing from her girlish naïveté, " you may be treated
as a *koolack* yourself and banished to Siberia or
Kotlas." [1]

" Nobody wants to marry a rich man nowadays,"
added one of the friends.

" Nor a poor one either, for that matter," retorted
Malanya, and again the three put their heads together in a fit of uproarious mirth.

" There now," said the mother, " you have heard
what they say." And shaking her head in distress she
turned upon the girls and, in a rising crescendo,
" Whom then do you want to marry? " she cried.
" You are afraid of a rich man, you don't want a poor
man. Who else is left? Do you expect always to remain young and attractive? You forget that there are
other girls growing up who will be younger and pret-
tier than you. They will receive all the attentions,
and the men will not even look at you. You will soon
be left out in the cold, a disgrace to yourselves and
your families, and there will be nobody to court you
except some grouchy old widower. And then what will
you say? "

Once upon a time such reproaches from her mother
would have crushed a girl; but now —

" In that case we'll go to town and work in the factories," said one of the girls. An innocent enough reply,
yet to me it was pregnant with meaning. In the old
days these girls were so timid and fearful of the out-

[1] A place of banishment in the old province of Vologda in the
far north.

side world. They shrank from the very thought of the city. The bazaars in their own little market town, where they could feast their eyes on flashy shawls and ginger cakes and white bread and trinkets, were the limit of their travels. And now here was this Malanya and her friends looking to the city as a place of deliverance.

" I want to go to town, anyway," cried Malanya again, " I am sick of mud and dullness."

" The *kolhoz* is the place where you'll end up, my dear, as we all shall," exclaimed her mother.

" If they build a nice one, the kind the organizer told us about, with a club-house, movie pictures, a park, an orchestra and a theater, we'll go of our own accord," said one of the girls.

" Yes," sobbed the mother, " and then you'll all be in mobs, working and eating together, going to the fields and coming back together, and meanwhile the men here will play round with other girls, and there will be all kinds of temptations and faithlessness."

" Then we'll play round with other men," retorted one of the friends.

" It may be better so," remarked Malanya non-chalantly, and the three again set off giggling. But this show of sophistication, a new thing in itself and purely the result of the Revolution, was too much for the mother.

" *Nu,*" she shouted, stamping her foot, " mind that tongue of yours, you naughty thing, or — Remember, I am still strong, stronger than you are."

But Malanya showed no concern at the threat.

An old woman in shoes and a homespun woolen coat and a bright kerchief wrapped turbanlike round her head came in, the grandmother of one of Malanya's friends, who lived just opposite. She shook hands all round and instantly plunged into the conversation.

" Nowadays," she exclaimed, " people need nothing — neither money, God, faith, devil, husbands, nor wives."

" How advanced you are getting, grandma! " remarked her granddaughter.

" Advanced rubbish," replied the old woman indignantly, "here is our countryman from America. Let him decide. Would any girl in the old days, after giving birth to a bastard or with one in her belly, go about with the other girls in the village to dances and spinning parties? She'd have buried her face for shame first. And now look at Matrena playing about in her condition as if nothing were going to happen."

" And remember Boris," added Malanya's mother.

" Yes, Boris," repeated the old woman. " That is another case for you. He went off one day to some village or other, and came home with a pretty wench, took her into the barn to sleep, and next morning he told everybody that she was his wife. He did not even go to the Soviet to get registered. That's why I said that people nowadays need nothing — neither wealth, church, nor virtue, nothing, nothing at all."

The girls seemed quite unimpressed. As before they exchanged amused glances at the complaints of their elders.

Presently two men came in, one a neighbor of Palahya's, an elderly *muzhik* with a grayish beard and heavy boots, the other, his son-in-law, a much younger man, clean-shaven, well-dressed and of an earnest demeanor.

" He's a Baptist," said the older man solemnly, " and he wants to ask you about the Baptists in America."

The younger man at once started plying me with questions. He had heard that there were millions of Baptists in America, and he would so much like to know something of their life and their manner of worship. Did they have to register their services at a government office as Baptists in Russia did? Were they forbidden to proselytize or to have schools, or to form their own coöperatives, and were their children, even when they worked the land with their own hands, deprived of citizenship? Did they believe in alcohol and smoking and in going into the army and in fighting wars?

Then he went on to tell us the story of his own conversion. He had been Orthodox, and, like all the Orthodox, he had since the Revolution been weakening in his faith. Once at a fair two men got drunk and started fighting, and one cracked an empty bottle over the other's head, knocking him unconscious, so that the police came and took him away to the hospital. A crowd gathered and the people began talking about the fight, an elderly woman arguing that if these men had had God in their hearts they would never have fought, for they would not have touched liquor. It was only infidels, she insisted, who had no respect for their own bodies and souls, and debased them with drink. She explained that she was a Baptist and talked about her faith. Baptists, she said, were not like Orthodox people — they knew what they believed and why they believed, and they never did anything for which they could not give a reason. Did an Orthodox Christian, she asked, know why every Wednesday and Friday he had to do without meat, milk and even eggs? Did he know why the priest spat and blew at the devil when there was a christening? Did he know why he kept so many holidays, sometimes three days or even more at a stretch, or what he was celebrating when he soused himself in drink? Orthodox people just did things, without knowing why they did them; but Baptists were different. They reasoned about everything. Well, this woman set him off thinking with the result that, some time after, he himself became a convert to the Baptist faith, and now he knew that real religion meant cleanliness, kindness to all living things, simple worship anywhere, in a house, in the open fields or even in a barn, industry, humility, abstaining from resistance and violence, no wars, no bloodshed, and the brotherhood of all peoples and all classes the world over. That was real religion.

" Good people, these Baptists," remarked the old woman. " They never offend anybody."

"And why should we offend anyone? " cried the man. " Didn't the Lord say 'Love thy neighbor as thyself ' ? "

He invited me to come to the meeting with him. Yes, they met every Sunday in one or other of their houses and the Soviets left them alone, though often enough Young Communists would come and argue with them. *Akh!* if only the Soviets would let them make converts! What real light they would bring to people — God's own light which warms the heart and rejoices the spirit and alone brings contentment and happiness!

When one listens to a Russian Protestant like this earnest young man it is easy to understand why the

Russian revolutionaries have changed their attitude toward the Protestant sects from one of benevolent patronage to implacable hostility. These people are filled with a passionate zeal, and they mean to abide by the tenets of their faith in their own way, which is utterly subversive of the basic tenets of the Revolution. They deny, for instance, the class struggle, the unforgivable sin in Soviet land. Therefore they renounce all hatred, of the *koolack,* of the private *entrepreneur,* of the *lishenetz* [2] and of all others who are out of tune with the existing scheme of things. Besides, they abjure the use of violence and war even against the enemies of the proletariat, and they hold out hopes of an inner peace which is incompatible with the spirit of militancy that the Revolution exacts.

Later on, I went out for a walk. The village was now humming with life. Young and old were outside in the street, sitting in groups on logs or planks in front of their houses, or sauntering up and down at their leisure. Boys and girls, in freshly greased boots and bright Sunday clothes, were strolling along in pairs or parties, their arms round one another's waists, gaily chattering and laughing and now and then breaking into song. A holiday spirit hovered over the village. Unlike Moscow or other towns, Sunday then still had a meaning here.

I was stopped by a number of peasants who had collected in front of the blacksmith's, where there was a pile of logs which made excellent seats. They invited me to " tell them about things " — of life in other lands, prices, goods, collectives, *technika* — everything. There were *kolhozniks* (members of the local *kolhoz*) among

---

[2] A person deprived of Soviet citizenship.

them, and a couple of them were wearing brand new rubbers which glistened in the sun. As there was no mud they obviously wore them for show. My presence soon attracted people, as any foreigner's does in a Russian village, and groups, almost crowds, gathered round me. It might have been a mass meeting. Taking advantage of the occasion I shifted the subject to that of their own local conditions, in the hope that I might have a chance of hearing what the peasant really thinks, be he *bedniak, seredniak,* or an actual or suspected *koolack,* if there were any about, and of course the *kolhoznik.* Here they were, all ready to hand, with ample time at their disposal and in a talkative mood.

" We are all in the dark nowadays," said a tall bony man with a pointed grayish beard.

" Waiting for light and not getting any," chimed in another, an old man leaning on a staff, with his hat so low over his eyes that you could hardly see them.

" *Nichevo,* it will come, this light," broke in a *kolhoznik,* a tall youth in a blouse with a collar and tie and rubbers.

His words were greeted with a loud laugh in which he heartily joined himself.

" You should have been here last winter, countryman of ours," cried another, a tall vigorous fellow, with bristling sandy moustaches and shrewd gray eyes, one of two brothers who ran the town windmill.

" Aye, there was excitement if you like," exclaimed several voices at the same time.

" And it is not over yet," someone added.

" No, indeed," cried another man.

" One thing at least we have now learned," said the old man with the staff, " and that is not to keep more than one cow or horse and at most only two pigs and a few sheep."

" Quite right, quite right," repeated the chorus, and there was something inhumanly bitter and hopeless underlying the gravity of their manner.

" They have taught us a lesson, one that we shall not soon forget."

The presence of the *kolhozniks* who are supposed to be, and often are, the local eyes and ears of the government, as well as its voice, did not in the least deter these peasants from speaking their minds without any show of reserve. As I listened to this resolve to keep only a single cow, one horse, two pigs and a few sheep, I realized why the Kremlin wants to collectivize the land in the shortest possible space of time. For, unless something happens to break this resolve, the production of meat and milk will be limited, and many urgently needed commodities will not be forthcoming for the outside market. The *muzhik* was on strike, and said so quite openly.

The discussion continued.

" A party of those special brigadiers [3] paid me a visit the other day," began a little man with a fuzzy brown beard and a toothless mouth. " After a look round off they went. And then, what do you think? One of them came back to find out if I was a *koolack*. I have an old straw cutter with which I have been earning ten or fifteen miserable roubles a year; well — I was charged with being an exploiter. It is a rusty old thing, this cutter; I have had it for at least fifteen years. So when the constable suggested that I was making money out

---

[3] Members of a voluntary group sent out on some special mission by Soviets or the Communist party.

of people, I laughed and told him that he could have the whole machine for the price of the iron in it. But the matter did not end there. 'How many cows have you got?' was the next question. 'One,' said I. 'Let me see it,' he snapped back. 'Very well,' I replied. So down we went to the barn, and as we were walking there I said to myself, 'what on earth will he say when he sees the young heifer? Will he call her a cow and confiscate her on the ground that I have lied to him?' But I kept cool. When we reached the cowhouse sure enough he at once exclaimed: 'Why there are two cows!' 'No,' said I, 'there is only one, the other is a heifer not yet two years old.' 'But she is with calf,' he cried. 'She certainly is,' I admitted. 'Then she is a cow, isn't she?' said he. 'Not yet,' said I, 'and she won't be one until she's had her calf.' 'And when will that be?' he asked. 'I am sure I don't know,' I protested, 'I was not at the pasture when she was served.' No more was said, but he looked and looked at that heifer. Then my old woman came in, and, father, you should just have heard what she had to say to him — Lord, how she talked! She called him names, she scolded him, she told him that he ought to be ashamed of himself for annoying poor hard-working people, and when he tried to answer she wouldn't hear a word. Once she actually spat at him. I was fairly scared. But he did absolutely nothing, nothing at all. Every time he opened his mouth she shouted him down, so he just had to listen."

"There's a *baba* for you," was the enthusiastic comment of the crowd. "But I was frightened all the same," continued the little man, "and all that night I couldn't sleep for wondering whether they would come back and confiscate the heifer and everything I had. But my

baba said that if they came she would break their heads
with a faggot. Through God's mercy they didn't come,
or she might have done something desperate."

"Yes, with you it went no further than fright," said
the old man with the staff, "but Demyan across the
way there, you know what they did to him!"

At the mention of the name a murmur of pity surged
through the crowd and several of the peasants shook
their heads.

"Think of it," continued the old man, "he lives with
his wife and a sister-in-law who is stone blind and quite
helpless. But for his support she would have died long
ago; he has been like a father to the poor thing. Yet
they pronounced him a *koolack* and stripped him of
everything he had. First they assessed his share of the
bread levy at three hundred poods, though he never
raised as much rye in his life. But they demanded it on
purpose so as to have an excuse for confiscating his
possessions, which they did, cleaning him out for good
and all. They took his eighteen-year-old horse, his
yearling, his one cow, his four pigs and all the oats and
unthrashed grain in his barn. Finally they sent Demyan himself to gaol for three weeks. As a favor they
let him keep three and a half poods of rye, no more.
They even took away the timber with which he meant
to repair his house and barns."

"And who was to blame? Why, the committee of the
poor in this very village," said a voice, and all eyes
were turned in the direction of the group of *kolhozniks*.
The latter, however, seemed quite unruffled. They went
on talking among themselves, and one of them laughed
outright.

"Why didn't they think of the blind girl, brother?"
asked someone.

" He has since been going round the government offices trying to get his case reviewed, and his property and rights as a citizen restored; but nothing has come of his efforts."

" Little they care for people's feelings. Human beings are nothing to them — nothing."

The *kolhoznik,* who had laughed, a man of about thirty, with blue eyes and an uncombed black moustache, turned to me.

" They tell you everything except the real reason why Demyan was dekoolackized," said he. " He hired outside labor, not merely on occasions when the law allows it, but for the purposes of exploitation, and he did some trading too."

There was a loud laugh. It was clear what the crowd thought of the *kolhoznik's* reply.

" Laugh away," he cried, rather irritably, " that's all you can do anyway, laugh and complain."

" Thank God at all events that we can still laugh, even if we can't talk freely," remarked the old man again.

At this the *kolhoznik* lost his temper.

" You old fool," he shouted, " who put a gag in your mouth? As though anybody could ever stop you talking," and turning to me he continued, " It is a good thing that you are here to see for yourself how they twist things . . . They talk and talk and talk, yet they have the impudence to say that they are not allowed to talk. What a people! "

" You know what happened last winter? " someone yelled.

" Well, what did happen? " shouted back the *kolhoznik.*

" We dared not speak at meetings. If we said anything that the organizers didn't like, they abused us, called us *koolacks,* and even threatened to put us in prison."

"We let the women do the talking," cried a voice from the back of the crowd.

"They did that in every village, just let the women talk."

"And how they did talk!"

"They went on day and night. The organizers had not a chance."

"If the organizer tried to stop them they made such a din that he had to call off the meeting."

"What is there to be proud of in that?" broke in another *kolhoznik.*

"Plenty of reason for us," screamed a middle-aged woman with a baby. "Our men folk," she complained to me, "had cold feet, so we decided that we'd do something on our own account, and many of us came with our babies on purpose, because we knew that the laws about women with babies would prevent their touching us."

"Are you utterly without shame?" broke in another *kolhoznik.* "There was only one constable of that kind here. Yet you talk as if they were all the same. He was a *peregibshtichik,*[4] he went beyond his instructions."

"That may be so, but in other villages they were often all of them, scoundrels," shouted another woman at the top of her voice. "I have a son in S—— and I know what the idiots did over there, and nobody attempted to interfere with them.

"But they had no right to do it," explained the *kol-*

---

[4] One who committed excesses.

hoznik with the unkempt moustache. " If you tell a story you ought to tell the whole story, and you know that some of those fellows who behaved so badly are now in gaol."

Feeling was now rising fast between the *kolhozniks* and their opponents. One thing was quite evident. The village was divided, not into *bedniaks* and *seredniaks* on the one side and the well-to-do on the other, but into *kolhozniks* and non-*kolhozniks*. The *kolhozniks* were " they " and the individualists were " we." This was certainly not the sort of split which the revolutionaries wanted to promote in the village — anything but, for it clove into warring factions the very forces that were supposed to amalgamate and jointly constitute the *opora* (the support) of the Revolution. But the mass of the villagers only saw in the *kolhoz* the power which had taken away their best pastures from them, had at one time even menaced them with the confiscation of their gardens, and, above all, had threatened to swallow them up themselves.

Presently a tall man with a ruddy face and a military bearing came up.

" Here is another liquidated *koolack,*" someone exclaimed. " *Nu,* Nikolai, tell our countryman what they did to you."

" *Nu,*" replied Nikolai with a wave of his hand, " that's an old story now, not worth repeating."

" Tell it, tell it, don't be afraid," several voices urged. Nikolai frowned.

" Last year," he began, " I thought of joining the *kolhoz,* but my wife threatened to kill herself if I did, so I did not. Well, you see me as I stand here? That's how they left me. Everything else they took away, except three poods of grain and a few sacks of potatoes which they allowed me to keep as a favor."

"The finest pair of horses in the village," a peasant close to me remarked, "three cows, ten sheep, twenty hens, a wagon, ploughs, they stripped him of everything, and of course they drove him out of his own house, and in freezing weather, too. Merciless."

"And we all know Nikolai," added the old man again. "Nobody in this village worked so hard or so honestly as he did. Ever since he was a little boy he has been the same. If on the way to his fields with a load of manure a piece were to fall off, he would go back and pick it up with his own hands, every bit of it and put it on the cart again. It was the same if any whisps fell off a load of hay, he would rake up every shred and put it back. He never left the smallest or the greenest potato in the field. Nothing was ever wasted in his house, that's the kind of man he was."

"Yes," said another man, "he ate and slept too little, was out in all kinds of weather, and never tippled as some of us do. He never, indeed, allowed himself the slightest luxury. Copeck upon copeck he put away, rouble upon rouble — all his neighbors will bear me out — and when he went to town he would not even permit himself the treat of a herring or an *abaranok* [5] — there is thrift for you!"

"It is all true, every word of it," cried several voices.

"If we had only known what was coming," said someone, "we would never have bothered to work and save to build up a respectable home. We'd just have loafed so that we might remain paupers, and then instead of things being taken away from us they'd be

[5] A wheat roll.

given to us. It is wonderful to be a pauper nowadays. You get everything for nothing, you pay no taxes, and you are the big *shishka* [6] in the village. But a man like Nikolai who has slaved and saved all his life now has to pay the penalty."

" Why then did he live like that? " came an indignant query from the fringe of the crowd. The entire assemblage turned to see who it was. " I don't know this Nikolai," continued the speaker, a young man in the early twenties, dressed for a holiday, with a cap and collar and tie and an up-to-date suit of clothes. I was told he was from a neighboring village, a student in some electrical *technikum* [7] on a visit to relations.

" I don't know Nikolai," he went on defiantly, " but I heard all that you had to say about him."

" Well, what of that? " said the old man.

" I'll tell you what," calmly replied the youth.

" Oh! dry up! " cried the old man impatiently.

" Plug up your ears, old boy," retorted the young fellow, " you need not listen if you don't want to. A lot of you people never want to hear any sense at all. But what I say is this. Here is Nikolai; the Soviets, you complain, have maltreated him. He has worked hard all his life to build up a place of his own. He denied himself everything, even a herring on market days. He'd pick up every bit of manure that fell off his wagon and every shred of hay that blew about his yard. An excellent citizen that — "

" No, a bandit," interrupted someone sarcastically, and a roar broke out from the crowd.

" An honorable citizen," continued the young man

6 Power.
7 Industrial School.

quite unperturbed, " the kind, at all events, that you hold in honor. But I ask you in all seriousness, what did he save for? You say yourselves that he was denying himself things all the time. He just saved. What for? For whom? Was it to take something to his grave with him? Why didn't he at least try to live? "

He paused as though for a reply, and it came.

" And what is the good of doing nothing and saving nothing after the fashion of rapscallions like you? "

" We try to live," replied the lad. " We buy clothes, books, and newspapers, and we study and do our best to understand the better life and to live it; that's what we do."

" And to push your elders into the grave," shouted a very old man. " Take me for example. I am sick. I have special wants. Sugar I must have, for instance, but do you imagine that I can get sugar? Not a bit of it. I am too old, I suppose, and you young scallywags think that it would be waste to give it to an old man like me."

" Join the *kolhoz*," suggested someone, " and you'll get sugar soon enough."

" As though there were not enough people already in the *kolhoz* to start quarreling! "

" They can do with a lot more."

" In the village of H—— the other day a man who preferred to run his own farm had a dispute with the chairman of the *kolhoz* over some question of pasture, whereupon the chairman pulled out his revolver and shot him dead."

The group of *kolhozniks,* who had thus far taken little part in the discussion, showed signs of resentment at this statement.

"And suppose there was shooting at H——"
shouted one of them. "Was there not shooting in this
village too last year? Was there not shooting in this
country before we even heard of the *kolhoz?* Why is it
always the *kolhoz* that is responsible? "

Someone tried to stop him, but he brushed him aside,
and turning to me he went on:

"Every time anything happens in the *kolhoz* they
yell themselves hoarse about it. They forget that the
same things happen outside the *kolhoz*. One of our men
tipped over a load of hay, and it was the talk of the
whole countryside for weeks. Two of our women
started a fight, and pulled each other's hair. That again
set everybody off laughing. The other day on my way
home, I noticed a horse that had come unhitched, and
I said to myself, if this is a *kolhoz* team everybody will
say that *kolhozniks* do not trouble to hitch up their
horses properly. But it so happened that it was Semko
there, so of course nobody had a word to say about it.
How they love to pitch into the *kolhoz*, but, *nichevo*,
they'll change their tune in time."

"That they will," cried another *kolhoznik*, "we'll
see who can raise the best crops, and who'll enjoy the
best life."

A tall woman with a hard face joined the crowd, and
an oldish man yelled out for fun:

"Here is the chief champion of the *kolhoz* in our
village."

"I? " protested the woman. "A champion of this
fresh torment that they are foisting on to us! "

"A paradise, auntie," someone on the outside
snapped.

"Paradise, of course," snarled back the woman,

"living by the bell. Did you see," she had turned to me, "the bell they have fixed up? They just live by it. They get up by it, eat by it, sleep by it, fight by it, and if anything should ever happen to that bell, they'd be more at a loss than little chickens which suddenly lose the old hen."

"She obviously doesn't like music," someone remarked facetiously.

"I certainly don't like bells," said auntie, "what a life in the *kolhoz*, always under someone's orders! Yesterday, for instance, I did no work. I just wanted a rest so I took one, and I ate more than I usually do, five times as much."

"*Zdorovo, zdorovo*,[8] exclaimed several voices. The woman smiled, pleased with the applause.

"Yes, I had five meals and there was nobody to say me nay. It was nobody's business. I was my own mistress. But in a *kolhoz*, how could I take a rest when I want to? I'd have to wait for the blessed bell before I could have a meal, and I could not have five meals unless the bell rang five times. That's the position. Then my little girl likes butter, but if I joined the *kolhoz* how could I get butter?"

"When our new cows come on we'll have plenty of it," interrupted a *kolhoznik*.

"But you have none now," she shouted back, "and my little girl wants butter at once, every day."

"When the harvest comes everything will be different," said another *kolhoznik*. "We'll have more than any of you and we'll fare better and live better. Just you wait and see, all you grousers."

"And supposing you do?" burst out Ilya, the pa-

---

[8] Well, well.

triarch of the village, a hardy old gentleman with a still upright carriage though nearing his century, "Would that be anything so unusual? You have got the best land in the village, the best pasture, the best grain for seed, the best horses, cows and pigs, raised by decent people with their own sweat and blood in this or other villages. You have wood and lumber from the State forests, tractors and other machines, credit from the government; everything, all the help, all the advantages. Where then will the miracle be if you succeed in raising better crops than we do? Why don't you perform a real miracle? Get the poorest land you can find, let the government impose on you half the burdens that it puts on us, do everything with your own hands, and then see what you can do."

"Yes, yes," chimed in a host of enthusiastic voices.

"Then let's see your miracle."

"Yes, a real miracle," repeated a host of others.

A *kolhoznik* began to say something, but Ilya interrupted him:

"And I say more. Give us the same privileges that you are enjoying, good land, machinery, credits, stock, and see if we don't even go one better than you. I know. When a man has his own things he will work his head off to get results, but when everything is pooled as it is in a *kolhoz*, he says to himself — 'I'll do as little as I can, for I'll get as much as the other fellow anyway.'"

"No use arguing with these people," muttered a *kolhoznik* to me, "they'll have their own way. They won't have anything new."

"We must reëducate you first," — it was the student again, "then you will change your attitude to-

wards labor. You will no longer say 'let the other
fellow do the work.'"

"Reëducate," sneered Ilya, "reëducate a *muzhik*.
You silly idiot. When you have lived as long as I have,
young man, you'll talk less nonsense. But I wanted to
say something else. The *kolhoz* is supposed to exploit
nobody. But did any landlord ever exploit people as it
does? Did any landlord ever take cows, pigs, horses,
wagons, timber and other things, too, from their owners
as the *kolhoz* has from these unfortunate *koolacks?* Yet
it, too, hires labor and far more than any *koolack* ever
did — exploitation!"

"Hear, hear," shouted a burly peasant, delighted.
And Ilya, stimulated by the attention he was attracting,
raced on with increasing fervor. "They talk about
exploitation. Well, look at the settlement of the
shliakhta [9] near here. Son of mine," he put his hands
across his chest and shook his head dolefully, "it was
as near a pogrom as anything I have ever seen in my
life. They were well-to-do people in this settlement,
cultured and industrious, and in the old days they
bought a lot of land from the neighboring landlords,
and they raised wonderful cattle, pigs, geese, sheep and
everything. They had machinery too. Of course they
employed hired assistance, so as to get the work done
properly, but they themselves and their wives and children worked harder than all the hired men. For a long
time the Soviets tried to break them with taxes, levies
of bread, fines, and cutting into their land, yet they still
lived on and prospered, for they were real hustlers and
good folk. Last winter, however, they were pronounced
koolacks, sixteen of them out of eighteen. To my dying

[9] Well-to-do Polish peasants.

day I shall never forget what I saw there last winter. I was on a visit to my nephew who had an allotment there. What a fate! Such wailing and shouting I never heard. They were one and all, men, women and children, yes even the newly born babies still at their mothers' breasts, packed off. They begged for mercy, some of the men blubbering like little children and pleading for their wives to be spared and allowed to remain so that they and the children could keep on living at home. Do you suppose that any notice was taken of their prayers? *Akh!* No more than a storm takes of the hay that has not been gathered from the field. Pity there was none. They all had to go, bundle up and get into the wagons and drive off to that awful place, Kotlas."

" But they were *koolacks,* uncle," shouted a *kolhoznik.*

" And *koolacks* have no place in a Soviet society," chimed in the student. " They are always against collectivization, against everything indeed."

" *Koolacks, koolacks,*" continued the old man. " Have then *koolacks* no feelings, have they no love for their wives and children? Do *koolacks* enjoy seeing their dear ones fall sick and die? They are now letting some of the women and children come back, if relations send for them or go to fetch them. Anisya from T—— has just returned. You ought to hear her talk! The poor thing, she went away with four children and only one has come back, three died up there. Another man from the same village has also come back with his wife. He was sent away illegally and permitted to return. But of his two children, one died on the way up there, and the other just as they got off the train the other day —

almost in sight of home. My son saw them in the market place. They had the body of the dead child in the
wagon wrapped up in a sack and covered with straw.
My son told me that the mother, poor little thing, cried
so wildly that the whole market place was upset. There
now," turning to the *kolhozniks* reproachfully.

"In a revolution you cannot stop just for a few
women and children," burst out the student.

The remark released an avalanche of abuse.

"You stop at nothing, nothing. . . ."

"Think of the grain you have shaken out of
us. . . ."

"And all the spying and denouncing by the
poor. . . ."

"*Koolack, koolack, koolack!*"

"Yes, *koolack, koolack, koolack.*"

"Everybody is a *koolack* who wants to keep his self-
respect."

"Yes, everybody, everybody, even if he has not a
shirt to his name."

"They scare you with words. . . ."

"And with threats. . . ."

The *kolhozniks* and the student tried to get in an
explanation, but the crowd was no longer in a mood to
listen. Carried away by a torrent of indignation they
would have no excuse. The wrath of the moment carried everything before it. Louder and louder became
their shouts as one after the other they jumped to their
feet, flourishing their arms and brandishing their sticks
as if to strike. The women, even more wrought up than
the men, shrieked their complaints and denunciations
at the top of their piercing voices. One man grabbed

me by the arm and begged me to follow him into a
corner where a friend from another village would tell
me of the *peregibi* [10] that the government organizers
had perpetrated there. Several people pushed up to me
and yelled their complaints into my face. The *kolhozniks* were as excited as the rest. The student jumped
over people's backs and mounting the pile of logs
shouted for order, but it was of no avail. Nobody
wanted order. Nobody wanted to listen. Everybody
seemed possessed. As no one took any notice of him
the student turned to the small group that had gathered
round me.

" It is always the same," he began, " they see nothing but evil in everything the Soviets do. They can't
get over the fate of the wives and children of the liquidated *koolacks*. Of course the women and children did
suffer. I was myself a special constable and helped to
dekoolackize people. It was not a pleasant job. But
neither is going to war and shooting and throwing
bombs and thrusting a bayonet into another man's
flesh, yet sometimes it has to be done. And this was war,
and is war. The *koolack* had to be got out of the way as
completely as an enemy at the front. He is the enemy
at the front. He is the enemy of the *kolhoz,* and wherever he could he struck at the *kolhoz* with all his might;
and that we just could not allow. And what pity did
these same *koolacks* show to women and children when
they had their bins loaded with rye and wheat and
would let none of it go to the city, where there were
people, millions of them, yes millions of women and children too, threatened with starvation? "

[10] Excesses or abuses.

" If the Soviets would pay them a decent price they would not stick to their grain," burst out one of his listeners.

" A decent price," shouted the student. " Didn't the Soviets pay the *koolack* a decent price? What did he want — blood? A decent price! In a revolution everybody has to work and suffer and sacrifice himself and help to build up the new society which is going to make everybody comfortable. But the *koolacks* thought only of themselves; all they wanted was to grab and grab and to keep their grabbings in their own hands. The rest of the country might perish — it was no affair of theirs. Think of the men and women in the cities sweating away at their work, and the *koolacks* holding the bread back from them. Where was their pity? *Koolack* children died — yes, but other children have been saved. And is it nothing that nurseries have been built, even in this village and in so many other villages round here? And what are these nurseries for but to keep the children well and happy, and to save them from disease and premature death? "

" Nobody said anything against the nurseries," someone interrupted.

" No," flashed back the student, " but you talk about *koolack* babies as though the Soviets tried intentionally to starve and kill them. Unreasoning creatures. The peasants want everything to happen at once. They would like the Soviets to take them into the *kolhoz* and immediately to shower gold and luxury upon them. Do wells dig themselves? Do barns build themselves? Do fields plough themselves? Do tractors make themselves? They forget that nothing comes without effort, without sacrifice. But, *nichevo,* they will learn, they will have to, and, babies or no babies, the *koolacks,* all of them, will have to go."

"We'll all go, we'll all perish," broke in the old man who had complained that he could get no sugar at the coöperative.

"You will if the *koolacks* are not liquidated — they'll swallow you all up and bring the bourgeois back and make slaves of you again. The *kolhoz* is your only salvation." The student finished.

The old man remained unimpressed.

"*Koolacks, koolacks,* that is all we hear nowadays," he answered. "I have lived through wars and epidemics and revolutions and droughts and what not. And this is what I say — if you have a rotten piece of stuff, how can you make a good hat? If you have a rotten piece of wood how can you make a good axle? Of course you can't. And if you have a rotten people how can you have order? Of course you can't, and we Russians are the rottenest people in the world, always against one another, always fighting one another. *Nu,*" and he despairingly waved his hand.

"That is the old way of talking, grandpa," said the student. "It has no meaning any more. But you are not to blame. You are too old to learn."

Later on I went with a crowd of boys for a swim. The student came along too. Afterwards, when we were stretching ourselves on the grass in the sun, he returned to the charge.

"Do you know what the chief trouble is with our *muzhiks?*" he said. "They all want to become *koolacks.* It is deep-rooted, in their very bones. Again and again I ask myself, why are they like that? Take that fellow, Nikolai, for instance, of whom they spoke with such pity. What had he all his life been sweating and saving for? What good did he get out of all his savings? And, you remember, the more he saved the more he wanted to save. Why, what for? "

He paused; I passed round the cigarettes, and as we smoked he went on.

" I have been thinking a good deal about the subject lately because of something that happened in my own village. The old landlord there had a wonderful black-smith, a plain *muzhik*, a *samouchka*,[11] but with an un-canny aptitude for mechanics. There was no machine, however complicated, even of foreign make, which he could not put right. Other landlords, when they had trouble with their machines, sent for him instead of for a professional mechanic. He was earning good money both from his own landlord and from others too. But he had the soul of a *koolack*. He never married and he lived all alone in a little house, did his own cooking, his own washing, his own mending, and all the time he kept on hoarding. He would never help any of his relations, not even his own brother and sister, and when his sister's children came to see him he never gave them so much as a ginger snap or a slice of white bread. He just saved and saved and hoarded and hoarded.

" The other day he got sick, and the *feldsher*[12] told him to stay in bed — he was too feverish to go about. The neighbors sent for his sister who lived about fif-teen versts away. When she approached the bedside, he shouted to her to leave the house at once. " You have come here to see me die," he screamed, " so that you can grab my property. But I won't die. I will outlive

[11] Self-educated man.
[12] Healer.

you and all your children and everyone else who wants
to lay hands on my possessions. Out with you, you
bitch." The poor woman went back and she had hardly
reached home when the old fellow died. With the help
of the police his relations searched the house and it was
amusing the things they found there — twenty-six axes,
fifty odd sickles, hundreds of nuts and bolts, a whole
stack of plough-points, piles of other spare parts — and
also sacks of horsehair and bristles and dried fish that
had begun to rot. His attic was also stuffed up with the
things he had been hoarding all his life — hoarding just
for the sake of hoarding, without any thought of using
them. Well, the old fellow had gold too. He bragged
while he was still alive that he had more than the landlords had, but neither his relations nor the police could
find it. They turned his house and the little barn and
shop upside down, but they could find the gold nowhere. Then they began to dig outside, and at last they
found it in some little iron buckets, and where do you
suppose they found it? Right under the earth closet!
Just fancy! The cunning old devil! And the question
I have been asking myself is, what good do these people get out of all this? One bucket of gold, two buckets
of gold, a sackful of axes, a carload of axes, a million
roubles, a billion roubles — why do people love hoarding? What pleasure do they get out of it? *Akh,* how
beastly! "

X

THE WHITE WEDDING

IN present-day Russia it is heresy to view with approval the old holidays. Spokesmen of the new régime see in them only a calculated effort of malign exploiters to bedevil the masses. In *The Calendar of Religious Holidays,* the author, F. Covalef, inveighs wrathfully against their nature and purposes. Holidays, he argues, were an occasion and an excuse for drunkenness and gluttony and all their accompanying evils. " On holidays," he writes, " it was drummed into the heads of the people that they must fulfill the commands of Christ, which in reality were the commands of the exploiting classes. . . . On holidays, with the aid of services and ceremonies, the priest and the exploiting classes hovering back of them, sought to prevent the unification of the toiling masses for the struggle against their oppressors. . . . The customs and ceremonials that pertain to the purely nature basis of holidays resulted in colossal damage to the people . . . served to perpetuate backward and unproductive methods of tillage and prevented man from wrenching himself free from poverty. . . . Now these customs and ceremonials hamper the spread of the *kolhoz* movement."

Further on, however, the writer points out that the old holidays were in some way rooted in an appreciation or fear of the forces of nature on which the welfare of farming folk depended. Eloquently he commends those Soviet organizations which, in their fight against religion, provided substitutes that linked the nature element of the old holidays to some present-day movement. " The day of Elijah," he says in speaking of the work of certain Soviets, " was turned into a day of electrification; Trinity into an arbor day; Pokrov into a harvest day and, in 1929, into a day of electrification. Easter was made the day of the first furrow, and in the future it ought to be the day of collective ploughing and sowing." Thus, in spite of Bolshevik bias the author is impelled to admit that there was an element in the old holidays which ministered to man's urge for festivity, excitement and romance.

Surely this was true of holidays in our village. Here, for example, was Christmas — the merriest of all festivals. Older people might find their chief diversion in drink, but youth cared little for mead or vodka. Instead, it abandoned itself to rounds of dances, song-fests and those minstrel-like parades which lent special lustiness to Christmas. There was the parade with the *Zvesda,* the star. Out of scantlings, boys would make a star-shaped wheel and cover it on both sides with gay-colored paper. Inside, they would insert candles and light them. Hoisting the star on top of a thin pole, they would revolve it by means of a string, causing it to whirl with brilliant illumination. Marching from house to house with this star and, turning it round and round, they would sing appropriate songs. The lady of the house usually rewarded them for their entertainment with a piece of pork, a boiled egg, griddle cakes or other peasant delicacies.

Equally exciting was the parade with the *koselchik*
— little goat. The boys would fashion the effigy of a
little goat out of sticks, boards and skins. One of them
would act as its official rider. From house to house
they would march, an accordion player or fiddler going with them. On entering a house the musicians would
play like mad on their instruments and the rider of
the *koselchik*, his hat decorated with brightly colored
paper, would dance around the room on his little goat,
violently tossing his head and flicking a shiny leather
whip. Then he would ask the lady of the house for a
mess of grain for the overworked and hungry creature,
and the request was always joyfully granted.

Both the star bearers and the goat riders never
missed a house in the village, whether peasant, Gipsy
or Jew. Sometimes, they would visit neighboring villages singing and shouting, and make the rounds of
the houses there, while similar parties of merry-makers
would come from other villages to ours.

Easter was less rollicking and more ceremonious
than Christmas. As if in emulation of nature which,
with the arrival of spring, resumed a festive appearance, the peasants would scrub and whitewash their
houses and paint the windows and the shutters, as on
no other occasion in the year. Those who could afford
it would decorate their lamps and windowsills with gay
colored tissue paper. The night before, at various places
in the street, there would be log fires which were kept
up until daylight, and folk would gather around and
regale themselves with gossip and ghost tales.

The chief diversion during the Easter holidays was
the game of *bitki* and what an exciting game it is! Two
men, each holding an egg, oppose each other. One man

exposes the small end of his egg, while the other, also
exposing the small end, taps lightly with his egg upon
the other until one breaks. Then the players turn the
eggs around, exposing the large ends and repeat the
tapping. The man whose egg breaks on both ends
forfeits it to his opponent; if both eggs break at one end
the players exchange them. There were men in the
village who all winter long prepared for this game.
They examined every egg before it went to market or
to the frying pan, sounding the strength of its shell by
lightly tapping the ends against their teeth. Any egg
which promised to be a winner, they would store
away for Easter. They would make the rounds of
market places in search of strong-shelled eggs and
pay for them from ten to fifty copecks apiece, an exorbitant price in the old days. Throughout the Easter
holidays, crowds would gather in the street, if the
weather permitted, otherwise in houses, their pockets
bulging with eggs and amidst excited talk and violent
gesturing would accept or fling out challenges and win
or lose egg after egg. Whatever the original reason for
this game and the pagan beliefs out of which it has
grown, it was a prolific source of fun and excitement.

Yet neither Christmas nor Easter could vie with
Trinity in sheer romantic appeal. Coming at the time
of the interval between the planting and the harvesting
of crops, it was as if built on a spirit of thanksgiving
for nature's bountifulness. Well do I remember with
what solicitude peasants would in the old days sweep
the streets and clean up the yards and set these out
with a double row of freshly cut birch saplings and
carpet the ground between with newly mowed grass.
They would twine leafy twigs around window-frames,

gateways, and fences. They would cover the ikons and the lamps inside their houses with garlands of flowers in season, chief of which was the gorgeous corn-flower. Dismal as the village might appear in ordinary times, on Trinity, clothed in a mantle of grass and foliage and flowers, it made a lovely picture.

The people, themselves, would partake of the brightness and gayety of nature. Dressed in their best, everybody would go to church, taking along flowers and freshly mowed grass. At certain parts of the services, the congregation would kneel down and make wreaths. These they would wear on the way home and then hang up on the ikons. They were supposed to be magic wreaths, possessed of power to keep away ill-luck from house and barn — that is from man and beast. In some parts of the country, girls in crowds would go to a nearby stream and amidst song and laughter would cast their wreaths into the waters and wait for results with fluttering hearts. If the wreaths floated away they would thrill with joy, for this was a sign that within the ensuing year they would be married. If the wreaths were caught in an eddy and whirled round and round in one place, their brows would cloud with disappointment, for that was a sign that their troth would be dissolved. If the wreath sank into the water their hearts too sank, for that meant that they would remain unwed, the worst possible fate for a peasant girl in the old days. I am not intending to trace the origin of these ancient practices, but one need be neither poet nor scientist to appreciate the urge for diversion and romance that went into their making.

The Bolsheviks, however, need not be alarmed over the stability of the ancient holidays and their multitudinous customs. The Revolution is fast gnawing away at their very roots and draining them of vitality. In our village the day of the *zvesda* and the *koselchik* was, I learned, at an end. Children of school age had not seen either. Other ceremonials were likewise disappearing. During the preceding Easter eve, only two bonfires were started and these were kept up only a short time. The people who gathered around them no longer diverted themselves with ghost tales, but engaged in a violent discussion of the one subject that never left their minds — the *kolhoz*. Peasants still played the game of *bitki*, but with ever diminishing zest, and there were young people who laughed at it as at something fit only for demented folk. It would not be long, I was assured, before *bitki* would go the way of the *zvesda* and the *koselchik* — into oblivion.

I did not, however, have to trust to mere hearsay to appreciate the collapse of the old scheme of things in holiday celebrations. Here was Trinity, and as I sauntered up and down the village I saw but faint attempts at the customary decorations. Not a yard could boast of the boulevard-like double row of saplings nor of the layers of grass that clothed the village in loveliness. A lone stick of brush, a few handfuls of grass carelessly scattered, a stray twig over a window was all that remained of the ancient ornamentation. Still people did observe it. They did not work and they dressed up in their best clothes. Few of them went to church and fewer still carried flowers. Also Trinity had remained the wedding season that it always was. True, this year, there were fewer weddings than usual — only four. Because of the uncertainties that the *kolhoz* had flung on them, youths were postponing marriage, and

besides they had become more worldly and were in
no hurry to rush into wedlock. Three of the four
scheduled weddings were red, that is secular, and the
fourth was white, with a religious ceremony. The white
wedding, perhaps the last in the village, roused my
chief interest and I invited myself as a guest there.

The bride was a blue-eyed girl of seventeen, with
flaxen hair, a round chin and a voice that was mildly
piercing. At the village dance the evening before the
wedding, she was as gay as any girl and frolicked about
with the boys with a freedom which in itself betokened
a new spirit among peasant girls.

Her mother, a woman of forty-two, with a wealth of
lustrous black hair and a handsome face, told me, between sobs, that she was sorry to have the girl marry
so young, especially in times like these when folks were
upset about everything. But America was to blame —
her husband had gone there before Anna was born
and refused to return home. Now and then he would
send a few dollars, but that did not relieve her of the
responsibility of managing the household. Had she
been in good health she would not have minded. But
of late she had been subject to headaches and back-
aches, and with the new order of things in the village,
her responsibilities, instead of lightening were growing
more arduous. She needed someone to share these responsibilities and who could do it more competently
than a man she could trust? Well, she knew Anna was
in love with Peter, and Peter, though only twenty, was
an exemplary youth, with fine work habits and of a
kindly disposition. He had wanted to wait until his
period of service in the Red Army was over, but he
yielded to persuasion and consented to an immediate

marriage. He would be a *Primak* — come to live with them and be the man in their house. His father had agreed to give him a wagon, a horse and a cow.

Early on the morning of the wedding, I went to the bride's house. The family had just finished breakfast, all but Anna, who, according to custom, was supposed to touch no food or drink until after the betrothal. Her mother and younger sister and her very old grandmother, were more excited than Anna herself. The grandmother, especially, was overjoyed that she had lived to see her granddaughter become betrothed to a good and worthy man. With tears in her eyes she assured me that she had been worried lest Anna and Peter, like so many young couples, forswear a church ceremony and she was so elated that they would be married by the little father.

As we were all sitting around the family table and talking, a matronly girl entered the house. She was the bridegroom's sister. Instantly Anna disappeared and soon returned with a gorgeously embroidered blouse. Unfolding it before me she asked how I liked it and, glowing with pride, explained that she had made it for Peter and that this was his wedding costume. Folding it gently, she gave it to Peter's sister who tucked it neatly under her arm and dashed out of the house.

Presently guests began to arrive, each with a contribution for the wedding feast — a pot of cheese, a dish of sour cream, a loaf or part of a loaf of black bread, a pan of boiled eggs, a sack of flour for griddle cakes, a roll of home-made sausage, a lump of boiled beef, raw salted pork and of course bottles of vodka and even more of homebrew. Setting these gifts on the table the guests seated themselves on the benches.

Those who found no seats stood up and soon the house was jammed with people, young and old, among whom were women with babies that were sucking from big uncovered breasts. The musicians came, two peasant boys with an accordion and a tambourine and instantly they broke into a merry tune. The playing struck a responsive chord in the guests and they burst into song, the older folks singing with as much enthusiasm as the young people:

> *Much ado with cabbage*
> *What with planting and with watering*
> *Love is even more trouble*
> *What with caring and forgetting.*

And again:

> *In a red house on the clearing*
> *My sweetheart promised to take me*
> *Pray, mother dear, see*
> *If he'll make a good son-in-law.*

A recess followed. The guests were waiting for the groom and were putting themselves into a fit mood to receive him. When he arrived, escorted by his sister and his groomsmen, he was greeted with the song:

> *Says little Peter, he says*
> *Why don't they bring my little Anna*
> *If they'd bring my little Anna*
> *She'd give me her right hand.*

Short and wiry, with light brown hair, mild blue eyes and wearing the blouse Anna had made for him, Peter, self-conscious and embarrassed, seated himself at the head of the table, surrounded by his groomsmen.

Nearby sat Nikita, one of the oldest men in the village,
and famed for his long beard and his ready wit. Tumbler of homebrew in hand, he recited a toast of welcome
to the groom; the other guests followed ending with
the salutation "to your health, bridegroom." Peter,
of course, was not supposed to touch food or drink
until after the return from church. His groomsmen
sought to persuade him to forget this ancient custom
but he staunchly refused to be persuaded. Once more
the guests burst into song, this time into the melancholy
strains of *"Sudba Neschastnaya"* (unhappy fate).
When the song was finished, Anna walked in on the
arms of her groomsmen. She wore a veil and her cheeks
were rouged. A buxom girl, with a ruddy complexion,
she needed no rouge; but since it was something new
in the village, something from the city, its use was
supposed to lend her special distinction. Looking
neither to right nor to left, she walked straight to the
place reserved for her on the bench facing Peter, and
he, without rising from his seat or removing his tight
fitting cap, greeted her with a smile. She returned his
smile and with a primness which was almost hauteur,
she proceeded to shake hands with the guests at the
table; the older people she kissed on the hand, not with
a touch of the lips but with a resounding smack. Once
more Nikita was on his feet with the inevitable tumbler
of homebrew in his hand. This time he recited a toast
to both bride and groom, wishing them happiness and
peace and above all a safe journey to church. Slyly
winking at Peter he ended with the words "May the
coachman forego the temptation of being too brave."
A fair enough warning, for custom has it that the
groom's coachman is to lash the horses into topmost

speed. Other guests repeated the warning, more in playful taunt than in earnest solicitude.

The feast continued. With no forks, no knives, no napkins, no plates, the guests helped themselves with their hands to the array of foods before them. They emptied flask after flask of vodka and homebrew. No sooner was one flask drained than another bobbed up on the table. Homebrew was forbidden by law yet nobody seemed worried about possible consequences. In reply to my question as to how they dared make it in the face of the existing ban, they laughed and assured me that as long as fields and swamps were endless, the Soviets could not see everything. Here, at any rate, the supply seemed inexhaustible, for fresh guests were arriving, bringing more and more flasks. Meanwhile the house was so crowded that guests stood in rows to the very doors. The windows were closed. The smoke of *mahorka,* peasant tobacco, filled the room with its nauseating stench and together with the odors of sweat, leather and alcohol, made the air so foul that I grew dizzy. But evidently none of the guests minded. Nobody fainted and nobody complained nor were their appetites impaired. They ate and drank with lusty relish, all but the bridal couple. They waited in silence, and Nikita, with his love of mischief, teased them endlessly — never, he exulted, were pork, beef, cheese, bread, griddle cakes so delicious; never again would they be so delicious and what a pity that they, bride and groom, so young, so innocent and so hungry, could taste not a morsel of all these delicacies. The teasing always is a part of the jollity of weddings.

Three wagons, filled with straw and covered with homespun blankets were driven into the yard. The

most distinctive was the one in which the groom was
to ride — the leading horse was one of the finest looking
in the village and the bow over its head was wreathed
with twigs, flowers and brightly colored paper. Now
with a bright sun shining it gleamed like an immense
crown. The coachman, a relative of the groom, sat at
the dashboard with his cap drawn so low as to con-
ceal his eyes, his feet tucked under him, his leather
whip shining like a steel weapon. It was evident that he
had had his share of drinks and was eager to live up
to the historic reputation of a man in his position and
drive on with all the speed that his voice and whip
could stir out of the horses. " Not too fast," cautioned
a friend of the groom, but in reply the coachman smiled
with contempt. He was in no mood for suggestions.
Soon the bride, escorted by her boy and girl attendants,
came forth and instantly the guests burst into song:

> *Oh watch the dust, the dust*
> *Little Anna goes to the altar*
> *To her fate she goes*
> *Her fate did not swim away with the water*
> *But followed her.*

And again in a spirit of jollity:

> *There goes the priest our little father*
> *Aye, there, open the church*
> *Marry these children in a good hour.*

While the songs continued, the bride's mother proceeded to bestow her blessing on the couple. With a loaf
of bread in one arm and with a sack of rye in her hand,
she walked round and round the bridal wagon scatter-

ing handfuls of grain in the air, now and then pausing
to offer a mouthful to the horse. When she finished the
groom and his party got into their wagon, the bride
and her escorts into theirs and a young married couple
and I into the remaining wagon. The musicians blared
forth a fresh tune, the guests chanted a lusty farewell
and as the horses started the bride scattered handfuls
of rye in the air. The wagon in which I rode led off in
the procession, but the groom's coachman lashed violently away at his horses and nearly upset us. My driver
protested with that volley of curses which drip so easily
from a peasant's lips. But the groom's coachman did
not bother to stop. Shouting furiously and flicking
his whip, he galloped on and on. Only several versts
away did he halt and wait for the other wagons, not,
however, out of a wish to be accommodating or sociable,
but to get into the picture which I had promised to
take of the procession.

The sun was hot, the sky was clear and all around as
far as the eye could see fields of rye were bowing to
and fro, like masses of Mohammedans in prayer.
Happy was the bride and happy was the groom and
happier still were their escorts, for they sang without
let-up.

> *Green grass mows well*
> *A cheerful girl loves well.*

As if in a spirit of mischief they followed with several
Soviet songs.

> *A white gown I shall don*
> *A yellow flower I shall pin on*
> *The little father shall not marry us*
> *Soviet alone shall unite us*

And again:

Aye, out in the field pretty corn flowers sway
With another lassie my sweetheart may be playing
But he will register [1] with me.

At last we reached our destination but the church
was closed. A crowd of children instantly surrounded
us, and were followed by groups of women who had
also come to see the wedding. We searched for the
priest in the churchyard but failed to find him. None
of the children and women could tell us where he was.
They had not seen him since services in the morning.
Without delay a party set off for his house. Soon they
returned with the news that they found the little father
asleep on a pile of straw in the barn. They wakened
him and he told them that he had waited for several
hours in the church but as not a single couple had come
to be wed, he went home, ate his midday meal and lay
down to sleep on the cool straw in the barn.

He was not long in arriving. His short, stocky bulk,
broad back and massive head with its sprinkling of red
hair around the chin, made him seem more like a merchant than a priest. He was a timid and reticent man,
loath to answer questions. He would not even express
an opinion as to why only one couple had come to be
married in church when, in the old days, the little
father of a parish like this, on a holiday like Trinity,
was so busy all day marrying people that he hardly
had time to breathe. One of the groomsmen urged
him to make haste and start the service, but on reaching the locked church door the little father remembered that the deacon had the keys. So now the

[1] I.e., Sign his name in the marriage register.

deacon had to be sent for, and when he came and un-
locked the door we all poured inside.

The priest retired into an inner chamber while the
deacon spread a strip of linen on the floor in the center
of the church. Over this linen he placed a faded homespun rug. The bridal couple were to stand on this rug.
Soon the priest reappeared and I gasped at the transformation he had effected. Garbed in silvery vestments,
with a crown on his head, he seemed to have risen in
stature. Apparently conscious of a fresh importance
and dignity he walked about with a fine stateliness of
which I never should have suspected him capable. His
timidity had fled and, though in the outside world he
might be scorned and cursed as an ill-omen, here he was
conscious of mastery. His voice harmonized with his new
bearing. Smooth, vibrant, dramatic, it was so powerful that, when he spoke the windows almost vibrated.
Like a man well versed in the art and mechanics of his
trade and enjoying the least detail, he proceeded with
the ceremony. With the ring of the bride in his hand
he made the sign of the cross over the groom and with
the ring of the groom, over the bride. Then, chanting
scriptural verses, he deposited the rings in a little brass
vial. Presently the deacon fetched two gilded crowns,
both set with gleaming jade stones. Giving them to
the groomsmen, who instantly lifted them over the
heads of bride and groom, the priest picked up a gilded
cross and a Bible. What a Bible it was! Printed in
large letters on heavy parchment and bound in blood-
red velvet and held in an ornately carved silver frame,
it seemed a symbol and a relic of the former wealth and
glory of the Orthodox church. The deacon lighted two
wax candles and the priest, after handing one to Peter
and the other to Anna, burst into a fresh chant, his

voice rolling sonorously through the vast spaces of this high-ceilinged edifice.

"*Peter, servant of God,*" he finally droned, "*is being wed to the handmaid of God, Anna. In the name of the Father, and the Son and the Holy Ghost.*" Turning to Anna, he repeated:

"*Anna, the handmaid of God, is being wed to the servant of God, Peter. In the name of the Father, and the Son and the Holy Ghost.*" Presently he moved backward and burst into a long chant.

"*Wherefore, Oh Lord, our God, who has sent forth thy truth upon thine inheritance and thy covenant unto thy servants, our Fathers, even thine elect from generation to generation, look thou upon thy servant Peter and upon thy handmaid Anna and establish and make stable their betrothal, in faith and in oneness of mind, in truth and in love. . . . By a ring was power given unto Joseph in Egypt; by a ring was Daniel glorified in the land of Babylon; by a ring was the uprightness of Tamar revealed; by a ring did our Heavenly Father show forth his bounty upon his Son.*"

Throughout this recital not a person in church stirred. Even the children seemed so impressed that they never made a move.

"Hast thou promised thyself to another bride?" the little father questioned Peter.

"I have not," came the low reply.

"Hast thou promised thyself to another groom?" repeated the priest turning to Anna.

"I have not," came her firm response.

"*Lord, my God,*" recited the priest, "*with honor and glory I marry you.*" Repeating these words several times he followed them with readings from his velvet covered Bible. When he finished, he put the Bible to the lips of the bride and groom and closed it. Forthwith the deacon fetched a flask of sacramental wine. Pouring it into two small vials, the priest offered a sip first to Peter, then to Anna and then twice more alternately to both.

Now they were ready for the march which is perhaps the most impressive feature of an Orthodox wedding. The priest led bride and groom, accompanied by their attendants. Trailing at the very end of the procession was a relative of the bride, holding a lighted wax candle, the bottom of which was wrapped in a piece of white linen and stuck through a hole in a crust of black bread. With a fresh flow of enthusiasm, the priest went on intoning:

"*Rejoice, Oh Isaiah! A virgin is with child and shall bear his Son Emmanuel, both God and Man. . . . Oh, holy martyrs who fought the good fight and have received your crowns, entreat ye the Lord that he will have mercy on our souls. . . . Glory to thee in Christ, our God, the Apostles Post, the martyrs joy. . . .*"

When the march halted the priest took the crown of the groom and laid it aside saying:

"*Be thou exalted, Oh Bridegroom, like unto Abraham; and be thou blessed like unto Isaac; and do thou multiply like unto Jacob, walking in peace and keeping the commandments of God in righteousness.*"

Then taking the bride's crown he continued:

"*And thou, Oh Bride, be thou exalted like unto Sarah and blessed like unto Rebecca and do thou multiply like unto Rachael and rejoice thou in thy husband, fulfilling the condition of the law for so it is pleasant unto God.*"

The couple were now wedded with all the pomp and

ritual of devout Orthodox followers. Someone burst
into a derisive laugh but the priest never bothered to
take notice. He seemed too conscious of his official
dignity and importance to be disturbed by a flitting
interference. He directed the wedded couple to a huge
ikon on the upper altar before which they were to
pray. Peter looked upset and did not move but Anna
jerked him by the arm and led him to the appointed
ikon. Kneeling down she made the sign of the cross
over her body and kissed the ikon. But Peter held
aloof.

" Did you see that? " one of his escorts turned to me.

" What does it mean? " I asked.

" He would not pray."

" And why not? " I further inquired.

" Ask him."

When they came down from the altar I did ask Peter
why he did not pray.

" I don't know how," was his astounding reply.

" But you are grown up," a woman who stood nearby
hurled at him with indignation.

"And what if I am? Nobody ever taught me to
pray." As if in boast he added, " And what's the good
of praying? Don't I keep well without it? " His words
exasperated the woman. Shaking her hand in wrath she
exclaimed:

" Oh, you wicked men! You heartless infidels, you
will feel sorry yet! Don't imagine that the Lord is not
hearing you. He will send a plague or a drouth and
then you will change! "

We drove back home and now bride and groom were
sitting together in the same wagon, their arms twined

around one another. The attendants once more took to singing.

> *We visited the little father*
> *Mead and vodka did we drink*
> *Little nuts did we shell*
> *Two children did we wed*
> *One highly precious*
> *The other highly prized*
> *Annushka highly precious*
> *Peter highly prized.*

We drove fast. The dust was rising in clouds, and song after song floated into the air. When we reached the home of the bride, the bridesmaids greeted Anna's mother with the chant:

> *Come, come, mamma dear, with the candles*
> *Thy little child has been wed*

Shaking the dust off our clothes we entered the house. The tables were freshly laid with food and drink. This time only the wedded couple and the party that followed them to church were to have a feast. So we crowded around the table and proceeded to help ourselves to homebrew and vodka and honey cakes and cheese and meat and the other delicacies. Presently some of the other guests, older people, began to dribble in. Stationing themselves before the table they chanted toasts to the wedded couple and emptied beaker after beaker of homebrew. Nikita also staggered in, his face flushed, his little eyes contracted, his hat pushed back exposing a lofty forehead that was seamed with deep lines. Approaching me he insisted that I drink with him to the health of the bride and then to the health of

the groom. Smelly and biting as was this brew, I compelled myself to keep Nikita company. But he seemed
determined to drink to the health of every guest in
the room, aye every person in the village and every
citizen, I thought, in the whole Soviet Union. This was
more than I had bargained for. But my refusal to keep
up with him stirred him to exasperation.

"You are not at all like your late lamented father,"
he chided, "who never would refuse one more drink.
What weaklings, what cowards people are getting to
be nowadays. *Akh*, what a world, what a world!"

He drew close, gulped down his homebrew and instantly refilled the tumbler. "Nothing is as it used to
be," he resumed. "A man of my years ought to know
something. Think of it — I am seventy-five, or maybe
eighty-five, I am not sure. Drink? Why at my wedding
we emptied not flasks but barrels, and not this insipid
samagon, but vodka with real flame in it. In those times
a wedding, my son, was a wedding and not an imitation
of child's play, and we caroused for days; we swam in
vodka, I tell you. And nowadays, *akh!*" He paused,
violently shook his head in disgust and in dismay and
continued:

"And when we are all herded into the *kolhoz* it will
be worse yet. But thank God, I am old, and shall not
be here to see it all. And now," lifting his tumbler so
that it hit the tip of his nose, "let us drink once more,
just once more, do not refuse, please, you American
devil." He moved so close that his needle-like beard
pricked my face and he forced his tumbler of homebrew to my lips.

"So I say," he picked up his indictment of the new
age, "people are not as strong as they used to be nor

as gay nor as human. Everything is getting tame. Do
you suppose that in my day when the groom first
went to the bride's house he could just walk or drive
into the yard as easily as Peter did this morning? Nay,
nay, his friends would not let him. They would lean on
the gate and yell at him to chase back home to his
mamma. No amount of pleading would avail him. He
would offer his friends money, bargain with them and
only when he paid them enough five and ten copeck
pieces to satisfy them, would they throw the gate open
and allow him to enter the yard. Then fresh troubles
faced him. The girls would hide the bride and would
not let him go near her. They would push him away
and scold and again he had to spend money. There was
excitement for you, there was living for you! And when
they started for church, do you suppose the young
people would let them ride on freely? They threw brush
and logs across the road and halted the journey and
again the groom had to pay lots of five and ten copeck
pieces to have the road cleared for him. And when they
came from church, do you suppose the bridal couple
could walk straight into the house? *Akh,* no, the bride's
mother had something to say about it. Wearing a sheepskin coat turned inside out, she would station herself
at the table near the door, with a tumbler of honey and
rolls in her hand. Bride and groom would approach
her and she would dip a roll into the honey and offer
it to the groom and as he made ready to snap it up with
his mouth, she would snatch it away and offer it to the
bride, and as she attempted to bite into it, she would
draw it away again. After teasing them like that, good
and plenty, she would thrust the roll into her own

mouth and then start teasing all over again, and every-body nearly died laughing."

He paused, looking reflectively at his tumbler, as though debating whether or not to touch it.

"It stands, it stands, this container of fire," he chattered away in a sing-song, "but soon it will stand no longer — it will be emptied." And turning to me he begged: "Once more, old friend, just once more for old time's sake, for your dear old father's sake who was such a good pal of mine. *Akh,* you wretch! You may never again have a chance to drink with me. Next year, if you come, I will be dead, I am sure I will be, so come, be comradelike — Whew" and he chanted merrily:

"Vodka, vodka, little vodka mine
Vodka, vodka, dear vodka mine"

"Fools," he philosophized, "are afraid of drink. Wise men are afraid only of women and not much of them. I am so much older than you are, eighty years old or maybe ninety; who knows? But my Lord, how much fire there is still in me. So here is a wedding for you. What a wedding! Nobody even drunk, excepting myself, and I am old-fashioned. Look around. There's the groom. Watch him, the little rascal, sitting at the table like a tamed rabbit eating and drinking and un-worried. He knows nothing will happen to him. But in my days, brother, they would grab the groom when he was not looking, carry him out into the yard to the trough, duck his head in water, duck it all the way up to his neck, even in winter. There was excitement for you. And there were tears too, ah, what tears, when the

korovey [2] was cut. The bride would loosen her hair and
her mother would singe it and tell her in song that she
was no longer a frivolous girl, but a woman with toil
and hardships ahead of her and a cruel master to rule
her. The bride would cry, ah, how she would cry and all
the women in the house would cry. And now, just wait
until they cut the *korovey* at this wedding. Maybe
Anna's mother will singe the bride's hair and maybe
she won't. But even if she does do you think anybody
will feel sorry and weep? Not even Anna will weep.
There, watch her giggling! She thinks I am an old fool
and maybe I am. But I know things. And really, why
should a bride nowadays weep? Take this Anna. Come
here in a few days and see who will be the master
of the house, and they are all getting to be like that
nowadays, these young women. Even their fathers can't
tell them things any more. And they call it a wedding,
Akh! "

He paused, swallowed another tumbler of homebrew, smacked his lips with a resounding noise and continued, " In a few years they won't even have such a
wedding. You are young and you will see with your own
eyes whether or not I am telling the truth. But I won't,
thank God I won't. I'll die soon — I can already smell
the approach of death. But no matter. I've had my
life. I have no regrets. Only mark my word when everybody is in the *kolhoz,* a boy and girl will just go to
bed and that's all that will be left of marriage. How
do I know it? Am I blind? Am I stupid? Have I seen
nothing of life? Think of my age, seventy-five, eighty-
five, ninety. Who knows? Hear me then — in the *kolhoz* people will get only enough grain for bread and

[2] Wedding Cake.

will they have any left for homebrew? Of course not.
And will they have any surplus of income for vodka?
Of course not. There now — no homebrew, no vodka,
no way of doing what you want to do and no wedding.
Don't you see? Haw, haw, haw! "

Violently he slapped me on the back and giggled,
his pungent breath beating against my face. Emptying
another tumbler of homebrew he staggered out into the
street and sauntered away, singing at the top of his
high baritone voice an old marching song in praise
of the Russian soldiers who pursued Napoleon out
of Moscow.

XI

THE KOLHOZ

ON my first visit to the village in 1923 the peasants had not even heard of *kolhoz*. Now it had become the most storm-stirring word in their everyday speech. Monster, scarecrow, redeemer, what was it? The older people could shout, fume, curse, but they could not dodge the challenge the *kolhoz* had thrust on them. Like the breath in their nostrils it was with them wherever they went. Its power, like a river at flood-time, was rising higher and higher, and growing more and more threatening. Last year at a mass meeting the peasants could shout: " We'll die and we won't go to the *kolhoz*," and the organizer could fling back: " You won't die, and you will go." Now in spite of protests, threats, fears, it had spread itself in massive defiance before their very doors.

The home of the secretary was temporarily the headquarters of the *kolhoz*. It was an ordinary peasant hut with a thatched roof and small windows located in the heart of the village. Inside no ikons hung in the place of honor above the head of the table. Instead the walls were adorned with the portraits of Lenine, Stalin, Kalinin and with agricultural charts and revolutionary posters. On the table were pencil, paper, books, and blotters. People singly, and in groups, kept surging in and out with messages, requests, complaints.

It was a little house but it always hummed with

life, and every *muzhik*, especially the individualist, watched it and listened· to all the talk and all the noises inside as if his eyes and ears were attentive to it alone. Whenever I passed it I could not help reflecting on its vast significance. It was made of lumber and straw. A bottle of kerosene spilled somewhere over the straw and a lighted match applied to it would reduce it to ashes in a few minutes. Yet what historic audacity it symbolized! What incomparable power it commanded! Surely no peasant could pass it without in his heart of hearts feeling that it had become the very arbiter of his destiny.

Here I must interrupt my narrative to examine briefly the structure and administration of the *kolhoz*, and at the outset I cannot emphasize too vigorously that, in distinction from the *sovhoz*, it is not a state enterprise. It is a coöperative association, legally incorporated and with a constitution defining in detail its functions and purposes. However intimate its relations with the state, however rigid the contractual obligations the latter may impose on it in return for the economic aid it offers in loans, machinery, expert advice, the *kolhoz* actually enjoys full powers of internal administration. Its acts, of course, must harmonize with the basic aims of the Revolution and with the immediate policies of the Soviet government, and it is under constant surveillance of the Soviets and the Party organization. In time its powers may be curtailed or expanded. One never can foretell what the next outbreak of the Revolution will bring. But at present (and anyone who has ever attended a mass meeting of a *kolhoz* has seen overwhelming proof of it) it does enjoy in local affairs an amazing amount of self-determination.

Because it is a coöperative association the final authority in the *kolhoz* is vested in its membership, which in Russian parlance means the mass meeting. The constitution provides that such a meeting be called at least once a month, and to make decisions valid no less than one half of the membership must be present. Only the mass meeting, for example, can admit or expel members, and only after it has sanctioned plans and proposals do they become effective. The voting is done not by secret ballot but by a show of hands, and once a year it holds elections at which it chooses two committees, known respectively as the administration, or executive, and the inspection committees. The first consists usually of nine members and selects the chairman, the secretary, and the treasurer. The second is composed of three members or rather not less than three. While the executive committee does all the planning and administering of the work and the life on the *kolhoz,* the inspection committee keeps a vigilant eye over its actions. Officially it is known as the " organ of internal control." It listens to grievances and complaints against the administration and with the consent of the mass meeting it may compel the latter to change tactics and methods of work. One of its chief duties is to review at the end of the year all the acts and plans of the administration and to check up all its financial accounts.

There are three types of *kolhozy,* though only two are of consequence. The third, known as the *tovarishtshestvo* (association), is losing ground and may in the near future be abandoned. The other two are the commune and the artel. Of these the commune is the higher or rather the highest social organization, and is the guidepost and the eventual objective of all *kol-hozy*. In the commune all individual income-yielding property disappears, and all productive resources — land, implements, stock, and buildings, are held in common. Of all the communes which I have visited in various parts of the land I cannot think of one where any of the members owned his own house or worked his own garden or milked his own cow, or raised his own hens. In a commune the only personal possessions a man has or may have are his immediate personal belongings such as clothes, sometimes house furnishings, and what savings he may have made out of his wages and out of the share of profit that may at the end of the year be disbursed among the members.

At present the communes are not in the foreground of the Soviet policy. Indeed Soviet authorities discourage their promulgation. In the winter of 1929–30 when Stalin and his followers finally resolved to end the forcible organization of *kolhozy*, they vigorously disavowed any aim to draw the peasant at once into a completely communized scheme of life. In proof of their good faith, they proclaimed the artel as the type of *kolhoz* best suited to existing conditions. Hence the artel is now enjoying widest popularity.

In the artel peasants pool their land, their work stock, their implements, their farm buildings, their accumulations or savings, in money or in kind. But they may maintain their individual homes and may keep a cow, hens, geese, ducks, pigs, sheep, and goats, though in numbers which must bear a fair proportion to their personal needs. They may also cultivate their own gardens and orchards. If they happen to have a surplus of produce they may dispose of it, preferably to the coöperative, but if they so choose, in the open market. Yet if in the estimate of their colleagues or local officials their transactions transgress the bounds of legitimacy, always an indefinable term, subject to local interpretations, they may be brought to account on the charge of speculation and made to suffer censure and fine and even expulsion from the *kolhoz* and a sentence in jail.

All the property that a newly admitted member brings to the *kolhoz* is appraised in terms of values that obtain in the coöperative market. The resulting sum is divided into three parts, entrance fee, indivisible fund and membership dues. The entrance fee runs from two to ten percent, the indivisible fund from one fourth to one half of the total amount, and the balance is reckoned as membership due. The first two shares remain the permanent possession of the *kolhoz*. Under no circumstances may the member claim them, even in the event of resignation or expulsion. Only the membership fee, for the present at any rate, remains his individual investment, bears dividends and on departure is subject to withdrawal.

Since the *kolhoz* is supposed to demonstrate its economic superiority to individual land-holding the compensation of members overshadows in importance all other problems. In the artels such compensation is derived from three sources: wages, dividends and profits. All members receive wages, though not all are entitled to dividends, and profits may not always be available for distribution. Wages are usually mapped out tentatively at the beginning of the year and are based on estimates of the possible returns from all the enterprises of the *kolhoz*. Only in the autumn when crops are harvested and the income is definitely ascertained are the wage-scales finally affirmed. Payment differs radically from the system that obtains in the factory. Members may draw an advance in cash or in kind to the amount of sixty percent and the balance they receive at the end of the year, when the crops have been gathered.

To sustain individual interest in the *kolhoz* wages are scaled according to the type of work a member performs and the degree of skill with which he performs it, though in no event must the highest wage be more than double that of the lowest. Exceptions may be made in the case of specialists — engineers, high-grade mechanics and *agronoms*. At present the idea of piece work is winning nation-wide favor, and it is only a question of time when it will supersede all existing wage-scales. But since differentiation in earnings such as piece work is sure to bring about conflicts with the basic Communist theory of equality of income, it is impossible to foretell just how long such differentiation will be practiced. Women are supposed to receive the same wages as men for the same work.

The question of the division of income is still in a state of experimentation. The Moscow *kolhoztsentr* (national *kolhoz* body) has worked out a general scheme for the year of 1930. According to this scheme five percent of the income from crops and stock including dairy products, is to be set aside as dividends on the properties that the individual members have turned in to the *kolhoz*. Taxes, insurance, reserves for possible mishaps, and for seed are figured out on the basis of prevailing conditions and needs of the *kolhoz*, and provided for accordingly. These sums are then deducted from the gross income and ten percent of the remainder is appropriated for the indivisible fund; five percent for social needs, such as a nursery, cultural work, a community kitchen in the field during busy periods, and the support of the old and the disabled. Special needs that may arise may be taken care of by special appropriations. The balance after all above items are covered, is distributed as wages and profits among the members.

The *kolhoz* may not dispose of any of its produce to private parties. It must sell to the government. In a year of average yield in the grain growing regions from one fourth to one third of the harvest, and in the non-grain growing regions only one eighth are sold to the government. The exact amounts of these so-called grain collections are determined by special committees and depend entirely on local productivity. Usually also about one fourth of the harvests are set aside for seeds and reserves and a definite amount for stock-feeding. The remainder of the grain is divided among the members and its cost is deducted from their wages. If the remainder is more than the members actually need for themselves the *kolhoz* is obliged to sell it to the government. It is not supposed to keep an " idle " surplus on hand.

The above scheme, however, is intended as a guiding principle rather than as a fixed rule. In a booklet that attempts to explain in popular language the ruling of the *kolhoztsentr* and the principle underlying the question of distribution of income in the *kolhoz,* and the first edition of which was printed in 300,000 copies, I find the following significant passage:

The mass meeting of the *kolhoz* is the real master of its income, and only this mass meeting can decide how to divide it and how much to apportion to each fund. The *kolhoztsentr* is merely offering the general suggestions that the income is to be divided in accord with the quality and amount of the work of its members. . . . It is necessary to reach a condition where every member knows where and for what purpose *kolhoz* moneys are spent and what income each family is to receive and what the financial condition of the *kolhoz* is at the beginning of the new economic year. Only when each member of the *kolhoz* knows its material condition will it be possible to strengthen the *kolhoz*. That is why the problem of income distribution must be discussed and decided in all of its details at the mass meeting.

This of course does not preclude the possibility of pressure of all kinds being exerted by Party and governmental agencies to effect this distribution in a manner to harmonize with prevailing Soviet needs and policies. Indeed, with the growth of the *kolhoz* and with its rise to prosperity, sharp conflicts between the Soviets and the peasants, the sharpest yet known, may break out over the problem of the division of income.

Membership is open to all men and women sixteen years of age or older, who have not lost citizenship rights. Soviet citizenship is not obligatory — foreigners are as eagerly admitted to the *kolhoz* as native sons. No less than fifteen families, unrelated by blood-ties, are required for the formation of a *kolhoz*, and the tendency is to expand them into large enterprises. There are endless *kolhozy*, especially in the so-called grain regions, with a constituency of thousands of families.

As I watched the men and women who are out in

the field organizing *kolhozy* I was again and again reminded of agents for the chautauqua in the days when that institution was a flourishing American enterprise. However different the purposes of the *kolhoz* from those of the chautauqua, the technic of the organizers of both bear intimate resemblance to one another. The chautauqua agent like the Soviet organizer receives extensive and eloquent coaching before he leaves for field work, and the one like the other is made to realize by their coaches that whatever happens they must "get those signatures on the dotted line," and bring in contracts. Both agents on arriving in a community seek the leading citizens and first attempt to interest them in their respective projects. But a difference as wide as the sky separates their conceptions as to what constitutes a leading citizen. The chautauqua agent finds the leading banker, the lumberman, the shop-keeper and others of the well-to-do group, sometimes also the influential clergyman and schoolman, especially if they happen to be in good standing with the above-mentioned group. The Soviet agent would have nothing but anathemas for such citizens, excepting possibly the schoolman. He would not demean himself by even crossing their threshold. To him the *batrak* — hired laborer, or the *bedniak* — the poor man, are the people of chief consequence, and the poorer they are the greater his respect for them. When he reaches a village it is these people that he first attempts to interest in the *kolhoz*.

There is also a colossal difference in the line of argumentation that the Soviet and chautauqua crusaders for a higher life pursue. The chautauqua agent has only one weapon in his arsenal — moral suasion. The Soviet

organizer almost forswears this weapon. At best it
is only incidental, and for the simple reason that to
the hard-headed *muzhik*, it would have little meaning
and less appeal. He relies essentially on the material
advantages that the *kolhoz* holds forth. He drums
away at the increased harvests that collectivization
would make possible. He outlines in detail the numerous privileges that the government extends to members
of the *kolhoz*. There is the question of taxes. During
the years of 1930–31 and 1931–32 the *kolhoz* and its
individual members are exempted from all levies on
food-producing stock. There is the question of indebtedness to the government. Again *kolhoz* members are
favored. The indebtedness they had incurred prior to
April 1930, whether as arrears in taxes or administrative and judicial fines, are on entering the *kolhoz* wiped
out. There is the question of credits. Again the *kolhoz*
enjoys superior advantages. For the purchase of machinery, stock, seeds, building materials for barns,
silos, houses, clubs and subsidiary industrial enterprises such as brick-yards, flour mills, cement works,
starch-factories, it obtains generous credits on reasonable terms. There is the question of manufactured
goods, always a source of irritation in the village. The
Soviet agitator promises to members of the *kolhoz* as
much consideration as to the poor. To the women he
holds out the lure of nurseries and children's homes
and, therefore, increased leisure for play and diversion.
To the young he emphasizes the advantages of play-
grounds, entertainment, freedom of education in all
schools and colleges and possible advancement to posi-
tions of highest responsibility in large Soviet enterprises. To all candidates and particularly to the aged

he offers assurance of security and care in time of illness and disability. Thus in all his arguments the Soviet agent stresses mainly the purely material and hedonistic advantages that the *kolhoz* will yield.

When the selling discussions are over the Soviet organizer like the chautauqua agent proceeds to read and to explain to the initial nucleus of possible followers the terms of the contract. Then with the support of this nucleus he seeks to draw the rest of the eligible population into the enterprise.

In his indirect mode of approach the Soviet agent has an overwhelming advantage over the chautauqua organizer. In event of failure to evoke a response, the chautauqua man can hold out no threats to the immediate welfare of anyone in the community. At worst he can express regrets at the unwillingness or inability of the people to bring to their town the " sweetness and light," which his particular chautauqua program might offer. But the Soviet agent has a mighty club to swing over his listeners. He can and does remind them not only of the difference in the taxation of the individualist farmers and of the *kolhoz* and of the greater difficulty they face in obtaining city goods, but of their hopeless position when they attain the stature of *koolack*. These warnings and admonitions make clear to the peasants that the road to more than modest advancement through individual effort is cruelly barred. For this, if for no other reason, the so-called freedom of choice which is supposed to guide the peasant in his entrance into a collective farm, is often only a name and his actual entry a result of forcible persuasion.

When discussions are at an end, both the chautauqua organizer and the Soviet agent proceed to gather signatures. In canvassing for these both realize that the first are the hardest to secure. Yet here the chautauqua organizer has a decided advantage over the Soviet agent. When the banker and the leading merchants have put down their names on the contract the less well-to-do citizens are easily swung into following their example. But in Russian villages it often happens that the industrious middle peasant, when he sees the names of the *batraks* and the ne'er-do-wells in the community on the contract (which is the constitution of the *kolhoz*), he shrinks from joining. He prefers to wait until, as he says, "the more decent people" have endorsed the scheme. It smacks, of course, of counter-revolution to speak disrespectfully of a *batrak* or a *bedniak*, who in Soviet sociology are the pick of the citizenry and entitled to the best that there is in the world. But the hard-headed *seredniak* follows his own intuitions and his own judgments. In my own village man after man assured me that he would join the *kolhoz* if only more of the "*prilichnye ludi*," decent folk, would do so.

Compared to the general run of *kolhozy* the one in my village was rather small. Only twenty-nine families out of one hundred and eighty, and seven individual members had joined. The total population consisted of one hundred and sixty-three souls. Though numerically small the *kolhoz* members constituted a powerful group in the community and had the political support of all nearby Soviets and all Party organizations. Seven hundred hectares of the richest land lying closest to the village with the finest pastures and the best water, made up the acreage of the *kolhoz*, and no sooner was this land measured out than it was divided not into the ancient three-field system, but into eight different fields so as to make possible proper rotation of crops and the use of machinery.

One evening the leaders of the *kolhoz* and I met for a conference. The chairman, a man in the thirties, was once a playmate of mine. A tall bony man with a lofty forehead and brown eyes and given to emphatic gesturing, he had at one time trained himself to be a *feldsher* — a healer. He was a man of little education, easily excitable and tactless in handling recalcitrant members, but of unimpeachable honesty, and he pushed the work in the *kolhoz* with energy if not always with wisdom. The secretary was also present. A handsome man in the twenties, with glowing eyes that were overhung with heavy brows, and with a finely wrought mouth, he was the best educated man in the village, and in contrast to the chairman, was suave and calm, never given to explosive speech or to violent gesturing. The other men of the administration had likewise come including the two brothers who were respectively members of the Party and of the *Komsomol*.

As the evening wore on other members of the *kolhoz* and neighboring peasants straggled into the house and soon the place was packed with eager-minded visitors. Sitting on benches, on the oven or standing row on row to the very door they listened with impassioned interest to every word that passed between me and the leaders of the *kolhoz*. With a frankness that was as admirable as it was touching the latter unfolded to me their plans, ambitions and especially their difficulties. Their chief trouble, they confessed, was lack of unity and good fellowship among their members. And that was in part due to their own poor management, but what could they do?

Mere *muzhiks* of little culture, without experience in operating a large enterprise like the *kolhoz,* and favored with little counsel from the outside, they had to grope along as best they could. The best talent of the Soviets and the Party was being flung into the large *kolhozy* in the district, and they would simply have to wait until new talent had been developed and could be spared for their *kolhoz.* Meanwhile jealousy and carelessness were only too common among their members and that was damaging in a double way, retarding the progress of the *kolhoz* and discrediting it in the eyes of the individual- ists, who always only too readily pounced on their mis- takes and failures and magnified them into signs of imminent collapse.

Yet in spite of all their shortcomings they had done much more plowing and seeding per person than they ever had as individualists or than any of the other individualists in the village had. That they had done their work better than the individualists was evidenced by the superior condition of their crops. They had thirty-one milch cows, and in about two years they hoped to have over two hundred. Sixty more they would acquire in the autumn. They would not be scrub cows either, such as the individualists owned, but animals of the best breeding available in the region. They had al- ready secured a ten year loan at four percent from the regional *kolhoz* body to be used in the purchase of these cows. They were raising all their calves except those condemned as unfit by the district veterinary. They had thirty-seven in the field, of which twenty-seven were heifers. The two bulls that they owned were among the best in the whole countryside and were serving the cows of half of the peasantry in their Soviet district at one rouble a calf. Helping to breed better stock without any profit to themselves was part of the social work that had been assigned to them. They had twenty-six horses and they needed no more. The tractor station in another *kolhoz* only six versts away, and the nearby *sovhoz* only three versts away, helped them out with machines — tractors, reapers, mowers, thrashing outfits. Although they were not as well advanced in their building program as other *kolhozy* in the region they had launched something that the village had never before known. They had already finished two immense grain barns, larger in size than any that the best landlord in the old days could boast of. Now they were putting up two cow stables each with a capacity of from one hundred to one hundred and fifty heads. These were carefully planned with the proper amount of cubic space per animal to insure health, and with many large windows on all sides so that the stalls would be amply lighted — much better lighted, in fact, than any of the houses in the village. They had likewise begun a horse stable of huge dimensions, and toward autumn they would start a pig sty with a capacity of at least a hundred sows. Their intention was to specialize in dairying and in hog-raising and later in large scale poultry farming. Soon they would begin to make silos, and by next year they hoped to have their barns surrounded with silos, all of them packed with rich fodder for winter use. They planned to set out an orchard of ten or twenty hectares at an early date.

They worked on a basis of wages, the summer rates being sixty copecks a day for minors and a minimum of ninety copecks and a maximum of one rouble and eighty copecks for adults. Slowly, however, they were putting all work on a piece basis, which in the long run would be more satisfactory to the individual members and would be of greater benefit to the *kolhoz*. Members who had no cows of their own purchased their milk from the *kolhoz* at the price of six copecks per liter. They also bought bread from the *kolhoz* at cost. They had as yet little meat to sell to their members — but in time as their young stock, especially the pigs, fattened, they hoped to be in a position to provide meat for those members who had none of their own. Even now, however, there were occasions when they had meat for their members, and they charged only ten roubles per pood for the live pig and eighty-three copecks a kilo for pork, which was about one tenth the price in the open market. Of course they were encouraging members to raise their own meat and eggs and to cultivate their own gardens and have their own cows.

The grain allowances per person were ample for their needs and varied from one pood for a newly born child to eighteen poods for a working adult. At the end of the year when accounts were drawn up, if there was a surplus grain available, each member could demand payment to the amount of eighty percent of his remaining wages in grain, this in addition to the regular allowance.

In their cultural life they could boast of no outstanding achievements. They had no club-house and that alone hindered the unfoldment of an ambitious cultural program. Still they had opened a Red Corner with a library and a reading room. They were subscribing to eight publications, and in autumn when they had sold their crops they would subscribe to many more.

Their library was small and it was thanks to Antosh, who had since gone from the village, that it had been started. Without taking counsel with anyone, he wrote a letter to Krupskaya, Lenine's widow, informing her of the cultural backwardness of the village and asking her to offer help in the promotion of its cultural standing. A short time later he received several boxes of books to the value of two hundred and fifty roubles, as a contribution from some society with which Krupskaya was associated. At first these books were the property of the village, but now they had been turned over to the *kolhoz,* though anyone might make use of them. They had since bought other books all of which were in constant circulation, for people were reading now more than they ever read in their lives. Perhaps some labor union would send them a supply of books as a gift, and if their income allowed they might buy some with their own money. Then itinerant motion picture shows were regularly visiting the village now, and in winter when school opened the dramatic circle would present performances once or twice a month. They might even install a radio in the Red Corner, and tune in on lectures and concerts broadcast from Moscow and other cities.

In their own modest way they were doing their utmost to realize the social purposes of the *kolhoz*. If a member was ill and needed medical service he obtained it free. They were too poor to maintain a healer of their own and while the chairman of the *kolhoz* had once trained for a *feldsher* he was out of practice and with the exception of first aid emergencies, he refused to offer medical aid to people. Usually a member who was sick was sent on a *kolhoz* team to see a physician.

Neither the consultation nor the medicine cost him a copeck, and if it was necessary for him to visit a specialist in a large city even in Moscow the *kolhoz* paid his railroad fare. Throughout the period of his illness he drew wages in full. A woman likewise if she was a regular member of the *kolhoz* enjoyed the same maternity privileges as the proletarian woman in the city. For a month before and for a month after her confinement she was released from work without loss of pay. Except for the first-born, she received a premium for every newly born child. Small as the premium was, only fifteen roubles, which she could obtain in cash or in kind, even in grain, it was a substantial help to a peasant woman who was not accustomed to city luxuries. Then there was also the nursery to which they admitted without charge not only their own children but those of the poor families who had not joined the *kolhoz*. The nursery functioned only during summer months, but as soon as they had attained a measure of economic solidity they would have it open throughout the year. If only they had enough man-power and lumber and nails, they would proceed immediately with the building of a nursery. Considering existing difficulties it might be a year or two before they would be in a position to build it.

All in all they were moving forward. The city of course could facilitate their task, if it would hasten more manufactured goods to the village. The amounts that were now coming to the local coöperative were not enough. People did not want money, they wanted goods. If the Soviet and Party leaders would hurry along increased supplies of these — they would pour fresh hope and fresh energy into the *kolhoz!* However, small as their *kolhoz* was and overburdened as it was with shortcomings, they could at least boast of one thing, their crops were incomparably superior to those of any individualist in the village. When these were gathered and divided according to plan, people would have an opportunity to ascertain whether or not the *kolhoz* was making life easier, richer and more secure. The autumn would tell the story. Perhaps I would come again?

I promised that I would.

XII

THE NEW AND THE OLD

SULLEN as were the older peasants in our village and reluctant as they were to join the *kolhoz*, there were times when they would say, " If we had a *kolhoz* like the one in C—— we wouldn't mind joining. There is a *kolhoz* for you, with a real *poriadok*." [1] Man after man urged me to visit C—— and note the difference between the *kolhoz* there and the one at their doors. In other villages peasants echoed this praise of the *kolhoz* at C——. It was the most famed *kolhoz* in the whole countryside.

I had known the village of C—— since boyhood. One of the largest villages in the district, it was even farther removed from the railroad than our village. In the old days its name was identified with a wealthy landlord's estate, which boasted a flour mill run by water power, a vodka brewery and one of the choicest orchards in the province. C—— therefore had always been a village of note in our district.

It was within easy walking distance from our village and as soon as I found the time I went there. With its log huts, its falling fences, its pigs and chickens strutting up and down the street and tumbling at will in and out of the houses, it was in its outward aspect as dismal and primitive a village as any in the district.

[1] Order.

The *kolhoz*, however, was located on the lands outside of the village, and I had no more than come within view of it than I grew aware of an energy and a feverishness which are not common to peasant folk. Rows of buildings were in process of construction. Teams loaded with lumber, bricks, stone, straw, clattered up and down the roads. The buzz of saws and the thumping of axes and hammers resounded in the air and the peasants, singly and in groups, with preoccupied mien, and with tools on their backs, were moving about from place to place. Here, as nowhere in the whole countryside, life seethed with action.

I went to the administration building and without knocking at the door, as is the custom in Russian villages, I walked into the office of the chairman of the *kolhoz*. Two young men, one bareheaded and one with a cap drawn low over his eyes, were seated at a long table with their backs towards me. Both were poring over papers, one of them loudly computing figures. They did not hear me enter and I did not at once speak to them. I surveyed the office — a small room, smelling of freshly cut pine and of freshly dug dirt. The walls were still bare logs and were hung with rows of lithographs of Soviet officials, most conspicuous of which was the one of the famed Cossack cavalry commander, Boodenny. A bookshelf loaded with paper-covered books, two tables, benches instead of chairs, a bed which signified that this office was also somebody's bedroom and a hanging lamp with a smoky chimney, were all the pieces of furniture in the office. Two large windows, facing a far-stretching park, and now open, admitted light and air and also flies.

I addressed the two preoccupied men and both instantly turned around and invited me to sit down. They had heard, they said, of my presence in this part of the world and had wondered if I would pay them a visit. They even thought of sending someone to invite me to come, and now that I was here, they would gladly put themselves at my disposal. One of them was the chairman of the *kolhoz*. He was a young peasant, about thirty, from a nearby village, with a bulb-like nose and a face in which pock-marks vied for supremacy with freckles. I had heard of him in other villages, for peasants spoke of him as of a man of courage and good humor, who never lost his temper and never scolded people. His associate, a handsome youth of about twenty-two, also a peasant, with deep blue eyes, flaxen hair and a face dusky with sunburn, was the *kolhoz* bookkeeper. Instantly the bookkeeper disappeared and soon returned with a pitcher of milk and a plate heaped with huge slices of fresh black bread. The chairman pushed these towards me and urged me to help myself.

" I suppose," he said, " you have heard a lot of wailing among the peasants? "

" Considerable," I replied. He exchanged a knowing look with the bookkeeper and both smiled.

" If you lived here," he said, " all the time as we have, you would hear a lot more. Wouldn't he, Kostia? " he turned to the bookkeeper.

" Indeed he would, indeed," answered Kostia.

" Peasants," continued the chairman, " have got to wail or they wouldn't be peasants. I have lived with them all my life, and having an uncle who is the champion wailer in this part of the world if not in the whole

Soviet union, I know whereof I am speaking." And he laughed heartily.

Rising, he beckoned to me to follow him. " Come," he said, " let's look over this place."

Once on the outside we paused before the row of new houses which stretched in a line with the administration building.

" These," explained my guide, " have all been built within the past year; they are all dwelling houses for our members."

They were log houses with thatched roofs, higher than peasant huts and with larger windows. We entered several of them. Made up into one and two room apartments, meagerly furnished, and with the walls still bare, they were surprisingly clean with nowhere a mark of the presence of pigs and chickens. The windows, however, true to peasant tradition, were shut and the air was stuffy, though not weighted with the usual smells.

After inspecting the houses we went to the cattle yard. Here four enormous barns, the largest I had ever seen, all newly built, towered before us. Three of these, explained my guide, were for cows and one for horses. Huge-dimensioned as were the cow stables, they were not fitted up into separate stalls, and ropes fastened to logs took the place of stanchions. But here were space, light and air. The huge windows, the high ceilings, the clean floors, contrasted markedly with the barns of peasants which always were windowless, with low ceilings and always heavily matted with manure.

Each barn had space for one hundred and fifty to two hundred cows and in less than a year my guide assured me would be filled to capacity. By the end of the Five Year Plan the *kolhoz* would own eight hundred milch cows — twice the number the entire village had ever possessed. Real milch cows they would be, for, American like, they would weed out and slaughter the ones that did not give enough milk to make their keep profitable. They were done with perpetuating scrub breeds of cattle, and they were likewise done with disregarding the question of proper feeding, for nothing was so ruinous to the peasant as his neglect of this aspect of farming. In winter he fed his cows straw mixed with hay, or else straw cut into chaff and scattered lightly with potato peelings or bran and soaked in hot water — food which would make the best cow shrink on her milk. But on the *kolhoz* they were now building silos, which not a single landlord in this part of the country had, in the old days, thought of introducing.

When I saw the silos I could hardly restrain a laugh — they seemed so amusing — for they were only deep holes in the ground! Smilingly my companion remarked, " I know that they are not like American silos, but in the absence of building materials, these are the best we can have. Some day we shall build real silos, like in your country. Give us time, *tovarishtsh.*"

We crossed this barnyard and came to another where stood an immense building. On entering we saw a brick fireplace, over which an enormous kettle of potatoes was boiling. Two girls, barefooted, and in white aprons, and with spades, were mashing the steaming potatoes. This, explained the chairman, was a piggery and the two girls were preparing supper for the pigs. It was a modern pig sty with large windows, a cement floor and running water for all necessary purposes and with a separate stall for every sow. Though at present they had only one hundred and fifty sows, chiefly English Berkshires, by autumn, explained the chairman, with good luck in raising the young pigs, they hoped to have them increased to two hundred and fifty, which was the capacity of the piggery. In another year they would build another as large as this one, and dairying, and pig and poultry raising were to be the chief enterprises of the *kolhoz*. In walking across the piggery I observed that unlike peasant pig sties, which like peasant cow stables and other barns, are cleaned twice a year, in spring and in autumn, here not a stall but was freshly cleaned and heavily bedded down with dry straw.

We continued our inspection tour and presently strolled into a park. Oak, birch, maple, evergreens, sturdy and rugged, stretched over a large area and gave one the impression of a forest. The pride of the landlord who had once inhabited the estate, the park had been the scene of many gay festivities, from which peasants, of course, always were barred. Now it was open to any peasant who cared to come, regardless of whether or not he was a member of the *kolhoz*. Overhung with the heavy limbs of birches, was a stage, from the top of which fluttered a red flag, and all around were rows of benches. In summer the park was the center of the social and cultural life of the *kolhoz* and hardly a rest day but something was taking place there — a lecture, a mass meeting, a dramatic performance, a motion picture show or some other entertainment.

We left the park, and presently found ourselves on a big field, where gangs of men were busily at work on new buildings. One of these was to be a coöperative shop, another a hospital, a third a schoolhouse, a fourth a nursery. By autumn, all these buildings would be open for use and in another year, in this very locality, a huge club-house would be erected. Because of its proximity to the park, this field, explained my guide, was ideally situated for a center of their cultural and social life, and since the field was large, it would enable them in the future to put up other buildings that they might need for cultural purposes.

We marched on and presently came to a huge field set out, as far as the eye could see, with fruit trees. "We planted this orchard," explained the chairman, "only last spring. There are forty hectares of it; next spring we shall probably plant twenty more, and we aren't going to let these trees grow up in wild confusion as most peasants do. We have engaged two specialists to take care of them. In a few years, if you come back, we shall treat you to the choicest fruits you have ever eaten." As we walked about examining some of the trees — apples, pears, cherries, plums, the chairman was visibly elated with the fine growth they were making.

" And now," he said, " there is something else that I want to show you — something with a rich and amusing history." He led me back through the park to a building standing as if aloof from all the others. We walked in and found ourselves facing several rows of oil burning incubators. A young girl, in sandals and bare legs, and with a red kerchief draped neatly over her head, was in attendance. The chairman introduced me to her as their poultry expert. He explained that she was not a member of the *kolhoz* but had come to spend the summer with them. In autumn she would return to her studies in the agricultural college in Voronezh. Her home was in Kozakstan, in Russian Central Asia. A pleasant girl, with a sunburned face and a matronly manner, she showed us the inside of several incubators, and explained her methods of hatching chickens. Since her arrival on the *kolhoz*, she had already hatched several thousand of them and she was sure, that before returning to school, she would turn out at least two more hatchings.

When we finished examining the incubators, we walked outside and lay down on the grass in the shade of a mighty oak.

" Now, I have got to tell you the history of these incubators," began the chairman, " and you will learn something of the problems we have been facing on this *kolhoz* and also gain an insight into the mentality of our *muzhik*. Only a verst away from here we have a place which was formerly a small estate of a landlord. It is ideally suited for poultry farming and so we decided to convert it into the poultry branch of the *kolhoz*. We wanted to do things in a big way, with no loss of time and decided to provide ourselves with several incubators. We called a mass meeting and explained the plan to our members and you should have heard them roar with protest. They wouldn't hear of the idea of hatching chickens in an incubator. Nobody, as far as they knew, had ever done it, not even the landlords in the old days. It was not natural, they shouted, to do anything of the sort and they prophesied failure for the enterprise. They were sure we would be merely throwing away precious eggs and waste large sums of money. We, of course, sought to argue with them and to point out the amazing results that incubators had given in your country, but they would not listen. They didn't care what happened in America. There, they argued, the eggs might be different. But in Russia, in their village, no — they would tolerate no such nonsense as an effort to hatch chickens in machines. They heartily approved of the plan of making poultry raising one of the chief enterprises of the *kolhoz*, but they insisted that we hatch our chickens in the old-fashioned way — through setting hens. Machines, they scoffed, could never take the place of hens.

" We argued and argued and finally, with reluctance, they assented to the experiment. They warned us, however, that nothing good would come of it and that if we failed, they never would forgive us. But we of the administration went ahead and ordered two incubators, small ones, each with a capacity of seven hundred eggs. When we got them we looked them over and then discovered that none of us knew anything about them. That did not discourage us. We got some books, explaining how to operate incubators and set to work. Meanwhile the *muzhiks* persisted in reminding us that we were engaged in a futile enterprise and every day they would ask us when our lifeless machine would turn out its brood of live chickens. And do you know, we had the rottenest luck imaginable. We hatched only one percent of the eggs, and you should have been here and heard these *muzhiks* scold us. They heaped on us reproaches and curses and even threatened to report us to higher authorities for deliberate mismanagement. It taxed all our courage and ingenuity to pacify them and the news of our failure spread in other villages and we were the laughing stock all over the countryside. A wretched experience it was for us but we didn't give up hope of retrieving ourselves with the peasants. We had to for our own sake as well as for the sake of the *kolhoz* movement.

" This spring, at one of the mass meetings, I broached the subject of incubators again. I expected to be howled down and I was. But I had set my heart on the project and I was determined to go through with it. Frankness, as you know, is the basis of our dealings with peasants, and very frankly I told them that the reason we had failed was because none of us had had any experience with incubators and I argued that if we were to obtain the services of a person, specially trained in the job, we could not help being successful. I read to them letters in the newspapers, describing the successes other *kolhozy* had had with incubators. In the end they consented to another trial and warned me that if this time the effort should result in failure, they would have to do something desperate.

" At once I wrote to the agricultural academy in Voronezh where they have one of the finest poultry schools in the country, requesting that they send us a senior from their poultry school, who had had experience with incubators. So they sent us this *tovarishtsh,*" pointing at the girl beside us, " and when she came I told her what a serious job she was facing. She said nothing and proceeded to work and, ah, how she did work, didn't you, *tovarishtsh?* " The girl smiled, blushed, but said nothing. " And do you know," continued the chairman with enthusiasm, " her initial hatching was seventy percent of the eggs she used. At first the peasants were incredulous. One after another came around to convince himself of the facts and when they saw the chickens they were dumb with astonishment. Then it was our turn to do some twitting, and believe me, we lost no opportunity in doing so. The second hatching was equally good. And do you know what's happening now? At our last mass meeting the peasants in one voice yelled for more and more incubators. There is a situation for you."

We returned to the office. " How do you like the *kolhoz?* " asked the bookkeeper.

" An impressive place," I replied.

" And remember, all the new buildings that you have seen have been put up within the past year."

" That's right," added the chairman. " This *kolhoz* is several years old but only within the past year has it taken on real life and this is nothing compared to what we are hoping to make of it in the next few years. We have got a big program — electrification, a brick factory, a new flour mill, new houses, a playground, an orchestra. Our plans are endless."

The bookkeeper, at the request of the chairman, went out to bring some more milk and soon returned with milk, bread, cheese and butter. After the lengthy inspection trip the food was welcome and the chairman and I ate with voracious appetites. As we ate we talked.

" What do the peasants think of it? " I asked. " Are they satisfied? " Both of my companions chuckled.

" They are grumbling a lot," remarked the bookkeeper.

" They always will grumble," said the chairman with good-natured indifference.

" And what are they grumbling about? " I asked.

"Actually," said the bookkeeper, "some of them are grumbling because we are not getting enough incubators." Again both men chuckled.

"They don't like the idea," continued the chairman, "of our not slaughtering more stock than we do so they could have more meat than they have been getting and, of course, they are disgruntled because of the shortage of textiles and tobacco and other city products. Peasants will always find an excuse for fault-finding."

"But the thing to do," the chairman again picked up, "is to go ahead with the job and convince them, through actual achievement, that under individual land holding, it would be impossible to obtain the same results as on a *kolhoz*. There is our problem in a nutshell. You have been around the villages here and you have heard the peasants rail at the *kolhoz* and prophesy doom for everybody in it, but compare their houses to ours, their barns to ours, their pigs to ours, their cows to ours, their crops to ours — anything and everything and draw your own conclusions as to where the future of our Soviet Union lies. And remember, we are just beginning."

"If we took stock of the *muzhik's* grumbling," said the bookkeeper, "we would be like the landlord from Vyatka of whom I have recently read. Maybe you have heard the story? A rich landlord he was, in possession of a vast estate, but the climate of Vyatka was too severe for him and he moved to Italy. Once after a long absence he returned home and observing the wretched life of the peasants on his estate, he decided to do something for them. He built fine stone cottages and turned them over to the peasants so they could have clean and comfortable homes. And do you know what happened? The peasants converted the cottages into lavatories and pig pens. In disgust the landlord packed up his things and returned to Italy.

" Of course, being a *bourzhui*," added the chairman, " he fled from reality. But we have no notion of fleeing to Italy, or America or any other place. We'll remain right here and continue our work, won't we, Kostia? "

" Of course we will." Again both men chuckled heartily.

Late in the afternoon on my way home I again passed through the village. With the impressions of the *kolhoz* fresh in my mind, life here seemed so still, so ancient. The weight of time and inertia was pressing with a heavy hand on everything — the houses, the street, the fences, the strutting pigs and chickens and even the people. All seemed so dilapidated, so forlorn, so dismally out of tune with the roar of energy and effort in the new world that was being built at its very doorstep.

In passing one of the yards I saw an old man leaning on a gateway. He was bareheaded and barefooted and his hair ashen gray and matted, swept down the back of his head and got lost inside the collar of his linen shirt. I greeted him and he invited me to stop. He asked if I would have a drink of milk, and without waiting for a reply called to his *baba* inside of the house to bring out a jar of milk " for an American guest." Instantly a crowd of children tumbled out of the house, and were followed by a number of grown folk, men and women. They all gathered around me and stared with the intent eagerness with which *muzhiks* always regard a foreigner.

The old man's wife, a short shrunken woman with a careworn face and dressed in homespun, came out with an earthen jar and a tarnished tin cup. In spite of my protests that I had had my fill of milk on the *kolhoz*, she and the others around insisted that I have some more. " Do not offend a dark-minded man by refusing his hospitality," a middle-aged stranger remarked. There was nothing to do but to comply. Several other passersby stopped. A string of teams drawing freshly cut timber also halted and the drivers joined the assemblage. An American amongst them — *akh* — what a surprise!

They all wondered what I thought of their *kolhoz*. I told them that it was a very impressive place.

" We are building a lot," remarked one of the drivers.

" Indeed," I replied, " more than on any other *kolhoz* in the region."

" Yes," the old man shook his head," they are building a new America there. They even have an incubator. Did you see it? "

" And how did you like the silos? " someone else broke in.

" And the new piggery? "

" This is a real *kolhoz*, isn't it? " another of the drivers chimed in.

" Real, real, well said," the old man echoed with a pronounced tinge of bitterness.

Presently another man joined us, also advanced in years, with a staff in one hand and with the other holding a sack that was slung over his back.

" A *bezboshnik* (an atheist)," someone hastened to enlighten me.

" What I say," the newcomer instantly broke into

speech, " is that we peasants have three enemies, the capitalist, the devil and God."

" Hear him, hear him," remarked the woman of the house with a sneer.

" Three enemies," the newcomer continued, " one of them, the devil, we have already gotten rid of. Nobody believes in the devil any more. The other, the capitalist, we shall soon clean out. God still remains and he too's got to go."

A ripple of laughter spread in the crowd.

" Fie on you! " exclaimed the old woman. She spat in disgust and departed. The children burst into a loud laugh.

" You are all laughing at me, but here is a man who comes from a cultured land," the newcomer addressed the crowd, " he's been around the world, let him tell us if it is not the devil, the capitalists and God that are keeping the poor people everywhere in slavery."

" He wanted to have our parish church closed," the old man remarked.

" I burned my ikons, too," added the newcomer with self satisfaction, " everybody ought to do the same. I went around telling people in my own village to join me and to make a real bonfire of the ikons and burn up God, and then they would be free people."

" Free people! " the old man jibed, " as though anybody could ever make the *muzhik* free."

" Well said, well said," another man piped in. " The *muzhik* will never have any luck. In the *kolhoz,* out of the *kolhoz,* he is lost anyway."

" Are you a member of the *kolhoz?* " I asked the last speaker.

" I am," he replied. " What else is there to do? "

"They don't let you live if you're not," one of the teamsters added.

"They don't, they don't," several voices echoed in unison.

"And now that they are all going into the *kolhoz*," someone else volunteered, "they are just getting to be enemies of one another, they quarrel and fight and what not."

"*Nu, nichevo*," calmly remarked the atheist, "times will be better if only we lose our old ideas and start with new ones. We have to be emancipated first."

The teamsters who were drawing timber for the *kol-hoz* departed. Several others including the atheist also left, for chore time was drawing near. The old man invited me to follow him into the house. We sat down at the table and while his wife was busying herself with making a fire on which to cook supper, we talked away.

"What do you think will come out of it all — this atheism and this *kolhoz?*" the old man asked.

"That is what I want to know," I replied.

"*Akh*, brother," he sighed, "if only we knew what the end of it would be, if only we knew!"

"Still," I ventured, "they are putting up such fine buildings on the *kolhoz*."

"The finest we have ever seen in these parts," the old man added, "and funny isn't it, the more they build, the worse life is. Now they won't even slaughter a calf or a pig and a lot of the *kolhoz* folk have to go without meat. But they have to work just the same, aye harder, for they are after them now, haw, haw, haw, how strict they are getting to be there! And why, why did they have to have it all? Didn't we get along well without all these fine buildings and incubators and silos and what not? People at least had peace and now they have no peace, no life, nothing . . ."

"Stop grumbling so much," his wife broke in, "be lucky that they have not dekoolackized you. They came very nearly doing it. It would have been worse if they had sent you up north."

"Who says it would not have been?" the old man protested, with feeling. "But I cannot help these thoughts coming to my mind. They promise us everything for tomorrow and who cares for tomorrow? Supposing there is no tomorrow? Supposing I die before tomorrow comes? Don't you see? Oh, it is no good, no good — our *muzhik* is just going to perish."

Darkness had descended over the village. People were returning from work. Cows, sheep, pigs, were being driven from pasture. Fires were peeping out of the windows and the stillness which was so dispiriting when I first came from the *kolhoz* was now broken. . . .

Two sturdy youths entered the house. They were the old man's sons, both like their father members of the *kolhoz*.

"They are helping with all the building on the *kolhoz* — carpenters," the old man said by way of introducing me to the youths.

"All you hear is that they are building, building," he continued with feeling. "But can we eat buildings, can we wear buildings, can we resole our boots with buildings? Why don't they take time off and give us more sugar, more soap, more meat, more textiles — things that we need and cannot get along without? Building! Whew! For what, for whom?"

"The pigs, the cows, the sheep," answered the woman with bitterness.

"They'll build houses, too," one of the youths explained.

"And supposing they do — who wants their houses, or anything else that they are offering?" the old man demanded.

The youths sat down at the table and their mother served them boiled potatoes, sour milk and bread.

"Thank God," she said, "they let us keep a few things for ourselves — a cow, a pig, a few chickens and our garden. . . ."

"Thank God for that," the old man agreed, "without anything of our own we'd feel as though we didn't belong anywhere at all, and yet they say that possessions are no good. They are all the time telling us that. Lecturer after lecturer is coming and telling us that we ought to forget possessions and have everything in common. Why then is the desire for it in our blood? Why?"

One of the sons winked at me and smiled, but said nothing.

"*Nu,* maybe it will work out well," went on the old man, "but all I know is that now, things are bad, very bad, worse than ever, by Jove! much worse. It is work and work and work and no reward, no joy. They are building, building, building, but they are not bringing happiness to people. Yes they will have everything on the *kolhoz,* big cow stables, big piggeries, big incubators, big silos, big machines and maybe big houses. But people won't have any independence, won't have any happiness. They'll be like the pigs and the cows — in stalls and in stanchions."

Both sons looked at me and smiled but said nothing in reply.

XIII

THE KOOLACK

THE four men in my village who had been de-koolackized had one thing to solace them — they were allowed to remain in their native countryside, three of them in the village. But Ivan Bulatov, who lived in a village which I had not visited since my boyhood days, had a more stern ordeal to endure. He had been stripped of his possessions, and exiled north to a lumber camp. Only thanks to the efforts of his son, a former soldier in the Red Army and a member of a trade union in the town where he was working, was he finally allowed to return home.

Sheer accident had brought me to Ivan Bulatov's village. I ran there once for shelter from a threatening storm, which however blew over after a swift and mild rainpour. I stopped in the blacksmith shop and it was there that I heard of Bulatov. Peasants commented on his good fortune in having a son who had been in the Red Army and was a member of a trade union. Otherwise, they felt, he might never have been allowed to come back. From the conversation of the peasants I gathered that during the months of exile Ivan had failed in health. He coughed and complained of aches all over his body, and had become so subdued, that he seldom visited neighbors, and spoke little, as though he were ashamed of his experience or afraid of people.

Quietly I slipped away from the blacksmith shop and made my way to Ivan Bulatov's home. The heavy gateway in the yard was closed. I climbed over and tried the door of the house. It was barred. I searched the sheds and the barns, and finding nobody around, I made my way to the orchard immediately in the rear of the yard. There beneath a lop-sided apple tree, sitting on a log and sewing a patch on a pair of freshly laundered linen trousers, sat a young woman. Dark-haired with a straight nose, a flushed face and a full-lipped mouth, and sporting a blue skirt, a white waist and a string of beads, she was astoundingly attractive. Beside her in a two-wheeled cart with a hooded cover over it, to keep off the sun and flies, lay a baby asleep. I thought that I had come to the wrong place, for there was nothing about this young woman suggestive of sorrow or misfortune such as one would expect to find in the home of a dekoolackized peasant even though he had been retrieved to his possessions. Indeed, this woman appeared a symbol of cheer and opulence.

I spoke to her and she did not at once answer my greetings. My approach seemed to nettle her and she surveyed me with distrustful eyes. I asked her if this was the home of Ivan Bulatov and instead of replying she inquired why I wanted to know, and without allowing me time to answer asked whether I was from the *rik* — the district Soviet. I sensed at once that she suspected me of being an official with perhaps unpleasant tidings, and I hastened to assure her that I was a native from the nearby village of B——, the son of so and so, and now as an American writer I was wandering about the native countryside looking up interesting people. My explanation seemed to reassure her, and as if in apology for her suspicion of me, she explained that rumors had been afloat that some of the officials in the *rik* were displeased with the return of her father-in-law and his wife and were planning to take steps to have them exiled again. That was why she had wondered if I were a Soviet official. She further informed me that Ivan and her husband had gone off to a swamp to dig up stumps for firewood, but that they would be back by dusk.

Our conversation awakened the baby and instantly she dropped her work and began to rock the little wagon, and when that did not help, she leaned over, opened her waist, and with hugs and kisses and words of endearment proceeded to suckle the disturbed child. Soon it became quiet, and she drew the cover over it, carted the little wagon into a shady nook beneath the overhanging eaves of an adjoining barn, and, returning to her seat on the log, resumed her sewing.

" Maybe you are hungry," she inquired, " would you like a drink of milk? "

I thanked her and told her that I did not care for food, and she proposed that I stay over and have supper with them, and at the table the old folks would tell me a lot of exciting things.

" Ah, I am so glad," she continued in a spirit of confidence, " that my husband gave up farming and became a carpenter and went to town and joined the trade union. Otherwise father and mother might never have come back and we too might have been banished."

" How long have they been back? " I questioned.

" A little over a month," she replied, " and they are so broken up. The least disturbance upsets them and they cry like children. They are so afraid of being sent back, though my husband assured them they would never again be molested."

Somewhere from the rear of the orchard a raucous voice fell on our ears.

"Anna, who is it you are talking to? "

"It is mother-in-law," explained the young woman and to the latter she replied, "A stranger who wants to see father."

The older woman came over, barefooted, with her face and clothes browned with a fine layer of dust. She was a big-boned person with a broad face, sloping shoulders and a dry skin. Her mouth was open exposing two misshapen upper teeth and she breathed audibly. She surveyed me with undue sharpness as though mistrustful of the purpose of my visit.

"And why do you want to see my husband? " she demanded sullenly. The young woman hastened to explain who I was, and why I had come and assured her that I was not from the *rik*. Stolid and hard-faced and as though loath to believe her daughter-in-law, the old woman continued to stare sharply at me. Her eyes grew moist and she began to sob and wipe her tears with shaking and calloused fingers.

Instantly the young woman jumped up and put her arms round her.

"Don't, little mother, please don't," she cried, seeking to cheer the older woman, "this is only a friendly guest from a foreign land come to honor us with a visit. He is not from the *rik* nor from the *raikom*.[1] "

"Ah, little son," the older woman turned to me, "if they'll only let us remain here — we'd be so content —

[1] Communist district Committee.

anything but to go away from our own people, our own home, our own land, to such a far, far away place as that terrible Kotlas! "

" There, there, little mother," soothed the younger woman again, "don't be afraid. Don't believe any rumors. Nikolai is a member of the trade union and they would not lie to him, and you have seen the papers, they cannot be wrong. Nobody will touch you."

" God grant that you are right," muttered the older woman. " Ah, what a *nakazanye* [2] it was, Lord have mercy," and she made the sign of the cross over her body. Wiping her eyes with her apron and saying she must go back to her work, winnowing rye with a scoop, she walked off with the slow measured step of old age.

Promising to call in the evening I bade Anna farewell and departed. " Do come to supper," she repeated as I started off. To pass away the time I walked leisurely round the village, then went in swimming with a crowd of the most hilarious boys I had ever encountered in the Russian countryside, and at dusk I went back to Ivan Bulatov's house. The old man was at home and so was his son, and what a contrast the two made, not merely in years but in appearance. Ivan was lean with a bent back, a bristly beard and haunted eyes, and seemed timid and crestfallen, while the son was short, stocky, with abundant light hair, and magnificent teeth. He bubbled with cheerfulness. His clear blue eyes overhung with thick lashes, sparkled with good humor and danced gaily as he spoke.

" The women," said the older man with a feeling of humility, " have told me about you, and I am so happy that you came. *Akh,* an American condescending to

2 Punishment.

honor a dirty *muzhik* like me and a *koolack* at that!
Thank you so much, so much." He smiled sadly, showing a mouth as toothless as that of his wife, and led me
to the table. The women instantly brought food, black
bread, boiled potatoes, sour milk, raw salt pork. We
ate peasant fashion with wooden spoons and out of
the same big earthen dish. A dusky light fell over us
from a hanging lamp and flies swarmed around continuously.

Hardly had we begun eating when Ivan, without
waiting for any questioning, proceeded to tell me the
story of his life. He spoke with feeling as though
eager to assure me that, in spite of the stigmatization
and punishment to which he had been subject, he was
a harmless creature, with some sense of decency inside
of him and too insignificant and feeble to perpetrate
evil against his fellow men.

He came from a poor family. In his boyhood he was
a *batrak* — hired man — on a large estate, working for
fifteen roubles a year which not he but his father would
always collect. He married and, after his father died,
he and his brother divided their land, each receiving
three dessiatins. His first three children died and left
him and his wife desolate. The fourth, a girl, grew up
well, married and was now living with her husband in a
nearby village. A fifth child, this son of his, Nikolai,
came next. They were poor but happy. Now they at
least had children, and an heir and something vital to
live for. But luck was against him. One misfortune after
another visited him, his horse died, a fire destroyed his
house and barns and burned four grown pigs to death.
Left with one toothless old cow he began working for
others by the day and saving every copeck he was earn-

ing. When he had five roubles he bought two calves and fed them the milk of the old cow, and again misfortune struck him — both calves and the cow died. By that time his Nikolai had reached the age when he could be hired out as a shepherd, and a neighboring village engaged his services for the summer, paying him twenty pounds of rye for each head of cattle he pastured. It was little enough but it was something and it helped along. On Sundays and holidays he would relieve the boy so that he could go home, see his mother and play around with his friends.

Then the Revolution came, nearby a *sovhoz* was started and there he worked on his spare days. With the few roubles he got together he bought from a peasant an old wool-carding machine, and then his real troubles began. Why had not God struck him dead before he ever bought the machine! Why hadn't he smashed it to pieces with an axe before he ever set it up? He had bought it of course with the hope of earning a few extra roubles with which to stock up his little farm and thus make possible a better living for his family. It had never occurred to him that an honest effort to improve the welfare of those so near and dear to him would be deemed a crime punishable with banishment to a far, far away wilderness. O, God, what a fool he had been!

Well, he set the machine to working and in the winter he earned one hundred and fifty roubles. With this money he bought two cows, raised a third, and also two horses.

For the first time in his life things began to look bright. He had seven dessiatins of tillable land and three more of meadow and he was not of the loafing kind, was not given to idling around. When he had no work on his own place he would hire out to the *sovhoz* and turn his time and his energies to some benefit to himself. All was well and he was so happy and hopeful.

Then the Soviets started the campaign against *koolacks* . . . and having three cows, two horses, a wool-carding machine and a newly built house, they imposed on him an individualistic tax. He had thought of buying a straw-cutting machine and what luck that he had not done so, else they might never have allowed him to return home. These devilish machines! Would to God they had all burned before any decent *muzhik* thought of coming into possession of them! O, these cursed machines!

Then the *kolhoz* movement reached his village and troubles came to him. Happy with his family on his own land, he saw no reason for scrapping his individualistic household, joining a *kolhoz* and losing his independence. He did not go around agitating against the *kolhoz*, the Soviets had not even accused him of that. He merely refused to join and when neighbors asked him what he thought of it he would tell them that he didn't see how it could be a success with so many "dark" and ignorant people working the land jointly. He was sure they would be quarreling and fighting more than working.

Soviet officials reprimanded him for his attitude, but he was no hypocrite. He would not lie to anyone, least of all to himself. In their dislike of his attitude they launched a fresh attack on him. They levied a tax of one hundred and fifty roubles on his wool-carding machine, and in addition imposed three hundred poods of rye as his share of the grain collection. He could

not possibly meet such an exorbitant obligation. He
protested that he never had raised in any one year as
much rye as he was supposed to sell to the government.
But the officials would not listen. He appealed to a
higher power and again in vain. He did not know what
to do and waited. He could not imagine that they would
actually insist on his delivering more grain to the co-
operatives than he had harvested. But they did, and
evidently only on purpose to have an excuse to crush
him. Distraught and agonized and fearing the worst he
was at a loss to know what to do or to whom to turn
for help. He thought of making a trip to the city and
discussing the matter with his son. But he kept putting
it off and one evening a group of brigadiers came,
showed him a paper and said that he was to be dekoolackized. His wife and he wept and pleaded with
them to be merciful, but they paid no heed to pleas
and tears, and proceeded to confiscate his possessions,
— cows, horses, sheep, geese, wagons, grain, wool-
carding machine, potatoes — everything, and also told
him to be ready by next morning to start for the north.

" Little son mine," he continued amidst sobs, " I told
them that I had a son who had been in the Red Army
and was now a proletarian and a member of a trade
union and therefore I was entitled to some consideration. I begged them to have mercy on my old *baba* —
and at least leave her here. But my words fell on deaf
ears. They insisted that I'd have to go to exile."

"*Milenky moy,*" [3] he continued with increasing tears,
" I had never been away from this village, not any
farther than the town of P——, where I would go to the
fairs. I had never lived among any other people but

[3] My Beloved.

my own, had never known any other people except the few Jews that came in and out . . . and the Gipsies that wander along our highways, and of a sudden I was to part from everything and everybody I knew. With my bare hands so to speak, with only five poods of rye and a few poods of other foods, I was to journey to that cursed Kotlas way up north. O, dearest, you should have been here " . . . he broke down and whimpered and his wife joined him, and it took the combined efforts of both son and daughter-in-law to calm them.

" The *baba* baked up biscuits and we started for town . . . and every step of the way we salted the earth with our tears. . . . I could have gotten off and kissed every particle of this dear earth of ours. Never, never again was I to see my village; never, never was I to walk or ride on this rutty road. I wouldn't even be buried among my own folk in my native soil but far, far away, among strangers! O, what a fate, what a fate for my old age. . . . And what was my sin? I had never killed anyone, I had never robbed anyone. I had never quarreled with anyone. . . . Ask my neighbors, hear what they have to say about me. Let the *bedniaks* themselves speak up and say whether or not I had ever done anyone harm. . . . If a man was poor and couldn't pay me for his wool-carding, I would wait, and some of them never would pay. . . . And if a man was in trouble, needed milk for a sick baby, I was the first to offer it and never charge a copeck for it. . . . I tried to live on terms of peace and helpfulness with my neighbors. And yet because I had a wool-carding machine, and because I hired some people to help me in the harvesting and in the threshing, which wouldn't have been necessary had my son remained at home, I was a *koolack*, a beast, a monster that had to be crushed."

"*Nu* father," Nikolai interposed impatiently, "enough of your complaining — it is Revolution and in Revolution don't expect favors from the government. . . ."

"Who was expecting favors? Who? I only wanted to be let alone — to live out my days with my wife in toil and in peace, that was all I wanted . . . and is that a crime? How could the Soviets who promised us so much when they came into power — how could they all of a sudden become so cruel, so inexpressibly cruel?"

"Such were the times, and there were mistakes, abuses by local authority. . . ." commented Nikolai.

"Yes and we were being crucified. . . . I tell you it was a nightmare, our trip was. We were packed into a *teploushka* [4] like cattle and there were so many of us. At night we could hardly stretch out and there were women and children who cried and just would not let us sleep. Now and then they would unhook us at some Godforsaken station and leave us there for hours and hours until another train would come along and pick us up . . . and oh, the stories that people told, the cruelties that they had to endure at the time of dekoolackization. . . . And hear me, hear me," he leaned so close now that I could feel his warm breath on my face, "there was one party of people who were told that they could bring along cereals and flour and potatoes on their wagons to the railroad station, and of course they did, and were happy in the thought that at least they would

4 Freight Car.

not starve on the journey north, and do you know what happened, do you know? O, God, how could people be so beastly? Why, all the food that these dekoolackized *muzhiks* brought to the station was packed into two special freight cars, and when the train started the freight cars did not follow, they were unhooked and the food was kept back. Imagine that."

" Father, O father," Nikolai protested again, " there were scoundrels who committed a lot of *peregibi* [5] and surely our guest having been in Moscow knows about it."

"·O, hush, Nikolai," said his wife, " let father finish his say."

" But it is necessary to explain that the government was not to blame for that," countered Nikolai earnestly, " else our guest might misunderstand."

" Have it your way then," continued the old man, " let it be *peregibi*. But that did not help the poor creatures who started with their families for the north, did it? And when we got there we were herded into camps without any accommodations — and children died, and I thought my wife and I would die, and really we shouldn't have minded death. We were so inexpressibly lonely, and our health was bad, mine especially, I began to cough and to have chills. . . . Ah, my friend, it was a nightmare. . . . But thank God, my son did not desert me, he is a proletarian and a member of a trade union and he began bustling about and after three months I was allowed to come back . . . and when we returned to this village and saw the fields again and the marshes and the native herds of stock and the little shepherds, I tell you, we cried with happiness, I blub-

[5] Abuses or excesses.

bered worse than an old woman — they all laughed at me, but I could not help myself. It seemed like coming back to life after you have been dead, that is what it seemed like."

"I suppose in your country, they do not treat *koolacks* like that, do they?" asked Anna. . . .

"Here, too, not everybody was treated like that," remarked Nikolai, "again I must say there were abuses, small-minded fellows who disregarded the instructions of the Party. . . ."

"Yes, but think of the hundreds and thousands who did not have a son like mine, and who had to remain there and will never be allowed to come back, think of that?" demanded Ivan, and turning to me he pursued, "and remember again that we are only *muzhiks,* 'dark' and inexperienced and so simple. When we live long in one place and have a family we are like an oak, get rooted deep in the very soil on which we live, and when we are pulled up we just wilt and fade. But, thank God, we are back," and turning to the ikons immediately above him he crossed himself and exclaimed: "*Hospodi pomilui.*" [6]

"He and mamma," said Nikolai now with a twinkle of good-natured censure "have become dreadfully religious since they have been back."

"And why shouldn't we?" queried the mother.

"Yes, why shouldn't we?" interceded Ivan. "It was God's will that we should come back, that's why we are back."

Nikolai winked at me and smiled but said nothing.

We finished eating. Anna and Nikolai crowded close to examine my camera, an object of never-ceasing won-

[6] Lord have Mercy!

der to peasants. If I would only take their picture, at least of their son, they would be so happy!

Then Anna and the mother stepped out to finish their chores and we three men remained alone in the house.

" If he had his accordion," said Ivan pointing to Nikolai, " he could play something for you, he is the best accordion player in the countryside, but they confiscated that, and have not returned it."

" I am trying to get it back," remarked Nikolai.

" Get it back! " replied Ivan with a sneer, " by this time some *kolhoznik* has probably ripped it to pieces. You know what they do with confiscated property, they turn it over to the *kolhoz* — everything."

" *Naplevat*," [7] Nikolai exclaimed, " I'll buy a new accordion soon."

Ivan also walked out and Nikolai, bubbling with mirth as was his nature, bombarded me with questions about life in foreign lands and particularly in America, and then proceeded to tell me how happy he was with his Anna and how nicely fixed he was in the city with a job and everything. I congratulated him on having won the heart of so lovable a girl and he blushing and giggling assured me that he had no easy task in winning her. She was a girl from this very village and he had loved her since his thirteenth year. They would always go to dances and parties together, and when she got to be seventeen suitors came to her from all surrounding villages, and one of them, the son of a peasant who had fifteen cows and three horses, had nearly won her. " I was nineteen then," he continued his narrative. " I didn't want to be married before serving my term in the army, and I was quite heart-broken when I learned

[7] The Devil take it!

that Anna had about decided to accept that rich suitor. So one evening while we were at a dance I called her outside and we went for a walk to the little wood out there beyond the village and we sat down on the grass. It was a lovely night with a full moon and I told her that I loved her and did not want her to marry that rich fellow, and she said that she didn't want to marry him either, because she didn't love him, she loved only me, but her parents and friends were giving her no peace and urging her to accept this well-to-do suitor. I was cheered to hear these words and felt hopeful. So I asked her if she would marry me, and she said no. I was stunned. The answer was so unexpected, because she had said that she loved only me! I asked her why she would not marry me and she refused to answer. I put my arms round her and squeezed her so hard that she cried — it hurt her so — and I told her that if she didn't marry me, something would happen, because I couldn't endure the idea of her marrying someone else. So she cried a lot and told me that she really loved me and only me, and would never love anyone else, but that she was so poor and had hardly any dowry, and she knew that my father was very proud of me because I was so handy with tools and was a good musician, and wouldn't allow me to marry a poor girl. I must admit there is much of the *koolack* in my father and he had always been wanting me to marry a girl with a rich dowry. But I loved Anna, I didn't want riches — the devil with riches. So I said to her, 'Let's fool father, fool him proper,' and she said, 'How?' and I said, 'I have seventy-five roubles saved up, and you take it and buy yarns and weave a lot of linens and blankets and we'll tell the old man that that is your dowry.' And she said, 'but he will want a cow and a horse and a wagon and I have none of these,' and I said, ' leave that to me — I'll talk the old man out of everything else.' And she was so happy and so was I, and we kissed and embraced and promised to love one another always and she agreed to send word to her rich suitor that she didn't want him and wouldn't marry him.

" Well, the old man grumbled because I wasn't getting as big a dowry as I deserved, but I won him over and that autumn we got married. Now both father and mother really love her, because she has been like a daughter to them, and — " blushing and laughing heartily as if overcome with joy — " we are just too happy for words. It is so wonderful to be in love like that, on my word it is, and Anna is interested in things too, goes to meetings and lectures and does social work — fits in beautifully with the life of a proletarian. In a few days, as soon as we get the old folks settled, we'll go back to the city and you must come and visit us and spend an evening with us. . . . Ah, she is one in a million, my Anna is," and he rolled back his fine head and laughed with happiness.

Soon the women and Ivan returned to the house. We gossiped away of trivial things, and then I bade them farewell and started for home. I had no more than reached the gateway when I heard Ivan calling after me to wait. It was late, lights in the village were out and *muzhiks* had gone to sleep. Only dogs were about, barking furiously.

" Excuse me, my friend," Ivan began as if in apology, "I know so little about the world and about the big people in Moscow and what they want us ' dark ' *muzhiks* to do. But you are a learned man, and surely you know those people, and dearest — hear me, perhaps it is not true that they are going to make another investigation and try to send me up north again. My son says it is not, and he is a clever boy, with a wise head. But my *baba* and I are so frightened. Sometimes we get up in the middle of the night thinking investigators have come to put us out of the house, and we cry so. Oh, if we only had any assurance that they would not bother us again, if only we did. And this is what I want to ask of you, and please do forgive me for bothering you, a stranger, with my personal troubles — if you ever see the big men in Moscow, Rykov or Stalin, please tell them that I, Ivan Bulatov will never have any wool-carding or any other kind of machine, and will never have more than one horse and one cow and one pig, aye, I might even get along without a horse, the devil with a horse, if only they would leave me alone."

I assured him that he need entertain no fears of exile now that he had been allowed to return home. But my words failed to comfort him.

" Maybe you are right, my little son," he countered, " but maybe you are wrong. I have only a few more years to live. I am not so very old, only fifty-six, but I am so broken up, and I am growing feebler from day to day, and I'd rather be shot than be exiled again. I tell you I'll throw myself out of the window if they put me on a train for the north. I want no riches, I want no accumulations. Please tell it to Stalin, maybe he doesn't even know what these local officials are doing, and he ought to know — yes, he ought to know about me. I want to remain in my own little hut, on my own little piece of land and work it with what little strength

I have and with what help my wife can offer. I want to live out my years in peace, and die on my own bed and be buried in my native village. Please, my dear, tell it to the big people in Moscow, do not forget, and I shall always remember you and pray for you."

He turned away and blubbered.

XIV

THE PUZZLED LITTLE FATHER

IN the old days the landlord, the *uriadnik* (con-stable), the priest, sometimes the school-teacher, though differing in their social position and in their cultural attainments, were the chief living links be-tween the Russian countryside and the outside Russian world. In importance and universality the priest over-shadowed all the others, even the *uriadnik* who, though constantly before the eyes of the populace, was only a petty official, of little education and subject to constant territorial shiftings. Neither his official position nor his glittering uniform invested him with that sense of mys-tery and power which hovered about the priest.

The *batushka*, little father, maintained no intimate personal associations with his people. Always his rela-tions with them were official, as of superior with in-feriors. His calling imposed on him no social obliga-tions toward his parishioners. He was in no sense a minister and except during confessions, which were obligatory, people would not unburden themselves to him of their troubles or go to him for solace from per-sonal sorrow. Yet he seemed as much a part of the vil-lage scene as the sky and the fields — as ever-present and as aloof. One could not imagine a village without its parish priest any more than a peasant house without ikons, or a river without water. The little father seemed as indispensable to the wholeness of life as the elements of nature. The peasant might cherish little respect for him, hold him in contempt, curse him, view him on occasions as an evil omen — but without him a funeral was no funeral, a wedding no wedding, a christening no christening, a Sunday no Sunday, a holiday no holiday. Essentially a pagan, the peasant accepted his priest as part of the absolute forces that ruled his destiny, all life. . . .

There were all manner of priests in the Russian villages, of varying degree of education and of varying repute with their parishioners. *Batushka* Timofey, for example, in our parish enjoyed the esteem of his people. Mild-mannered and soft-spoken he was devoted to wife and children and had escaped the bibulous reputation so many of his colleagues had acquired. No ugly rumors floated about him as about the little father in the adjoining parish who loved vodka more than his good name and whose behavior in other respects was not above reproach.

Batushka Timofey was a landlord of parts in possession of forty dessiatins of land, a fine herd of cattle, a flock of sheep and some splendid horses on which he and his children could often be seen on our roads riding in saddles or driving in a factory-made carriage. Neither he nor any child of his ever engaged in heavy labor — man-power was so cheap in the villages — but they all loved to putter around the garden, and the orchard, and the little father himself gloried in looking after his bees.

He lived in a huge house which with its shingled roof and large windows towered handsomely over the dwarfed huts in the midst of which it stood. Fronted by a magnificent orchard it was set off from the neighbor-

ing world by a high fence with the boards so close together that not even children could crawl through and
tamper with the fruit. Like the house, the orchard was
vastly superior to those of the surrounding peasants,
for the little father and his wife, like nearly all priests
in Russia, understood fruit-growing better than

CHRIST, WITH THE FIGURE OF CAPITAL BEHIND HIM, TELLING POV-
ERTY " CONSIDER THE LILIES OF THE FIELD " [1]

muzhiks. In summer as one passed this orchard the
luscious fruits, so near and yet so far, glistened tempt-
ingly in the sun. The *batushka* was a kindly man, and
when children peered enviously through the fence and
he happened to see them, he would hand out to them an
apple, a pear or plum.

An idyllic life *batushka* Timofey lived as did every

[1] The cartoons reproduced in this chapter have appeared in
various anti-religious Soviet publications and are the work of D. Moor,
the most popular Bolshevik cartoonist.

village priest in pre-revolutionary Russia, peaceful, leisurely, abundant, with hardly a care in the world. Indeed, was there a class of officials in old Russia further removed from the travails and vexations of daily life than were the village priests?

I remembered the *batushka* so well that on my first visit to the old home I went to call on him. He lived three versts away in the village which was the seat of his parish. When he came to the door I did not know him. In the eighteen years of my absence he had changed beyond recognition. Shrunken and bony with his long hair sparse and matted and hanging over his back like a dirty rag, with his face thin and brittle as though the skin were frozen or dried up and on the point of cracking, and with a loose linen smock falling over his boots below the knees and accentuating the pallor of his features and the frailty of his body, he seemed a mere skeleton of his former self. Even his teeth were gone and his gums were black as though lacerated by disease. Except for his eyes, which had retained some of their ancient sparkle, he seemed drained of vitality and void of a sense of self-importance, even of self-confidence. As I saw him now decrepit and crestfallen, he seemed a mere memory of the stalwart and joyous-hearted little father that I had known in my boyhood days.

He did not recognize me and stared at me with apprehension as though I were a messenger of sad tidings. He held the door half closed as if hesitating to admit me. I introduced myself mentioning my father's name and instantly he threw the door open and welcomed me. He had mistaken me, he said, for someone he was loath to meet — a Soviet official with information as to whether or not he could remain in his house. He had received an order to vacate it, but had appealed to a higher power and was daily expecting a reply to the appeal.

"Thank God," he remarked with a sense of relief, "it is not he. . . . My heart was pounding so wildly as I stood at the door facing you that I thought I'd collapse." He fell into a seat and put both hands over his heart as though to calm it. "But there is no telling — the day is long yet and the night still longer, anything may happen. It is not like in the old days when months and years passed and all remained the same. Nowadays much may happen in one day, aye in one hour, very much. But ah, tell me something of yourself, your mother, your brothers and sisters — what a long time you have been away, a very, very long time!"

We were in the dining room, and it was bare now, with few pieces of furniture and still fewer furnishings. The floor was unwashed and crusted over with bits of mud. The paint on the walls was peeling and in the corner right over the ikons a spider was weaving a web. As if in answer to the multitude of queries that came to me he hastened to explain: "You see how changed everything is! We have not a single servant any more, cannot afford one and besides, it is dangerous, they would call us exploiters and parasites and would surely put us out of the house, and the *matushka* — well, she is getting too old to do hard work, and so we let things slip." Eyeing me searchingly he continued, "You have not been here long? Ah! So you know little yet" — and leaning close as though to confide a secret, he remarked, "it is better to have things neglected — windows unwashed, floor unscrubbed, even hair uncombed — they'll respect you more if you look wretched. . . . That's the truth," and he laughed bitterly.

His wife came in and I gasped when I saw how she had faded. Her eyelids had contracted so that her once pretty eyes were barely open, and her face was crisscrossed with deep lines. Bareheaded and barefooted and puffing at a fat cigarette rolled peasant-fashion in coarse wrapping paper, she made a sorrowful picture. Only when she spoke did she seem like her old self, alert and animated. After greeting me with a burst of endearments she rushed off and soon returned with a sizzling samovar which she set on the table. The little father invited me to come to the table and as he was pouring tea he kept up a flow of melancholy chatter. . . .

"It is well that you have come back, very well, and now you can see with your own eyes what is happening here — the world turned upside down . . . we have lost everything — see how bare this room is? . . . the whole house is like that . . . we have sold everything for food, for bread, we had to . . . and the orchard, dear, that too is gone now, nationalized and we are not supposed to get one wormy apple. The watchman is a good man, a Jew . . . every morning when he picks the fruit off the ground he brings us in a hatful. . . . We have no tea. We have not had any in a long time . . . we use dried apples instead, soak them in hot water . . . please excuse such tea . . . an inventive people, aren't we?" He looked up with the hurt expression of a boy who is on the point of committing an indiscretion.

"We have no sugar either — please do excuse us — we just haven't got it. Imagine, little son — a *batushka* without sugar!"

It was hard to imagine a Russian priest without all

the sugar he ever would want for tea and for all other purposes. He surveyed the table with his eyes and on espying a little paper box in the folds of a coarse towel that covered a loaf of black bread, he reached for it and opened it. " But ah — things are not so very bad, here is something, our daughter has sent it with her boy who came yesterday for a visit here." He thrust a little white pill into my glass. " It is very sweet, sweeter than sugar — saccharine, but sh-sh — not a word to any-one, little son, it is forbidden to have saccharine. . . ."

" Eat the bread," pleaded the *matushka,* " black bread, it is the only kind we have now and thank God for that, and here, take an apple, it tastes good with bread. . . ."

" You should have come to us in former times," the *batushka* resumed, " then we could have entertained you fittingly, Russian fashion, with a broad heart. . . ."

" Aye, indeed, we could," the *matushka* chimed in with enthusiasm as though happy at the mere recollection of better days, " then we had sugar, tea, jams, meats, closets bursting with food and all from our own estate — everything our own. . . ."

" And now nothing," he continued, " black bread, apples, hot water and saccharine as long as it will last which will be only a few days. . . . *Ekh, Bozhe moy,*[2] if only they would not try to put us out of the house! "

" Then we might as well dig our graves. . . ."

" Surely," I ventured, " some peasant will offer you shelter? "

" Perhaps — I hope so — I have done them no evil. I have always been kind to them. But the peasants have changed."

[2] My Lord.

"Indeed they have, they are not as hospitable as they once were. . . ."

"Not as interested either. . . . Imagine it, when my land was taken not a man mumbled a word in protest; when my orchard was confiscated again they were silent, and now that I am being driven from my house, nobody bothers to help me. I might as well have been a stranger instead of a life-long neighbor and the priest of this parish. . . . O, you don't know what a Revolution does to people. . . ."

"You have had no Revolution in America — a Soviet Revolution?"

"No."

"Then you cannot imagine how people can change."

"*Nu*," mumbled the *batushka*, "let us not grumble too much — It is God's will. He gives and He takes. He blesses and He punishes, so let it be. . . ."

While on my way over I had formulated an endless series of questions I had planned to put to him. But now when I saw him in his neglected house stripped of the once luxurious furnishings and himself so decrepit, so humbled, so subdued, and his wife, once so comely and jovial, now so withered and resigned, I lost all desire for serious discussion. What else but sorrow could they speak of? No words they would utter could convey the wretchedness of their plight as eloquently as did the mere sight of them in their now barren and neglected home, from which they might at any hour be driven. . . .

Seven years had passed since that memorable day. Not long did *batushka* Timofey and his wife have to endure their agony. Both died within a short period soon after my visit. Now a red flag floated over their

THUS SAITH THE LORD

house. It had been turned into a community club and into the headquarters of the local *kolhoz*. The church was still there with its spacious grounds and its lovely park in which children were now running races and playing games. As I gazed at it I wondered how much longer it would endure? During the preceding winter meetings had been held to consider the advisability of closing it, but nothing had happened. Yet a church must have support, and whence was it to come in the future?

The man who had succeeded little father Timofey, an imposing fellow with a red beard and a thunderous voice, fled after a few months. He was not earning enough to support himself, and now this man's brother had come. He too was red-haired and with a magnificent voice, but what else could be said of him? To most questions he would answer with a shrug of the shoulders or with the brief "I don't know," and not because he was cowed, but because he was dismally uninformed. He had not graduated from a seminary. He had been a mere deacon in a country church, and only because of his voice and his love of music had he been elevated to the priesthood. He confessed to me that he never read any books. He never had heard of Tolstoy! With the older priests all over Russia growing older and older and with death fast thinning their ranks, the dignitaries of the church are drafting into service whomever they can recruit, even a man as innocent of knowledge as this new *batushka* in our parish.

Only one parish in my native countryside, in a little town some twenty versts away, enjoyed a semblance of prosperity. This parish owed its seeming strength not to sheer luck but to its geographic location and to the personality of its priest, *batushka* Dimitry. The town was a trading center in a fertile valley and on market days, twice a week, its public square was thronged with visiting peasants. The trading folk, hating the Soviets, gave generously toward the support of the church. It was the only place of refuge they had left. There they could gather with some degree of safety, talk and engage in an activity, worship, which was in itself a slap at the Soviets.

Batushka Dimitry was shrewd enough to take advantage of this special condition. Besides, he was a man of some culture. He had always read books and magazines and had kept himself informed of events in the world. And he was fearless. He never shrank from an encounter with an intellectual foe, whether Communist or Baptist. He visited the club-house of the Communists, which was formerly his home, and greedily read the publications which came there, especially the *Bezbozhnik,* the atheist journal. In the early years of the Revolution he had appeared in public debate with local Communists and once with a visiting Party man from some far-away place. From peasants in various villages I learned of the excitement that this debate had caused. Father Dimitry had asked his opponent, who had maintained that man is master of his own destiny and owes no allegiance to any supernatural powers, why had not any man, including Communists, fashioned with their own hands sunshine, rain or stars? The Communist replied that it was not God but nature that had created all these things, whereupon little father Dimitry countered, much to the amusement of the non-Communist portion of the public, by asking who made nature? A watch, he argued, had to have a maker, a house had to have a maker, even a Revolution had to have a maker. Who then was the maker of nature? The Communist argued that nature made itself, and a lot of people laughed and thought that the priest had the best of the argument.

I had heard so much about *batushka* Dimitry that I went to see him. When I arrived at his house I found the gateway locked, and the only response my continued rapping evoked was the infuriated barking of several dogs.

Shortly afterwards I strayed into a village where there was a funeral. An old man, I was informed, while out in the pasture feeding a bull, was gored to death. It was a white funeral, that is one conducted by a priest, and I learned that the priest who had come to officiate was little father Dimitry. I went to the funeral. Few people were there and they were mostly of the immediate family of the deceased and some older neighbors. The body after being washed was fitted out in the man's Sunday attire with a white linen shirt and an upstanding collar that swathed neck and chin. It lay on a bench with the face exposed. At its head a wax candle was burning, stuck in a box of rye. The priest was solemnly intoning " eternal memory," and several peasants were crossing themselves. There was no pronounced grief. There seldom is among peasants when the deceased happens to be an older person. Only one *muzhik*, a boyhood friend of the dead man, stood with bowed head and now and then wiped his tears. When the corpse was put into the casket this man, on kissing the body farewell held his lips long over the cheek of his departed comrade. When he lifted his head he murmured sorrowfully, " Farewell, my friend, farewell, O, happy man, happy man."

After the funeral I went with the priest to his home, which he had built on a plot of land that the Soviet had assigned to him when his house was confiscated. He introduced me to his wife, a heavy red-faced woman with a kindly smile and coarse hands. Both took me around their garden and with marked pride showed me their beds of vegetables and roses. " My *matushka*," said the little father, " is a big *spetz* [3] — all that you see is her work. I help her some but she is the boss and does most of the work. We don't dare hire outside labor, we might lose the land and it would cost too much."

"Yes," said the *matushka* with excitement, " I am a *spetz,* my father was an expert gardener in the city of Vladimir and I learned things from him. When they took everything away from us, they thought that we'd get lost and would forfeit our land and have to give it up. But I can make things grow — cucumbers, potatoes, cabbage, beets, turnips, berries, everything. This garden and our cow and the dozen odd hens we have give us the things we need, and we get along. The most important thing is not to lose one's courage and not to give up one's faith. . . . If one has faith and courage one can live and one has something to live for. Don't you agree? "

She left us and hastened to start the samovar, and then the three of us sat down round a table in the garden drinking tea and eating freshly made raspberry jam, cakes and sausage. Here in this house there was no evidence of destitution. Yet as our conversation continued I sensed in the priest's words anxiety for his future. He spoke gravely of the new crisis he was facing now, when private trade was completely snuffed

[3] Specialist.

out and his chief supporters were too poor to make their usual contributions. Had it not been for them he never could have raised the two thousand roubles that he had spent on renovating the church. That was over a year ago. Now it would have been impossible to raise the money, for some of these traders were in exile, others in jail and those who were around town were wracking their minds as to what to do now with all pursuits shut to them. As for the peasants, well —

"*Matushka,*" said the priest, "tell him what happened last Sunday."

"A man came last Sunday afternoon," she said, "to have a baby christened. He had always been a member of our parish, and when he brought the baby into the house he said, '*Batushka,* this is my sixth and it is the last I shall have christened!'"

"Imagine a *muzhik* speaking like that," the priest interrupted.

"And the *batushka,*" she continued, "asked him why he would not christen any more babies and he said he was going into the *kolhoz.* So the *batushka* told him that the law does not interfere with the christening of babies, even if a man is a member of a *kolhoz,* and mentioned the names of several *kolhozniks* who had him christen their babies, and the man only smiled and said in a *kolhoz* there was a new order and there was no need for priests, for religion or for christenings."

"And do you suppose he was wrong?" exclaimed the priest. "In the *kolhoz* there will be no place for religion, perhaps that is one reason the Communists are pushing it so vigorously, they want to kill religion and bury it, and they won't even put a monument over its grave."

"Yes, it is the truth, my dear," sighed the *matushka.*

"Only the other day," the priest continued, "I met the chairman of the local Soviet — I have talked to him several times — and he said to me, '*Batushka,* you had better give up your profession, disavow the church and God and get yourself a job, or it will go bad with you. The *kolhoz*,' he said, ' will kill all need for your profession.' And I asked him, ' What sort of a job might I find? ' And what do you suppose he said? ' Sweep the streets.' "

" The wretch," burst out the woman with exasperation, "think of him speaking so impudently to a *batushka!* "

" Yes," nodded the priest dolefully, " that is what I am facing now — the breakdown of private trade, the impoverishment and dispersal of my chief supporters and the invasion of the *kolhoz* with its power to soak atheist ideas into the very blood of people. What future can there be for me? "

" But maybe," interceded the woman, "the Lord will make them see the truth yet — their pigs have been dying in the *kolhozy*."

" Yes, that is true, Siberian plague has been sweeping the countryside and killing off a lot of pigs."

" It may be a visitation," the woman remarked with a feeling of awe not unmingled with hope. " O, Lord, what a world, what a world! "

" Yes, indeed, what a world," agreed the little father and lapsed into reflection.

" *Nu, nichevo*," said the woman rising and patting him gently on the back, " let the whole world turn against Him, but we won't. We can always earn our bread, even if nobody comes to church any more and we have to close its doors. We can work and raise our food as indeed we are already doing and not so badly. Isn't that so, *batushka?*" and she smiled and patted him again and walked out. He arose, walked reflectively up and down the room, then halted at the door. Looking around as if to see if anyone was near, he beckoned to me to follow him to a window opposite the door. There we sat down on a newly-made bench.

"You see," he began in a subdued voice as though not wishing his wife to hear him, "I have to be careful in the presence of the *matushka,* because she gets easily upset, and she is such a firm believer. But I tell you of late I have been asking myself a lot of questions. I cannot run away from these questions — they pursue me by day and by night. But I cannot answer them, and it is so impossible nowadays for a man like me to get to the saintly leaders of the church, to the really wise men of God, and discuss things with them and have them solve my perplexities."

He looked out of the door again to make sure his wife was beyond hearing distance. "Hear me. In the very old days when the Israelites went against Him, He appeared before them through their prophets and made His will and His power manifest. When they sinned He chastised them, and brought them to His feet. Think of Moses and of Aaron and of the others, to whom He would reveal Himself. Think of the visitations with which He plagued Pharaoh so as to lighten the task of Moses. You see what I mean? In those days God made Himself known, He spoke to His people, censured, punished them, destroyed their possessions. And now? Please, I beg of you, never mention a word of what I am saying, not a word, for it may go bad with me. It is counter-revolution to wish failure for the

Soviets. It might mean death, and they are terribly
heartless with priests and traders. It is only to you,
an American, that I dare speak as I do, and I have got
to speak to somebody or I sometimes feel as though
these thoughts will choke me. I dare not whisper a
word to my wife — she would be so upset. But —
think of it, the whole youth of our land is drenched in

THE LORD DELIVERING A SERMON TO ADAM AND EVE

contempt for Him and His church, and all over the
country He and faith in Him are impudently mocked
and spat upon — and nothing happens.

" The other day I heard someone say that a meteor
had fallen somewhere in the wilderness of Siberia and
blasted up by the roots miles of big timber. In Siberia
in the wilderness, where nobody was made to feel His
power and His will! Do you see? Why did not it fall
somewhere else, say — over the Kremlin? Why does
not He emerge and assert Himself as He did in days
of old? Why doesn't He reveal Himself to someone
worthy of His trust? I am sure there are such people
left yet. Why then doesn't He transmit through them

His wishes to all of us, the Bolsheviks and the other infidels and in such a way that they couldn't doubt His being, or His power? Don't you suppose if He made Himself known, people would flock back to Him? Of course they would. They would bow in repentance and promise to believe and obey and worship. Yet here we are, His servants — waiting, waiting, and nothing happens. The heavens are silent, the earth is silent, the stars are silent, everything is silent." He paused, scratched his head and looking back once more to see whether his wife was near, he continued:

"Sometimes I say to myself if He does not care why should we? Isn't He expecting too much of us? Doesn't He see that we alone, with our human frailties and imperfections, can achieve little? And for Him with His power it would have been easy to do something big and decisive. Or is He merely trying us out, to see how much we can endure? Perhaps, who knows? But it is so hard, so very hard on us, His servants! "

Presently the *matushka* returned with a broad smile and in her hands a fat Rhode Island hen. "What a beauty! What a marvellous layer, and such large eggs too. I'll make you an omelette of her eggs and maybe you'll think you are home again. Please be in no hurry to go." Humming a merry tune she dashed out of the room, and forthwith we could hear the crackling of a fire in the kitchen.

"Now please don't misunderstand me," the priest resumed. I am no infidel. I believe in my God and in my Christ, I have sacrificed everything for Him. My eldest son has abandoned me because I am a priest. He would not come home to see me any more, is ashamed of me, and nearly broke the heart of my *matushka.* Yes, I have worn my crown of thorns, I am still wearing it, and won't hesitate to die wearing it, — only it would have been so easy for Him to nip the whole thing, and bring people back to their senses. Without God, without faith, without an acceptance of something outside of one's mortal flesh — what is life? How much better is man without religion, without God, than the cow that is crossing the street yonder, or the pig that is rooting the ground over across in the yard? How much better? What sort of a life is it when you know that all ends when you die, that all your earthly sufferings are in vain, and that all those you have always loved and cherished you will never see again, and that you and everybody are turned into dust to the end of time? Once in a discussion with a Communist, when I told him the things I am telling you, he laughed and said, 'Little father, when you die you will be only a piece of carrion, nothing else, fit for crows to fatten on.' I was so shocked I could hardly speak calmly to the man. . . . To think of such a nasty notion getting rooted in human minds. . . . Then what does all life mean? What is this world for? What are this earth and sky and stars and trees and grass and you and I and Lenin and Stalin and America, and everything, what is the purpose of it all? "

As he stopped we heard coming from the kitchen the sputter of grease in a frying pan.

XV

THE LANDLORD HERDSMAN

WELL did I remember Abram Terukhin as he looked in my boyhood days. Tall, shaved, well-dressed, cheerful, he was a landlord of parts and a merchant to boot. Whenever he passed our village on his way to the lakes where he operated fish concessions, he would stop at our house, for he was a lover of tea and we were among the few families in the village that owned a samovar. His arrival always caused a joyous commotion among us children, for we felt free and easy and intimate with him, and he would give us candy and pat us on the cheeks and treat us not with the condescension of other grown-ups but as equals. Though a Jew he was highly esteemed by the highest Czarist officials in the district. They could not help responding to his geniality and his many-sided talents, especially as a breeder of cattle. Not a landlord in the whole region could boast of as splendid herds as his were. Again and again at agricultural exhibitions his cattle won first honors.

He lived on an estate of several hundred dessiatins within easy reach of a small town. Since he was a Jew and might own no land, his estate was made up of fields which he rented from the nearby town, from surrounding peasants and from landlords. His house, set back from the highway, nestled within the embrace of a far-stretching and magnificent orchard. It was a huge house of many rooms with high ceilings, large windows, a spacious porch and it was always freshly painted and decorated. The lawn was kept clear of refuse and was brightened with flower-beds.

A man of means, he would hire special tutors for his children to prepare them for entrance to the Russian High-Schools. Though Jews were admitted by percentages, his children found the doors to these schools open, for he had "protection"; the director of the gymnasium and the mayor of the town and the representative of the nobility were his friends, and never hesitated to confer a personal favor on him.

On my previous visits to my native countryside I had heard nothing of him. I had not bothered to inquire. I had not even thought of him. But this time I learned casually that he had joined a *kolhoz*. Former landlords like former officials and *koolacks* are legally barred from *kolhozy*, but an exception was made in his case as in that of certain other Jews on the ground that, since they were victims of special repressions, they were not wholly to blame for engaging in so-called speculative and exploiting pursuits. Legally, therefore, there was nothing irregular or startling in Abram joining a *kolhoz*. But socially and spiritually the transition from his former to his present station in life, with all the accompanying conflicts and readjustments that the process involved, presented something striking and even challenging.

On learning that he was living on his old place, I went to see him. I had no more than reached the yard of his home than I grew aware of the change that had swept over the place. Washlines flapping with linens and all manner of clothes radiated like spokes in a wheel from the house to nearby trees. Sticks, bark, manure, rags, other débris lay scattered around the grass which was uneven, uncut and had in parts died out. The board fences had grown mossy and were tumbling; the wooden box over the well was sagging and the massive sweep that towered over it looked as if it had been pulled loose. The house itself with the paint faded from walls, windows and shutters, had lost its old luster, and had begun to droop. Even the spacious porch appeared shrunk and battered. Gone now were the old cleanliness, the old privacy, the old smartness. No longer was this place a retreat for gentlefolks. Its idyllic calm had given way to raucous noises. Women with bare feet and dishevelled hair, carrying armfuls of wood, pails of water or baskets of provender, were coming in and out of the house, and children, a little army of them, likewise barefooted, unwashed and half-clad raced noisily up and down the yard. They were the families of other *kolhozniks* who had moved into Abram's house.

I asked a little girl who was sitting on the ground playing with a baby where I might find Abram.

"Out in the fields," she replied, "pasturing the cows."

Pasturing the cows! So Abram was now a herdsman! I could not help thinking of the sense of reproach which the Russian word *pastukh* — herdsman — carried with it in the old days. If you wished to show contempt for a man's intelligence you called him a *pastukh*. It was a synonym for stupidity and degradation. Nowadays of course it had assumed a social loftiness comparable only to the word *dvoryanin* — nobleman — in the old days. In travelling about Russia I have met Soviet dignitaries who would boast with elation of the fact that at one time they or their parents had been mere herdsmen. Yet in spite of the volcanic reversal in social values, and the prestige that had now become attached to the word *pastukh,* I could not help cherishing a secret pity for a man like Abram who in the twilight of his life had come to nothing more exciting or more worthy of his talents than herding cattle and on the very land of which he had at one time been master.

I found him in the field stretched out on the grass with his chin cupped in his hands, watching a herd of fine cattle pulling at the rich grass of a far-spreading marsh. Bareheaded and barefooted with his trousers rolled up to his knees and his shirt-sleeves to his elbows, his hair closely clipped, his face swarthy from sunburn and mottled with wrinkles, he seemed a very old man. He was unshaved and not well washed. Beside him lay a long leather whip and a few paces away with its head almost hidden in the grass a black dog lay sleeping. I introduced myself to him, for never should I have recognized him nor he me. He sat up overcome with surprise and his face lighted up with a radiance that brought back some of his old attractiveness.

" I am an old man now," he remarked, " sixty-three and I look over seventy, don't I? " There was neither regret nor resentment in his voice, only resignation and even good humor. " Taking it easy in my old days, herding cattle," and pointing to his whip he added, " this is my tool, a sacred tool now, a proletarian tool, and he," pointing at the dog, " is my chief assistant.

I have another, a nice peasant boy, very clever and very alert, but sometimes he falls asleep and I cannot find him."

I sat down on the grass beside him and we plunged into talk. The sun was up high in the sky, a breeze was blowing over us, and all around the big herd of *kolhoz* cattle browsed with audible zeal in the rich grass of the lowlands. It was quiet all around save for the incessant warbling of larks which pierced the stillness with gayety.

" I suppose when you go back to America and tell your mother that I am now a herdsman she will wring her hands in sorrow and lament over my fate, and thank God that she did not remain in this land to see with her own eyes the downfall of so good a man as I was. Yes, your mother used to think I was a very good man," and he chuckled merrily. I thought he was straining himself to be good-humored but neither his voice nor his facial expression revealed any pretense. He seemed inhumanly void of regrets at the fall of his fortunes. " But really you must tell your mother that it is not so bad — do you know what it now means to be a shepherd? In the old days pious Jews did not honor their rabbi with as high fervor as society now honors a shepherd. Still," and he laughed again the joyous laugh of sheer amusement, " it is funny — everything is funny here, isn't it? A world upside down — only try to make your mother understand, so that she will laugh and not weep." Of a sudden assuming an air of earnestness and solemnity, he continued, " I never weep, never. I swear to you I don't. More — I am not so sure that it is not all for the best." He paused and looked at me with a penetration that was almost embarrassing, as though seeking to ascertain whether or not I was in accord with his opinion. " Living in Russia," he pursued once more, "makes a fellow ask a lot of questions, an awful lot of them, questions which in the old days would have seemed ridiculous. Now they pound away at you day and night and you don't rest until you find answers, and the answers come too, surprising answers, at which in the old days you would have laughed even more than at the questions. Maybe we are mad and idiotic, but maybe we were crazy in the old days, and are only now recovering our sanity and wisdom. You do understand what I mean? " Again he laughed his boyish good-natured laugh. . . . " Tell me, don't you think I seem queer to you? "

" And why do you ask? " I questioned.

" Because, my dear, you come from over there — from another world — where things are so utterly different, indeed as much so as would be a horse with the feet of a pig or a pig with the feet of a goose. I have never been in America, so I cannot speak of her, but I have travelled in Germany, used to go there to the baths in the old days, and now as I think of the world which Germany was, and compare it with our Russia, I shrug my shoulders and ask myself, is it really possible that such a world as Germany ever existed anywhere? Here you even lose the sense of time, a year seems like an age, a generation. It seems ages since I have been in Germany." Again he paused and again he laughed as though amused at his own words.

" Of course don't imagine it was easy to make this shift from the old to the new world, especially as I had a wife and children who could not forget the old life, the old ideas, the old standards and who were looking up to me as to a man of strength and wisdom and with power to perform the miracle of holding together undamaged the old world in which they lived. . . ."

A black cow had strayed into a nearby clover field and snatching his whip and flicking it violently Abram started after her. At the top of his voice he yelled at her to turn back. Meanwhile the whole herd scented the clover and started for it and Abram with the alertness of a lifelong herdsman and amid continuous snappings of the whip, turned them quickly back to the pasture. When he returned he was sweating and puffing hard and wiping his face with a soiled red handkerchief. He seemed younger now than when I first saw him.

" There is an old *muzhik* on this *kolhoz,* older than I am," he began again, "who used to work for me. He is a wholly illiterate man. A newspaper is good to him for only one thing — roll cigarettes in, and so are books. But he is no fool, he is quite a philosopher. When I joined the *kolhoz* he came to me and shook hands and congratulated me. ' Abram,' he said, ' you are a good man. You have done the right thing. You have shown that you don't think yourself superior, that you are ready to take pot luck with the rest of us — good and bad. And why, Abram,' he continued, ' should you want to be different from me for example? Why,' he said, ' should any man enjoy things that his neighbor has not got? ' In the old days had a man propounded such a question to me I'd have thought him a hopeless fool or maniac. I was reared in the idea that some people are better than others and are therefore entitled to better things. I questioned this idea no more than I did the presence of the stars or the sky or the coming of the seasons of the year. But I want you to know that now — I no longer dismiss such a question easily. . . . Now this old *muzhik* is no mere idiot or madman to me. Now I myself ask this question in all seriousness. Why should one man or group of men partake of joys and pleasures that others are denied? Why is it the poor man's fault if he has not the cunning, the energy, the luck, the education of the wealthy man? Why? Have you ever asked yourself that question? Answer it. Try. I have answered it. I am answering it all the time. I tell you I agree with that *muzhik* who once was only my hired man. These inequalities are wrong, desperately, brutally wrong. . . ." And as though wanting to show his ease and reconciliation he began to hum an old ditty in a soft resonant voice which in spirit harmonized pleasantly with the whispers of the breeze and the chirping of the tireless larks, a song of man's contentment with the world.

"Don't for a moment imagine that I am a Bolshevik," he resumed, "I am not. I don't know what I am. I don't care to know. The only thing I know is that I am not the Abram I once was, and what is more I would not want to be my old self again. If the Soviets came to me and told me that I could have back all that they took from me and could continue my old life in the old way, I would thank them and refuse. . . . Honestly I'd feel ashamed to be in my old boots. They would not fit me anyway — I have been going around barefooted too long. Do you understand? I am finished with the old life, finished for good and forever — thank God. . . ."

" And how about the wife and children? "

" Well, the children have long ago gone through their conversion and the wife — she is getting there slowly. . . ." He rose to a sitting posture and constantly pointing his finger at me as though to emphasize his words, continued:

" Consider my position in the early days of the Revolution. . . . It was very bad. . . . I thought I'd go mad. Army after army came here — and one thing I did know — for me as a Jew the coming of a White General or of the Poles could only be a calamity. In view of my position and my economic solidity, they might spare me personally. But I could not think of myself only. True, I never was pious, but when a *pogrom* occurred anywhere, I'd sink with grief, and neither the Whites nor the Poles could or would guarantee the Jews against *pogroms*. Only the Reds even in those hectic days of civil war were death on *pogrom*-makers. They protected the Jew as a Jew. And do you know what I did? I helped them. My whole family did, my estate was their underground headquarters. The Whites and the Poles had taken me for one of their own, because I was a landlord. But underground — right here on this land, in my cow stable, in my barns, in my cellar, was a whole organization busily undermining the power of the armies of occupation.

" Later when the Reds established themselves, I gave up most of my estate and kept for myself only as much as I and my family with a little outside help could work, in all about twenty dessiatins. From year to year, however, I realized that it was only a question of time when I'd be squeezed dry of everything. . . . Now it was a new tax, now a new self-obligation, now a fine. . . . They were milking me good and proper, and I was growing drier and drier, if you understand what I mean. I came dangerously close to being branded a *koolack*. I was threatened again and again with deprivation of citizenship rights. My oldest son left the family and started out for himself. He became an *agronom* and is now at work somewhere in Siberia and he would have nothing to do with us, was almost lost to us. My younger son sought to enter the university and though he is a good student and passed the examination with high standings, he was not admitted, and only because he was the son of a father who had been a landlord and was still regarded as a well-to-do farmer and employed hired help. Of course we all worked, worked hard. They could not say we lived off the labor of others, though in summer we did keep two peasant boys.

" So here was my condition, oldest son gone, youngest frustrated in his ambition, and I myself looked at askance and constantly threatened with deprivation of citizenship rights. Of course the local officials could not possibly do that. I was not without revolutionary deserts. It was no small thing for me in the days of the civil war to turn my estate into headquarters of the revolutionary secret organization. I have all the documents of those days. I'd go to Moscow if necessary and demand reinstatement. I'd stick around until it was done. I'd knock at the doors of everybody, even of Stalin if necessary.

" No, I was not afraid of the threats of local officials. All my life I had dealt with officials and I never had truckled to them. I never had pocketed my self-esteem. In the old days officials minded me more than I minded them. Of course I paid them a pretty penny for the privilege of enjoying a sense of security. As a Jew I always had to pay for every breath of free air that I breathed. The present-day official, however, is different. Sometimes he is stupid and brutal but he is honest and has faith in himself and knows what he wants. One after another they used to come here, these officials, not on friendly visits but to make a fresh appraisal of my belongings, inform me of a new levy I was to meet, go through my house and barns and write down everything they saw. Sometimes they would come and remind me that as an employer of two peasant boys I was getting to be a *koolack* and in time would suffer the doom of a *koolack*.

" I was growing very nervous, and every time a team would drive into our yard I would get panicky and suspect it was some official with more burdens and troubles for me. I could not examine my mail without trembling lest there be a new government document with a fresh penalty for some transgression. It was a hopeless situation. I knew that sooner or later they were sure to get the best of me. I sensed that the individualist farmer had no basis in a Soviet society, none whatever. Everything was gathering to crush him, and when the *kolhoz* movement began to sweep the land, I was sure I was right.

" And besides, as I have already told you, I could not escape from the millions of questions that the challenge of the Revolution was hurling at me. A fellow cannot run away from them, and he begins to wonder if he has a right to three cows and two horses and a goodly number of chickens and sheep when his neighbor has no cow, no horse, hardly any hens or any sheep.

He begins to ask himself if it is indeed right for him to have meat and butter and cheese and white bread and other things, when his neighbor lives only on cabbage soup and black bread. When the injustice of inequality in material enjoyment is hammered at you all the time, it sinks in, and makes you uneasy. It bothers not only your mind but your conscience. Well, I decided it was time to act. I would delay no longer. It was dangerous and it was uncomfortable.

"One evening last autumn I called my family to-gether for a conference. We sat around the table and I turned to them and said, ' My dears, it is time we did something and the only thing to do is to quit at once, completely and forever.' Well, tears were shed, plenty of them, and we talked, talked our hearts out all night, and finally we agreed that we would give up the old way of living and join a *kolhoz*. And mind we left no reservations in our minds, none whatever. I never act with reservations in important things in life. I will not fool myself. We decided we'd not only give up our land but everything. We'd have no individual property ex-cepting what we needed for our daily usage. ' We must tear up the old books,' I said to the family, ' and burn all the old records. We must start life all over again as though we were newly born, and there are to be no grumblings and no regrets and no sighing for the old days. Yes,' I said, ' we must start this new life with clean hands and with clean hearts.' And we did. We turned everything over to the *kolhoz*, every cow and calf and hen, every sack of grain and every spear of hay. We would not bother to take advantage of the law allowing a *kolhoznik* to have his own cow and his own hens, I would avail myself of no privileges. We even turned our house over to them to do with as they pleased. If they wanted us to move to some other place we'd move, and if they allowed us to keep for ourselves just one room, we'd be satisfied with that. And do you know after we had made our decisions we felt happy, regenerated, free of fears, suspicions, premonitions. We gave up everything we owned, but we gained peace of mind and reconciliation with our own inner selves.

" Of course we are not always happy. I am a *khosiain* — understand something about household economy and farming and I see all around me a colossal amount of blundering and wastage. But neither I nor my wife grumbles. Cheerfully we submit to the rules of the game. . . . Frankly, we don't have as good food now as we once had, and we don't dress as well. See me bare-footed and in these dirty and patched trousers? I am saving my shoes for winter, because it won't be easy to get new ones. I am wearing my old clothes as long as I can, or rather as long as my wife can make them hold together. We eat meat once a week or once in two weeks and we get little sugar . . . and little tea. But we have enough bread, and milk too, and cucumbers, and we get a pound of butter a week per person, and all the potatoes we want and now and then a few eggs, and we get along. My young son is now as good as any-body — he can say his father is a peasant, a *kolhoznik,* and he dare look everybody in the eyes. He is in Rostov working and preparing for the university, and this time he is not going to be kept out because of his father's social position. We have only two rooms for ourselves and our house is filled with neighbors some of whom are people we never before have known. We share our kitchen with three other families and our samovar with one other. But we have peace of mind. We are afraid of nothing and nobody, officials don't bother us, nobody points a finger of scorn at us, and we work regular hours without worry and excitement. Our neighbors might be a little more orderly — keep things in better condition and some of the children might be less careless, and not throw things around the premises as much as they do. But these are small things — we are used to them and besides I like children and now that my own are grown up I delight in playing games with them or watching them play by themselves. . . . That's how it is. . . ."

XVI

A NEW GIRL

SHE was in the barn milking a horned black cow when I first saw her, a sturdy girl with a flushed face that was lightly sprinkled with freckles, and with bobbed light-brown hair held in place by a narrow red ribbon. She appeared older than eighteen, which Abram had told me was her age. She was barefoot, and her gray gingham dress covered by a white apron reached only to her knees and exposed her bare finely curved legs. Her name was Vera.

Abram, who had spoken to me of her, regarded her as a real creation of the Revolution, as new to the Russian countryside as the *kolhoz* or the tractor, and as significant. So eager was he to have me meet her that he drove me out to the *kolhoz* on which she was living.

"Our chief," said the secretary of the *kolhoz*, introducing me to Vera.

"Don't believe him," she retorted with confusion, "I am only a milk-maid."

Our voices or our appearance or both frightened the cow she was milking. Amid a succession of sharp grunts the animal lurched forward, overturning Vera's stool and milk-pail and tearing her dress. Instantly she was on her feet, protesting that she was not hurt, and, holding together her torn dress, she dashed out of the barn. My companion was noticeably distressed.

" Poor child," he lamented, " she has so few clothes, and nowadays it is not easy even for us in the *kolhoz*, who are favored in the coöperative stores, to obtain material for new ones."

Soon Vera reappeared in another dress and apron. Self-possessed and smiling, as though the accident were a trifle, she proceeded with her milking. In Russia all the milking is done by women, and this *kolhoz*, which boasted over one hundred milch cows, was no exception. Vera, like all the milk-maids who were considered old enough to work full time, had to milk eight cows three times a day. Busy as she might be with social work, so the secretary of the *kolhoz* informed me, and regardless of the hour — sometimes it was dawn — at which she might return from a lecture or conference, she never missed a milking. Always, as soon as the cows were brought in from pasture, she was on hand for her duties.

The secretary gave me a brief account of her life. She came from a small town, the daughter of a tailor who had died in the early years of the Revolution, leaving a wife and three children, of whom she was the youngest. Because of her proletarian origin, the best in education was free to her, and she hastened to take advantage of the opportunity. She chose agriculture as her life-work and on graduating from an agricultural institute where she specialized in live stock, she had planned to continue her studies in the famous Timiryazev academy in Moscow, Russia's leading agricultural college. But the Party, in this case the *Komsomol*, blocked her plans. A loyal revolutionary, well versed in Party aims and principles, an energetic organizer, a good orator and with innate capacity for leadership, she was sent to this particular *kolhoz* to supervise its activities.

Officially she was milk-maid and live-stock expert. She worked at her job like any other member of the *kolhoz* and was paid no more than any other worker of her kind. But her real tasks, which began when her day's farm work was finished, were manifold and delicate, for this was no ordinary *kolhoz*. At the time of its origin, five years before, it was made up of ten families, all Jewish. Now, as the result of a great influx of members during the preceding spring, it had become a so-called "international" *kolhoz*, comprising fifty-seven families of which a majority were Jewish, but which included also Poles, Letts, Lithuanians and Russians. This racial heterogeneity and the social origin of the Jewish portion of the membership, who, prior to their settlement on the land, had been mainly petty shopkeepers, thrust daily upon Vera a host of problems. In addition to participating in purely economic affairs, she settled personal tilts between members, and worked for racial understanding and social harmony. All the cultural work of the community — lectures, readings, discussions, diversions — were under her direction, and so was the editing of the wall-newspaper, which made its appearance once a week or once every two weeks, and which, like all such newspapers, whether in a *kolhoz*, a shop, or a factory, was the medium through which members voiced their dissatisfactions, criticisms and demands. In her leisure hours she would visit nearby villages and hold meetings with a view to winning fresh converts to the *kolhoz* movement.

As I watched her milking I could hardly believe that this young, inexperienced-looking girl, just past adoles-

cence, was entrusted with so weighty a burden of responsibilities. I could not help speculating as to what
might have been her destiny in the old days, in the dismal little town where she was born. As the daughter of
a tailor she would have had no social standing in the
community. If she had attended school, it would have
been only long enough to learn to read and write and
to recite prayers in Hebrew. At an early age she would
have become a servant in some well-to-do family, or
an apprentice in her father's or some other shop. She
would have saved copeck on copeck until she had
gathered several hundred roubles; then matchmakers
would have visited her parents and sought to marry
her to some proletarian — a tailor, a carpenter, perhaps
even a shoemaker (who, for some reason or other, was
in the old days relegated to the lowest social position,
especially among Jews). If fortune had been kind to her
she might have become the wife of a petty trader, but
she could never have married a merchant of standing
or any other personage of importance, so sharp and
decisive were the lines of cleavage in the old Russian
social world. And only by virtue of membership in
some revolutionary group might she hope to become
the spouse of an intellectual.

After marriage, children would have come, and she
would have reared them in the same manner in which
she had been reared. The outside world and all that
it implied in mental development and emotional exhilaration would have remained as alien to her as a
foreign land.

Yet now, at eighteen, she was entrusted with a formidable task. The roads of advancement, though not
in a material sense, were everywhere open to her, and

she could traverse them as far as native ability and social obligations would allow. And there are numberless girls like Vera scattered over the vast Soviet domain. When one meets them, hears them speak, notes the flame of devotion in their eyes and in their voices, one realizes afresh what a double-armed power this Russian Revolution is: how on the one hand it stifles and on the other it redeems personality. Whether it does the one or the other depends upon whether one is an enemy and non-conformist, or a ward and supporter of the new dispensation. A cruel taskmaster, the Revolution recognizes no middle ground, holding that " he who is not with us is against us."

When the farm work was finished for the day, Vera, the secretary of the *kolhoz,* and I made our way to a pile of freshly cut logs outside of the barn and sat down.

" Vera," the secretary asked mischievously, " would you like to go for an automobile ride? "

" Would I! " she joyously exclaimed.

" This *tovarishtsh* has an automobile of his own," teased the secretary.

" Really? " she queried incredulously. " Here? " Whereupon the secretary chuckled and confessed that he was only teasing.

" She has a lot of ambitions. Tell him, Vera, what they are."

" They aren't so many," she remarked.

" Tell him," prompted the secretary.

" Well," she began reflectively, " I'd like to have just one long ride in an automobile, and so fast that I would have to shut my eyes, and I want to go to Moscow to study agriculture in the Timiryazev Acad-

emy, and I want to learn to fly, and I'd like to be a
good tractorist and know everything about a tractor —
take it all apart and put it together again."

" Is that all? " teased the secretary.

" Well," she added after some further reflection, " I
would like to see a real motion picture. I have only seen
little bits of ones."

In the little towns and villages in which she had spent
her life only the inferior motion pictures were shown.
I was astonished when she told me that she had never
seen " Potemkin " nor " The End of St. Petersburg "
nor " The Storm of Asia " nor " The Women of Rya-
zan," nor had she heard of Mary Pickford, Douglas
Fairbanks, Charlie Chaplin, the three screen heroes of
every school child of Moscow. As I watched her react
with child-like joy to the excitement of the moment,
I had the feeling that she was no political leader, no
revolutionary agitator, not yet a full-grown woman,
but a sturdy girl with an outgoing love of play, fun,
adventure.

" In America," she queried, " they have talking pictures? I suppose only in the big cities? "

"Everywhere," I said.

" Even in villages? "

" Yes."

" Indeed? " She shook her head in wonder. To the
secretary she remarked:

" There is *technika* for you. If only their proletarian
would hurry along with the Revolution, we might be
having talking pictures here on this *kolhoz.*"

" And just think of the shoes we'd have," added the
secretary. " You would not need to go barefooted, *Komsomolka,* and I might get a pair like those which Ford

or Rockefeller wears!" He chuckled. But Vera grew thoughtful.

"Tell me," she asked seriously, "what's the matter with the American proletarian? Why doesn't he start something? It is time he woke up."

"Do her a favor," pleaded the secretary, "tell her you believe in world revolution. She cannot bear to have anyone doubting its possibilities."

"Why should he lie to me?" she protested with resentment. "It is the truth I want."

The secretary winked at me and laughed; then, hearing someone call him, excused himself and left.

"Really, is there no chance of a revolution in America?" she asked in the sad spirit with which an American child might inquire, on Christmas eve, if there were a possibility of Santa Claus failing to make his appearance during the night.

"What do you think?" I countered.

"All countries must have revolutions."

"Why?"

"Because capitalism has outgrown its usefulness and must fall. That is clear enough, isn't it?"

Like their enemies in and outside of Russia, the revolutionaries are intolerant of differences of opinion affecting the basic dogmas of their faith. In asking for information they really seek confirmation. The young revolutionaries, being more impassioned than the older ones, are especially hostile to expressions of doubt as to the validity of Communist doctrine, particularly when these question the inevitability of a world revolution. Their minds are as closed to a skeptical attitude on this subject as are those of the religious Fundamentalists to a critical study of the Bible. From previous experiences I had learned that when the question of world revolution is up for discussion it is best to dismiss it. I tried to do so this time, but Vera insisted on explicit answers. When I offered them, arguing that in a highly industrialized society the middle class is so powerful that any attempt at a proletarian revolution would result in a butchery of the proletarian, she seemed nonplussed and disturbed. But not for long.

" I cannot agree with you," she finally retorted, " it is impossible. The proletarian must win. He simply must." Her mood changed and once more she was only a playful girl.

" There are so many questions," she said excitedly, " I want to ask you. Millions of questions. Tell me everything, everything about America."

" What especially interests you? "

" Well, what do the girls of my age do? "

" They go to school, read books, amuse themselves."

" How? "

" Theater, motion pictures, dances, games; some of them," I added after a pause, " go to church."

" What! " she exclaimed as if shocked. " Young girls like me go to church? How absurd. Why do they do it? "

" I suppose they get satisfaction out of it."

She dug a finger into her cheek, as was her habit when she grew thoughtful.

" Is satisfying one's self such a great thing? " and as if speaking to herself she continued, " I don't think so." Several times she shook her head as if reassuring herself that she was not in error.

" There is my brother," she proceeded, " once he was a nice lad, a devoted Party man, a real revolutionary; but something happened to him and he turned bad.

Now he drinks, and though he is married he has to send money to another woman by whom he has had a child, and when I ask him why he lives such a bad life he says he is trying to find this thing you just spoke of — satisfaction. Surely that is not a good reason — not even a good excuse, is it? " She paused again. " Or take these *muzhiks* in the villages. I go out to them often and argue with them about collectivization; I tell them that if they ever want to crawl out of their vermin-infested huts they had better join the collectives, because only the collective can raise them to a modern way of living. And what do you suppose they say? That they get satisfaction out of their way of living, and why should they change? There must be something besides satisfaction, mustn't there, to justify our ways? "

" You are an atheist, aren't you? " I asked.

She laughed.

" Why do you laugh? "

" That you should ask such a question. How can any sensible person be a believer? "

" Would you say that believers are fools? "

" If they are not fools they are at least terribly misguided," she flung back. " Capitalists keep drumming false ideas into their heads until they believe them."

" And you carefully analyze everything that you believe? " I challenged.

" Of course! " Then, as if feeling the need of further substantiation of her words, she added, " History, science, even nature is on our side."

She returned suddenly to the subject of the American girl, and bombarded me with a fresh volley of questions. How did American girls dress? How many dresses did they have at one time? How many hats and shoes?

She never had possessed more than three dresses at a time, she said, and but one pair of shoes — at the moment she had no shoes at all, only sandals. She did not expect to have shoes until autumn, when fresh supplies would come to the local coöperative store. And in all her lifetime she had never worn a hat. But such deprivations did not disturb her.

" We have more important things to buy now — machines! But some day when we are industrialized we shall have everything, dresses, shoes, hats. . . . What books do American girls read? "

" Travel, novels, plays, poetry."

" I suppose Marx and Lenin are forbidden in America? "

" No."

" And the *Pravda* and *Izvestia?* "

" Also permitted. "

" Really? "

She was so loath to believe in the truth of my words that she questioned me several times. Measuring everything in terms of the dictatorial Soviet standards under which she lived, she could not understand this tolerance of " capitalist masters " toward the chief prophets of the proletarian revolution and the leading journals of its dictatorship. It seemed to her equally incredible that in America one could travel without passports, without papers of identification, and that one did not need to register with the police in every place one visited. She had always thought, she confessed, that capitalist countries were at least as vigilant as the Soviets.

Once more she turned to the subject of the American girl.

" Do American girls earn their own living? "

" More and more of them are becoming economically independent."

" I am so glad," she remarked with elation. " It is so necessary for a woman to be free, and she can't be free if she has to depend for her bread on someone else, even her own father. What else do American girls do? "

" What else should they do? "

" I mean," she explained, " what purposes have they? What is their objective in life? "

" Themselves."

Nonplussed, she stared at me as though awaiting an explanation of my words. When I offered none, she remarked:

" Do you mean to say that they have no social purpose? "

" Not in the sense in which you use the words."

" Have they nothing outside of themselves to live for, something for society, for the masses? "

" In America things are different."

" So! " She shrugged her shoulders in bafflement. " And don't they miss a social purpose? " she questioned.

" Apparently not."

" How strange! " she exclaimed, and grew pensive again. After a prolonged pause she added, " No, I should never enjoy such a life, never! I'd feel so lost, so lonely. Living just for myself? Hm — never."

There was truth in her words. Such a girl would feel lost in an individualistic society. She would miss the group activities, the group purposes, and group passions of the Revolution. It would take an upheaval as mighty and as bloody as the one Russia had gone through, to win the revolutionary youth back to a feeling of contentment in an individualistic society. This fact alone would make the conquest of Russian territory by an alien power a gruesome tragedy for its present youth. Before there could be subjugation there would have to be conversion or extermination.

A young man riding a bicycle came up and joined us. He was shaved; he wore a neat blue blouse, a new cap and freshly polished low shoes; and he spoke, not the dialect of the region, but literary Russian. Vera introduced him as the teacher in the district school. He had come to escort her to a meeting in his schoolhouse, three versts away, at which she was to deliver a lecture.

" What will be your subject? " I asked.

" The theses of the industrial and agricultural policies that are to be submitted by Party leaders to the Sixteenth Congress of the Communist Party." Excusing herself, she pranced away to her room to make herself ready for the meeting.

It was a glorious evening with clear skies and balmy air — an evening for fun, play, song, dance — and yet this eighteen-year-old girl was to walk nearly two miles to address a group of boys and girls who like herself had worked all day in the field or barn, on a subject that would tax the mental energies of a keen-minded scholar.

Soon she came out ready to leave — washed, combed, wearing a light coat over her black dress, her legs bare above short socks and sandals.

" Please stay with us a few days," she begged me, " tomorrow is my rest day and I am going to the big meadow two versts away to pick a mess of sorrel. Maybe you'd come along and we could talk some more." Turning to the teacher she continued: " This *tovarishtsh* has been telling me interesting things about America — how different their young people are from us, so unbelievably different." She bade me goodnight and departed with the teacher.

Early the next afternoon, Vera and I started for the meadow. We turned from the highway into a footpath that cut across the immense rye field of the *kolhoz*. The stalks were so high that the ears of grain scratched our faces until the skin burned. When I complained of this, Vera laughingly chided me for being so sensitive to little things — so " unproletarianized," she teased. " You surely do need a revolution in America, if only to harden people like you. And still you say that the middle class is stronger than the proletarian and will cut him to pieces if he rises. I don't believe it. No, the proletarian must triumph."

We walked on until we reached the meadow. Sorrel was abundant, and it did not take us long to fill the basket. Then we retired to the shade of a stately birch by the roadside.

" I told my audience last night," she began, " all that I learned from you about American girls, and some of the girls at the meeting were strong for having as many dresses and hats and shoes as the Americans. *Bourgeois,* aren't they? And some of them actually admitted that they had four and five dresses and two pairs of shoes. Imagine that! Then we talked a lot about America, and decided that she isn't as great a country as we supposed. In only one thing is she great — in *technika*.[1] But though she has the best machines in the world, culturally she is not far advanced."

[1] Industrial development.

" And why do you say that? " I questioned.

" Because no country can be far advanced culturally when its young people live for themselves and believe in God and go to church."

A number of wagons passed us, loaded with logs and lumber which obviously had been parts of a building.

" Our teams," said Vera, hailing the drivers with a loud greeting.

" Where do they come from? " I asked.

" From some village where the property of *koolacks* has been liquidated. These are their houses and barns. The Soviet gave them to us."

The words *koolacks* and " liquidated " brought afresh to my mind the tragedy of the prosperous peasant in Russia. As I contemplated the teams plodding along this quiet road with the remains of households that were once astir with energy and sentiment and hope, I once more sensed the terrible inhumanity of the Revolution in its treatment of real or supposed enemies. Where now were the men and women and children who once inhabited these houses now being carted off in fragments as casually as if they were but fallen trees from a forest? My face must have betrayed my feelings, for Vera inquired why I looked so concerned.

" It was terrible, wasn't it, this liquidation of the *koolacks?* " I replied.

" Terrible? " she repeated without a trace of commiseration. " Nothing of the sort! "

" Think of throwing men and women and children out of their homes, stripping them of all possessions and means of livelihood, and exiling them to some far-away camp in the north or to some barren patch of land away from their own village! "

" You sound just like one of our own intelligents," she scoffed gently. " What do you suppose would happen to the Revolution if we were all like that? "

" But wasn't it a cruel procedure? " I persisted.

"Of course it was; but do you suppose it was a joy for us to go through the villages throwing people out of their homes and confiscating their possessions? We are not entirely bereft of feelings. One of my friends in our *raikom* told me that once while he was confiscating the possessions of a *koolack* a little girl of no more than three came up to him crying and begged, ' Uncle dear, please leave us enough bread so we won't die of hunger.' He was so upset that he had to run out of the house to hide his tears. There now! "

" Did he go back in and continue the liquidation? " I asked.

"Of course he did. He had to. The *koolack* is the *bourzhui* in the village, and he has to go." Then, as if feeling the need of further justification of procedure, unparalleled in history, she added, " It is either the *kolhoz* or the *koolack*. The two cannot live side by side. Don't you see? " She seemed grown up now, and formidable — a warrior on the firing line, sure and decisive and pitiless.

We drifted into a discussion of marriage.

" Would you marry a *bourzhui?* " I asked.

She threw back her head and chortled.

" What a foolish question! "

" Why is it foolish? "

" Because we have no more *bourzhuis,* or won't have, very soon."

" Supposing it was a foreign *bourzhui* that you fell in love with? "

" I am not so sure that I would let myself fall in love unless I could win him over to my views. I don't like to quarrel, and with a *bourzhui* I should always have to." After a pause she added, " But of course, rich as he might be, I'd never let him support me; of that I am sure. I'd work for my own living, as every woman should."

" Do you believe in marriage? "

" Marriage, hmm! " There was a sneer in her tone.

" If you were married, would you want your marriage registered? " I pursued.

" I should not care much whether it was or not."

" So you really don't believe in marriage? "

" I didn't say I didn't, and I didn't say I did," she hedged, and after a reflective pause she added, " If you will promise not to ask any more questions on this subject I will tell you what I believe."

" Well? "

" I believe in love."

" In free love? "

She stared at me uncomprehendingly.

" What sort of love is it if it isn't free? " she queried. " But it must be real love," she added after a pause. " Have you read the novel *Natalya Tarpova?* I am reading it now. Natalya, you know, is never satisfied with the man she marries, so she flits along from husband to husband. In the end she marries an engineer, a non-Party man. Do you suppose I have any sympathy for such a woman? Of course not. She is as bad as a harlot. She is a harlot. She does not know what true love, what true companionship is. You read a lot about such women in *bourgeois* literature. I am now reading *Anna Karenina*."

"Anna is not that kind of woman, is she?" I ventured.

"No, but she is too overcome with sensuality; and do you know why? Because she is not economically independent and she has nothing in the world to live for excepting herself and, only incidentally, her son. Consequently she has only her own satisfactions and her own emotions to think about."

Hearing her, so young, speak with such gravity and decisiveness on questions of so delicate and intricate a nature made her seem almost unreal, and for no known reason I laughed.

"Why do you laugh?" she asked reproachfully.

"You know so much."

"No, I don't."

"And you are so young."

"What difference does that make?" she flared back with resentment. "In a revolution the younger you are the more you have to know."

An elderly Jew passed us. He carried a scythe on his shoulder, and seemed so absorbed in reflection that he did not notice us. When Vera greeted him with a loud shout, he waved his hand but did not stop.

"Recently," she said, "I had a row with him. A shrewd old fellow he is. Our Commissary of Agriculture has issued orders prohibiting the slaughter of calves unless a veterinary has condemned them as unfit for breeding. We have to do this in order to make up for the slaughter of stock last winter. One night this little man sneaked two calves into the village and had them slaughtered by a Jewish *shokhet*. When I asked him why he had done it, he replied that he and several other Jews in the *kolhoz* wanted to have *kosher* meat.

That was all right. Anybody who wants *kosher* meat is entitled to the privilege of getting it, if it is obtainable. But this, you see, was something altogether different, a violation of the discipline of the *kolhoz* and of the instructions of the Commissary of Agriculture. That I could not overlook; so what do you suppose I did?"

" What? "

" Well, I lectured the old fellow and then I took the meat and gave it away to the Gentiles of the *kolhoz.*"

" Wasn't that cruel? " I asked.

" Cruel? Well, sometimes you have to be unkind. And what would you say to an incident like this? Once two Red soldiers stopped here and asked if they could buy two pounds of bread. They had been walking since morning and had about fifteen versts ahead of them before they got to camp. They were dusty and sweaty and hungry. I told them that we did not sell bread or anything else, but would give it to them, as much as they needed. I asked the man in charge of our food store to weigh out several pounds of bread for the soldiers. He gave them the bread, they offered him fifteen copecks, and he took the money. You have no idea how furious I was. To take fifteen copecks for bread from Red soldiers, who, if an enemy invaded our land, would be ready to give their lives! At another time a similar thing happened. A Red soldier stopped and asked if he could have a bowl of cottage cheese, and the clerk in charge of the food store accepted ten copecks from him. Luckily I happened to be on hand, and I directed him to return the money to the soldier and deduct ten copecks from my wages. You have no idea how deep-seated the trading instinct is in some people who have been engaged in business. They are all the time com-

plaining that everything is a failure, and only because
they cannot accumulate personal possessions. I don't
understand this craze for individual possessions. Supposing they had millions? They'd die; and then what?
When I was in school I was allowed a monthly stipend,
and most of the time I'd forget to collect it. Only when
the dining-room clerk would threaten to bar me from
the table if I did not pay my bills, would I go after it."
She paused and began to whistle a tune; and as I
watched her, so decisive and so impassioned, she again
seemed grown-up, remote, formidable.

" There is something else I must tell you," she began once more. " I am sure it will amuse you because
it concerns you. This morning as we were in the barn,
some of the men and women were talking about you.
They thought you were a strange sort of person — an
American, surely able to hire a horse and drive around
these villages, and yet you walked. And do you know
what they said? Don't be hurt now. They said that
you must be too stingy to pay for a horse — that's why
you walked; and they thought you were foolish to use
up your strength and wear out your shoes. Isn't that
amusing? But in the old days middle-class Jews had
such a dislike and disrespect for physical effort that
they seemed to regard even walking as a disgrace.
You have no idea how difficult it is to root out
the old notions from the minds of some of these
people."

" I suppose," I queried, " you often have to argue
with them? "

" Rather," she answered. " The other evening we
had a meeting to decide whether we were to build a
hen-house or a pigsty. I was the only one for the pig-

sty. Our Commissary of Agriculture is urging us constantly to concentrate on pig raising in order to lessen
the meat shortage, and we can do it with pigs faster
than with any other animals. The others were strong
for the hen-house on the ground that hens needed good
care and pigs could thrive anywhere. Even the *muzhiks,*
who have all their lives been raising pigs, gave this
argument. They laughed at me when I told them that
a pig is a very tender animal and must have a clean
place to live in; otherwise it easily succumbs to illness
and dies. For hours and hours I argued with them
until at last they agreed that I was right. Now we are
building quarters for two hundred sows."

" And what about the relationship between the Jews
and the Gentiles? " I asked.

" Oh, that isn't a serious problem. They are getting
more or less accustomed to one another. Of course,
once in a while old feelings of anti-semitism do crop
out, but we are fighting it. Something happened the
other day which may interest you. We received a supply
of textiles for our members, and of course we all turned
out to get our share. One peasant woman who had just
joined the *kolhoz* was displeased with the ration allotted
to her and scolded the clerk in our little shop, telling
him that the only reason she was not receiving more
was because she was not Jewish. I was so furious that I
almost cried. And you should have heard me talk to
her! Of course, I'd have been just as indignant if it
had been a Jewish woman who spoke with contempt of
a Gentile. It is so stupid, this racial prejudice on the
part of people who, for their own good, ought to be
comradely with one another. I can understand a class
struggle which is rooted in exploitation; but racial

conflicts are only the work of the *bourgeoisie,* who stop at nothing to keep the proletarian masses divided and dark."

"I suppose," I asked, shifting the conversation to another subject, "that you have learned to shoot?"

"I wouldn't be much of a *Komsomolka* if I hadn't.

"Would you go to the front in time of war?"

"Would I? They couldn't keep me from going."

"And you would fight?"

"Of course I would."

"With bayonet?"

"With anything."

"What a brave girl," I remarked.

"Brave nothing."

"But you are a woman, and so young."

She frowned. "What difference should that make?" she asked. "Why should only men do all the fighting?"

"Because," I replied tritely, "they are men."

"*Nu,* more *bourgeois* sentimentality."

"But men," I insisted, "have always done the fighting."

"Always!" she hurled back with exasperation, "How I hate the word! The very aim of our revolution is to smash this ' always,' this going back to the past for guidance and wisdom."

"Still," I persisted, "men are stronger than women."

"And what if they are? It is not strength alone that counts in war, is it? And besides, women can stand a lot. I have been out on campaigns in villages with girls and with boys, and I did not see that the boys endured hardships any better than the girls. The idea of men being fitted for this and women being fitted for that is *bourgeois* rubbish."

" But bayonet fighting," I pursued, " think what it means."

" All fighting is terrible," she replied, " but if the *bourzhuis* attack us, will they spare our women? Supposing a *bourzhui* army came to this place and discovered that I was a *Komsomolka,* would they keep their hands off me just because I am a girl? You cannot make me believe that. So why shouldn't we women fight and use bayonets if necessary to keep the *bourzhuis* out of here? "

There was no bravado in her words, only conviction and determination; and this time her very youthfulness added to her stature. One could not doubt that she would be as good as her word, and that if need arose she would shoulder a gun and wield a bayonet and kill or be killed in the same high spirit of martyrdom and exaltation with which men in an earlier age killed and died, not for their country, not even for their homes, but for their God. . . .

I was making copious notes of our conversation. She leaned over to watch me write, and said:

" Are you putting down everything I am saying? "

" I am trying to."

" Be sure that you don't misquote me," she warned, with a sudden coquettishness.

I promised that I wouldn't.

XVII

GIPSY ROSA

IN the course of my wanderings about my native
countryside I strayed one afternoon into a far-away
village on the edge of a forest, and on being told by the
peasants there that a Gipsy colony had settled only a
short distance away, I set out to visit it. I had no sooner
emerged from the forest into the clearing in full view
of the tents than a pack of dogs, barking fiercely, hurled
themselves toward me. Behind them a pack of wildly
shouting children also scurried forward. Someone called
the dogs back, but the children raced on until they
gathered about me — hideous-looking children, unwashed, unbarbered, almost unclad, with eruptions on
legs and faces, and with red, swollen eyes. Yet they were
the soul of hilarity. They pushed, crowded, shouted
with abandon.

" A copeck, uncle, for bread! "

" A copeck, uncle, for sugar! "

" A copeck, uncle, for cigarettes! "

I shook my head and told them that I had no money.
But rebuffs mean nothing to a Gipsy. I doled out a
handful of small coins, but still they clamored. Luckily,
as we drew near the camp, a bearded old man with a
huge whip shouted at them and they dispersed instantly like chickens pursued by a dog. The old man
greeted me affably, but I had hardly time to respond

before another army of solicitors swarmed round me, fortune-tellers, all women, many with babies in their arms or strapped to their breasts, and all talking at once. I walked on, protesting that I never had my fortune told. But they were determined to tell it in spite of me. One woman, old and gaunt, with sunken chest, hollow eyes and a red kerchief draped round her head, the image of the hag that figures so prominently in peasant folk tales of the region, trailed close behind me, tugging at my sleeve with her bony fingers.

" There is sorrow in your face," she chattered away dolefully, " a great sadness in your eyes. An evil man is on your trail, an evil woman is in your path, a great misfortune is in store for you, if — " She halted, smiled maliciously and putting a finger to her nose as if in threat, added: " I can rescue you with my cards. I have rescued hundreds like you, and to their dying day they blessed me and prayed for me." My resistance was fast ebbing, and she hastened to take advantage of my weakness. Swiftly she drew a pack of greasy cards from the ragged folds at her breast, shuffled them lightly and, picking them over one by one, proceeded to enlighten me as to my destiny. When she had finished, I gave her a half-rouble. She thanked me with a courteous bow, yet chided me for being niggardly.

Meanwhile the other women clustered about me and offered to tell my fortune all over again. I shook my head and marched on, but they followed along. I protested that I had no more money, but to no avail. I passed around cigarettes, but no sooner did they light these or tuck them away in their bosoms than they continued their pursuit. I do not know what would have happened if nature had not intervened. Fortunately a storm blew up, sudden and fierce. Thunder rocked the earth, and sheets of rain lashed violently against the tents. The women hastened to get under cover. So did I.

I dashed into a nearby tent, extended over a huge wagon. A dog chained to the hind wheel howled with fright as thunderclap followed thunderclap. Nearby, on a blanket spread over the ground, a handsome youth lay smoking a cigarette. He invited me to share the blanket with him. His interest in me quickened when he learned that I was from America. There were so many things he had always wanted to know about this far-away gold-swept America! " Tell me," he asked earnestly, " do handsome fellows get big dowries there? "

I answered that to the best of my knowledge the institution of dowry did not exist in America. He stared at me with suspicion, as if unable to believe my words. Ah, and he had thought that Americans were such a cultured people! What, then, did they do with all the money they had? A strange land! In a burst of confidence he informed me that he had just passed his twentieth birthday, and brides were already offering themselves to him — lots of brides, from all kinds of colonies. But he would bide his time. He would wait for the highest bidder — never would he marry a girl, however pretty she might be, unless she was ready to present him with at least a horse, a wagon and a dog.

In the midst of our discussion of these matters, a voice somewhere above me called out: " Are you perchance a doctor, Stranger? "

" My father," explained the youth. I looked up

and saw the head of an old man protruding from the top of the wagon, out of a pack of feather bedding.

"I'm terribly sick," he moaned. "My teeth ache, oh, how dreadfully! I keep putting snuff inside, and it burns, but it doesn't kill the pain." He was a big man, with a bushy beard spreading like a mask over his face. He sat up in the wagon, holding his swollen cheeks in his hands and wailing. "I cannot eat, I cannot sleep, I cannot sit and cannot lie down — O Lord, what affliction!"

The dog, which had been leaping about excitedly, suddenly broke loose from its chain and dashed out of the tent. The youth raised the tent flap and called to the animal; then, when it refused to come, he ran out after it. Taking advantage of his son's exit, the old man, with a secretive gesture, beckoned me to come close. "Tell me," he whispered, "are there doctors in America that can make an old man young again?" He had heard, he said, that there were such doctors in Russia, and that for ten roubles they would perform an operation which would make one younger by ten years. But he did not trust Russian doctors. It was terrible to be old; life was so joyless. He was seventy-five, and ah, how he would love to go back to forty-five — the best age of life, when one is neither wise nor foolish, neither hard nor soft, neither over-hungry for pleasure nor oversated with it, neither too much aflame nor too much congealed.

The rain had subsided, and the sun shone again. News that an American visitor was in the camp had spread rapidly, and Gipsies from other tents, men for the most part, came over to visit. They were as full of curiosity as were the peasants, and, like them, eager

to unload their woes. Times were hard, they told me,
and the Soviet authorities were showing no disposition
to make them easier, were in fact constantly making
things harder. They were driving the Gipsies from
field and forest, and harassing them in the market
places with fees and fines. Their incomes were shrink-
ing from day to day, while prices were swelling. It was
hard to earn bread.

"What about settling on the land, like the Jews?"
I suggested.

"Ah," replied one of them, a cross-eyed man with a
formidable moustache like that of a Cossack trailing
down his massive chin, "a *muzhik* has his land, and a
Gipsy, his horse. Do you understand? Our horse is
our land, our bread-box, our treasure. We are not
trained to till the land, and we are not as clever as
Jews; we cannot change so easily."

"My father," broke in another man, "once tamed
a wolf. He fed it milk and meat, fondled it, played with
it, made it his pet. But one day it got loose from its
chain and dashed away into the woods. It never came
back. We are like that. Try as hard as you please to
domesticate us, the first chance we get we run off to
the woods. It is in our blood, Stranger."

"Every bird picks up its food with its own beak,"
said another. "You cannot graft a hen's beak on a dove
or a heron's on a goose, or a duck's on an eagle. A
Gipsy has his own beak, and no other will fit him."

"Right, right," several voices assented in unison.

"The Soviets are never satisfied," one of them went
on. "Taxes we pay like others, more than others. We
join the army. We even register our horses, and in
time of war we shall have to let them go at whatever

price the government sees fit to offer us. Everything
we do as commanded, and yet they will not let us alone.
They are hounding us constantly. Only today a man
came and told us we should have to clear out of here.
The place is government property, he said, and no one
is allowed to make use of it. We pleaded with him, yet
he left without giving us assurance that we could stay.
What shall we do? They want us to be like other
people, but how can we? We are Gipsies; our blood is
not like theirs. We are wanderers, horse-traders — good
for nothing else. Tied down, we would be worse than a
bird in a cage.

" In the old days when times were bad for us in the
market place, when peasants had no money and would
neither buy nor trade horses, then our women would
work harder than ever. They could always get plenty
of business, for the Russians had more faith in them
than in other fortune-tellers. But now do you know
what has happened? People have no faith — they are
infidels. Even *muzhiks* no longer believe in God nor in
fortune-telling. Our women can earn nothing."

"How is it in America? " someone asked. " Do
people there believe in fortune-telling? "

" Some do," I responded.

" And is there a Soviet government in America,
too? "

" No."

" No? Ah! " They seemed puzzled and surprised.

" We thought," remarked the man with the moustache, " that the whole world had already gone Soviet."

" So horse-trading is free in America? "

" Free."

" And is wandering permitted also? "

" Yes."

" A Gipsy can buy in the stores as cheaply as anybody else? Everything — sugar, tea, leather, dry goods? "

" Certainly."

" How can you get to America? Is it beyond Bessarabia? "

" You go to America by water," I explained.

" Water? So! "

" Sure, by water! " exclaimed the youth with whom I had been talking during the storm. " Lots of water, big water, the ocean, bigger than the Volga. Is it not true, American? " He turned to me. I nodded.

The old man broke in plaintively.

" Couldn't we go in the wagon? " he asked. " Are there no bridges? Our horse is strong. He can take us far."

" How could there be bridges? " the young man said scornfully. " Of course we couldn't go in the wagon, we would have to go in boats."

" Then you are right, we can't go," the old man sighed, and sank into a thoughtful silence.

" Of course we can't," the young man continued. " It takes lots of money! And that is something we have not got. So we have to stay here." He jingled the few coins in his pocket as if to demonstrate their scarcity, while the old man shook his head sorrowfully.

" If there was only a way out — something we could do to placate these stubborn Soviets! " The old man spoke again with a distinct note of despair. " In the old days some high official or rich landlord would take a fancy to one of our girls, and through him we could obtain favors. We want to keep our race pure. Gipsies

are for Gipsies. But still, we would make an exception,
if we could get some good out of it for the tribe. We
would even agree to let one of our girls become the
wife of a Soviet official if he would use his influence to
make life easier for us. Do you know of such an
official in Moscow, a big man, with power to set laws
aside? "

" There is no use talking," drawled the young man,
" we are lost. We are like a beast in a trap."

"We are, we are," voices repeated in doleful re-
frain.

This despair of the Gipsies is by no means limited to
the groups I have described. Travel from one end of
the Soviet Union to the other — in Asia and in Europe
— and wherever Gipsies gather, you can hear them
voice their dark forebodings. And well they may. This
fierce Russian Revolution, which, like a war tank,
moves ever onward, flattening out everything in its
path, this Revolution which has shattered the foundation of religion, of private property, of the modern
family, which is daily turning to hilarious sport our
western conceptions of success and social achievement,
is at last reaching out for the Gipsy. In all respects he is
a symbol of a mode of life — of private trade, fortune-
telling, vagabondage, economic parasitism and, above
all, absence of social responsibility — which the Revolution is seeking to destroy. Of course, he is fighting
back with all the slyness and subtlety which centuries
of vagabondage and evasion of law have inculcated in
him. He has done so in the past in many lands, and
has never yet been defeated. But never before has he
faced so formidable an array of forces.

With all his loathing of certainty, security, monotony, the Gipsy cannot ignore the need of physical self-preservation, and under the Soviets it is growing increasingly difficult for him to eke out a livelihood through his customary occupations. The attack on private property has not only cut deep into his chief source of income — horse-trading — but has made people intolerant of idlers and of anyone who derives a livelihood from so-called non-productive activities. Peasants were never before so vindictive with Gipsy malefactors, real or imaginary, as they now are. Recently a Gipsy colony stopped for the night near a village on the outskirts of Moscow. The peasants ordered them off the land, and when the Gipsies refused to go, a battle ensued, with both parties using whips, sticks and knives freely. A squad of Moscow police had to be summoned to quell the conflict. In another place, also near Moscow, a Gipsy and his wife were accused of stealing a horse. They were lynched by a mob of local peasants, and their bodies burned. In another village in the south three horses had disappeared. Suspicion fell on a Gipsy colony that was camping in the vicinity. In the resulting clash between Gipsies and peasants, three Gipsies were murdered. Frequently the newspapers carry stories of peasant outbreaks against Gipsies. Indeed, the central government is often besieged with petitions from all over the country begging it to do something to keep the Gipsy off the highways and byways of the country.

Efforts are now being made to draw the Gipsies into so-called useful pursuits, chiefly into industry and into farming. The *kolhoz* movement has reached them, just as it has the Jews, and is upsetting their ancient ways no less implacably than it has those of the Jews.

And though only a small number of Gipsy youths have
been fired with zeal for social crusading among their
people, yet there are among them individuals who in
earnestness of purpose and in devotion to duty can
hold their own with the most ardent revolutionaries in
the land of the Soviets. Certainly Rosa can.

I met Rosa in a roundabout way, not in my native
countryside but in Moscow. My interest in Gipsies,
especially in the efforts to colonize them on collective
farms, led me to the discovery of a Gipsy club in
Moscow. Located on the ground floor of a fine building
in a remote part of the city, it is little known to people
outside of the Gipsy colony. There on Monday evenings
the members foregather for entertainment and social
diversion, which in the Gipsy definition mean chiefly
singing and dancing.[1] The choir of this club, the best of
its type in Russia, is made up solely of Gipsies, without
that admixture of portly Russian ex-baronesses and
former princesses who bulk so large in most Gipsy
choirs, whether in Moscow or in New York. This choir
is a tribal institution, and, like all such choirs, sings to
the accompaniment of a guitar; but it sings as no other
choir I have ever heard. Most of the songs begin in a
soft drawling monotone, more like a moan or a wail
than like a tune; it flows on and on, seemingly without
end and without purpose, lulling the listener, soothing
his emotions rather than stirring them. It is as if the
singers were too crushed to assert themselves, and preferred to edge away into the background, into the twilight. Of a sudden there is a pause, so brief that one is
hardly aware of it; and then the tempo changes, the

[1] In recent months Gipsy music and dancing has been prohibited
in Moscow.

pace quickens, heads sway, bodies rock, eyes glow, faces flame, voices swell higher and higher, gayer and gayer until a whirlpool of passion fills the air and carries one away into a vision of something extraordinarily barbaric and irresistibly alive. The song may be only about a horse, a fair, a forest, a stream, a starry night on the steppe, a frustrated love, a fulfilled love, but there is always this climax of riotous gayety or riotous sorrow, this explosion into thunderous rapture.

On and on the choir sings with joy, madness, fury; and then from behind the scenes or from the choir itself, a raven-haired man dashes out waving a white handkerchief, and flashes into a Gipsy *pliaska*.[2] Soon a woman joins him. Round and round they whirl, smiling, beckoning, calling out to one another and to the audience. The singers, as if surcharged with fresh energy, sing with increased passion and accompany the singing with violent clapping of their hands. The dancers respond to the mood of heightened fervor. They hop, jig, stamp the floor with their feet, scream with ecstasy, the woman constantly luring and eluding the man, he as if aflame with triumph or desire leaping into the air, whirling round and round, violently slapping his hands against his boots, his hips, his breast. Then, with an explosive shout and gesture, both halt. The dance is at an end, and the visitor wonders whether what he has just witnessed was actuality or illusion.

One evening the master of ceremonies introduced a special dancer from a camp on the outskirts of Moscow. He was a young man, with light-brown hair that fell in waves over his forehead and ears, and an af-

[2] Hop.

fectation of eccentricity so extreme as to make him appear absurd. When he appeared on the stage a titter ran through the hall. Then the guitar twanged and he glided easily, gracefully into the dance, his face stiff, his eyes wide open. Up and around he glided, rousing at first little interest and no enthusiasm. Of a sudden he cried out and began to whirl, slowly at first, then faster and faster, slapping his legs, his thighs, his breast, his arms; and now and then with a violent bang, the floor. The crowd sat breathless with excitement, and when he finished a volcanic burst of shouts and hand-clapping shook the auditorium.

In the midst of the applause I felt someone's hand on my shoulder. I turned, and before me stood the director of the club, with a girl. He introduced her as the Rosa of whom he had often spoken to me. We all sat down together, and when the entertainment was over and the auditorium cleared, a small group, principally Gipsy leaders, remained to converse with Rosa. She was only nineteen years of age, a tall fair-skinned girl, with black hair, brilliant eyes, perfect teeth and a radiant disposition. Even among the women of her own people, noted for their beauty and vivacity, she would have attracted instant attention. Her eyes sparkled as she talked and her voice vibrated with a rich resonance.

Rosa came from the city of Smolensk. Her father had settled down before she was born, so she had never developed the passion for wandering that possessed her people. The Revolution had caught her imagination when she was still too young to appreciate its significance, and she thrilled to the adventure it offered. She attended its schools and mass meetings, read its books, listened to its lectures, and was moved to join in its work. She saw her own people — vagabonds, despised, uncared for — out of tune with the new ideas and new purposes, their future dark and uncertain. She resolved to work among them. With funds which she managed to squeeze out of various Soviet organizations she opened an ice-cream factory to provide work for Gipsies. The plant waited, but laborers would not come. Her people refused to accept the jobs which Rosa offered them. They would not work indoors. Finally her father came to her rescue. He dropped his own work as a sausage-maker and, with the help of some friends, began to operate the ice-cream factory. Gradually other Gipsies were persuaded to work there, and the factory became an outstanding success. Rosa then opened a sausage shop, and that too was successful. She planned a modern dressmaking establishment, to be operated entirely by Gipsies, and undertook the stupendous task of teaching Gipsy girls to sew.

But the land claimed her at last. Out she sallied into camp after camp, spreading among the men and women the idea of becoming farmers instead of social outcasts, despised everywhere by everybody. Times were hard, Gipsies were discouraged, and some of them yielded to Rosa's persuasion. She organized one collective farm, then another, a third, fourth, fifth, sixth, seventh, and, wonder of wonders, so far not one had collapsed!

Rosa did not neglect the young people. She argued some of the parents into consenting to send their children to school, provided tuition would be free. Rosa assured them it would be. Now she had pupils, but no schoolhouse. After a lengthy search she found a vacant hut just outside of Smolensk. She scrubbed it clean, fitted it with benches and tables, and called it a schoolhouse. She had no books, insufficient paper, few pencils and very little else in the way of school supplies, but she opened school anyway. Then someone spread the rumor that schools for Gipsies were only a fresh trick of the Soviets to gain possession of horses and other Gipsy property; the Soviets might promise to waive the tuition-fee, but then agents would come and demand it anyway, and in case of default would confiscate everything the parents of school children possessed — Were not Soviet agents confiscating property in all the villages?

Rosa was furious. What right had anybody to doubt her word or her integrity? Had she ever cheated or tricked anyone? It was true that Soviet agents were confiscating property of peasants — but of what peasants? Of those who were hiding their grain or fighting collective farming or assaulting Soviet workers or damaging schoolhouses. But Gipsies, if they were law-abiding, had nothing to fear, Rosa assured them. After several stormy sessions she won her people over and proceeded to hold classes in her schoolhouse without further interruptions.

When I saw her she was in Moscow, trying to obtain from the central government increased appropriations for education and other cultural and social work among the Gipsies. She glowed with enthusiasm as she spoke to me of her work, her adventures, her plans for the future. She seemed the symbol of triumphant mankind, freed from doubt and terror. Then she told me the story of an experience of hers.

A colony of Gipsies — several hundred tents — had opened camp near Smolensk. Knowing many of the group, she went out to spend a night with them. In the evening the young people gathered before open fires — played the guitar, sang, danced and made merry until late in the night. The memory of the music and dancing were like wine to Rosa. Her eyes sparkled and her voice rose with excitement as she went on. " It was so good to be alive, to feel one's blood heated up, one's very soul afire. I shall never forget that evening. I felt so magnificently happy. Long after everyone had gone to sleep I still lay awake thinking — oh, of everything, and principally of the beauty of all life and all nature.

" Of a sudden I felt panicky. All my happiness went dead and I was plunged in gloom. I asked myself what right did the Soviet government or I myself have to interfere with this superb happiness of my people? What if these people were poor and ragged and unwashed? What did it matter if they had no future? There was joy in their lives which they would lose if they changed. Was it not wisdom, after all, which for hundreds of years had made them resist so strenuously all efforts to modernize them? They were only seeking that which we all want — happiness. Could they ever find, in a settled life, the satisfaction they knew as vagabonds? I was distracted and felt like a criminal who had come to steal their greatest treasure. For a time I was sick at heart and hated myself. What could I give them in exchange for this witchery, this beauty spread out beneath the moon and the stars, the trees and the grass? With my own hand I was helping to destroy it. I was sorry at the moment that I myself had not cultivated a love of vagabondage and won the romance, the peace, the excitement which my people knew."

As if to collect her thoughts, she paused, but not for long. Lifting her face and smiling with good-humored amusement, she continued: "But it was only a passing mood, I assure you, a fancy, born of weak-heartedness. I came to earth quickly enough. I was too good a revolutionary to allow myself to be affected for long by sentimental misgivings. I realized of course that these Gipsies might have joy, but sorrow they could not escape. Theirs was after all a dreadful life — they were so helpless, so desolate, so filthy. They lived like dogs, really, in flower-filled fields under star-dotted skies without seeing or understanding the beauty of the world around them. Ignorance and poverty were their daily companions. Risk and uncertainty were their everyday lot. No, I thought, there was no hope for them in vagabondage — no salvation in their resistance to science and knowledge. Deliverance, I felt convinced, could come only through enlightenment, through productive work, through becoming part of this great society of laboring citizens that we are building in Russia. My task then was clear — to help civilize and modernize these eternal wanderers, to bring them in touch with all the advanced thought of the world, so that they could enjoy all the fruits of this thought. Don't you think I was right?"

THE FAREWELL VISIT

BY the end of August, after a summer's wandering over collective farms in various parts of the land, I went back to the old village and I had no more than arrived there when rains set in. Day and night it rained, now in caressing drizzles and now in stinging showers. The peasants sulked and cursed. Some of them had not yet drawn in all their oats and others feared the wetness would rot potatoes and they shuddered at the thought of facing the winter without their *kartoshka.*[1]

One morning the sun came out bright and warm and the village breathed in relief and made ready to rush to the fields. But towards noon, heavy clouds swept the skies, a cold wind tore through the air and with thunder and lightning for accompaniment, a shower crashed down. It grew so cold that people donned their woolen *svitkas.*[2] It got so wet that older folk complained of pains and aches. The street had turned into a river of mud, so deep at the upper end that sheep had to be carried across. In the hollows wagons sank to the hubs and walking had become an art and a science, or perhaps only an exercise in acrobatics. With no sidewalks, no pavements, not even the customary piles of brush to fill up the worst holes, one had to pick his way with caution, step by step, as in a swamp, when jumping

[1] Potatoes. [2] Cloaks.

from bog to bog. In places, unless one was barefooted or in heavy boots, one could make his way across by climbing monkey-like over the fences.

With the autumn weather descending prematurely, the village was as if sunk in dreariness. The endless gray skies and the endless black mud had blotted out all color and all brightness. The very air seemed as if choked with gloom, which spoiled the mood of the people. They moved about with little verve. Even the young folk were without their wonted animation. The dogs likewise had drooped in spirit, and did not leap after passers-by with their customary ferocity but were content to show their ill-temper with a whine or growl. Never before, in all my visits to the old village, had I been so profoundly aware of its dullness and desolation and its remoteness from the comfort and exhilaration of the outside world.

Question after question pounded at my mind. Why hadn't these *muzhiks* laid out sidewalks, if only of boards or logs or piles of brush? Why hadn't they paved their yards? Why hadn't they put footscrapers on their doorsteps, so that on entering the house, people could remove the layers of mud from their boots or their bare feet? Why hadn't they cobbled the streets? Poverty was no explanation and hardly an excuse. If they had joined hands they could, with little ado, rid themselves of this mud and the ugliness and discomfort that it invited. Why hadn't they done so? Why, even in matters of desperate importance, were their powers of initiative so stunted? Why were even so-called *koolacks* content to follow the custom and the routine of their ancestors? Why the inertia, or laziness, or stupidity, or whatever you chose to call it?

The answer, however, became obvious when I thought of the peasants' past, of the ages and ages of isolation and monotony in which he lived and of his dark subservience to a medieval-minded gentry. Cut off from contact with the outside world, there was nothing in his life, save the little stimulus that the *zemstvos* provided, to light up his imagination and set ablaze his creative impulses. With mud and toil and filth and ignorance for daily and life-long companions, his chief means of escape from himself and from the world was vodka, and what a terrible guzzler of this fiery liquid he had become.

Depressing as was the village in this inclement weather, it was not without a fund of fresh news and gossip. On my arrival peasant after peasant hastened to give account of the events that had transpired in the months of my absence. At the coöperative there was still a shortage of tobacco, textiles and nails, but kerosene was more abundant and so was soap and more ample than ever was the supply of cosmetics, including rouge. The most exciting event that had happened since my last visit was the installation of a radio at the *kolhoz* headquarters. A trade union of shop clerks in the nearest city which had taken up a *shefstvo* [3] of the *kolhoz*, had offered sixty-five roubles towards the purchase of the radio and the *kolhoz* made up the balance. Unfortunately, nobody in the *kolhoz* or in the village understood the mechanics of the radio and whenever anything went wrong, which happened often, they had to send for a repair man, five miles away. Still when it functioned well they could tune in on Moscow and other cities, and in time they hoped to be able to connect

[3] Patronage.

with foreign countries. With a gush of pride nearly everybody in the village asked me to be sure and see the radio and tell them how it compared with radios in America. Even individualists were anticipating a more cheerful winter because of the diversions the radio would furnish.

Something else that was new had come to the village — underwear. Handkerchiefs, collars, ties, cosmetics, which were utterly unknown in my boyhood days, had already become familiar, and now underwear had made its appearance. The first shipment consisted of one pair of drawers and the whole village turned out to buy them. A woman was the first person in the queue and so she got the drawers. She tried them on and decided that she didn't care for them, so she ripped them up and made herself a blouse. That, however, did not allay the interest of the people in the new garment. Several shipments of complete suits of underwear had come to the local coöperative, and no sooner would the news of their arrival spread than crowds would come to buy them. The village was becoming underwear conscious.

The *kolhoz*, however, was still the chief topic of discussion. No end of tales did individualists have to narrate of the disorder and mismanagement that prevailed there. Once a group of men had gone to the swamp some forty versts away to cut hay. After several days' work they returned, their job barely begun. The chairman was delirious with exasperation. What would happen with the new drove of cattle coming in autumn if the swamp hay remained uncut? He denounced and cursed his lackadaisical colleagues and pleaded with them to go back and finish the haying, but they stubbornly refused. In desperation he picked out one of the fattest bull calves on the *kolhoz* and disregarding the order of the Commissary of Agriculture to slaughter no stock that was fit for breeding, he butchered it and offered all the meat to the striking men. That broke their resistance and they returned to their jobs. What sort of system was it, demanded the individualists with malicious joy, if the chairman had to bribe his own associates to keep them at their work? Why didn't the individualists need a bribe to attend to their tasks? What would happen to the individualists if they loafed, like members of the *kolhoz*, who, often enough, in the heat of harvesting, with a bumper crop of rye on their hands, would stretch out in the field and go to sleep?

Indeed, what would have happened to the *kolhoz* rye if the individualists hadn't come to the rescue? Of course, the *kolhoz* paid them well for their work — allotted to them pieces of meadow which they were only too happy to have. Yet the fact remained that so many of the people on the *kolhoz* were like overfed pigs, and when they got out into the field, they searched for shady nooks, and lay down to rest. Why was it so, cried the individualists, and why had the *kolhoz* people allowed their garden to choke with weeds? And why, when the administration of the *kolhoz*, in an effort to combat lassitude, had adopted piece work, did the official who divided the grain acreage into units, attempt to cheat some of his own associates? The group with which his wife was to work was assigned hectares which were smaller in area than the others, and when the women in the other groups, suspecting chicanery, checked up on these measurements with their own belts, they were, naturally enough, scandalized. Why, demanded the individualists, should there be such disorders and deceptions in the *kolhoz,* and what would happen if these continued?

Once more, the *kolhoz* officials invited me for a conference so that I could hear their side of the story. Frankly enough, they admitted the charge of disorder and mismanagement and internal dissentions. Some of the members just wouldn't fit into the new scheme of things — some but not all. Others there were, who had the good of the *kolhoz* at heart and toiled away with energy and devotion. Was it of no significance that as old a woman as Ulyana, growing nigh to seventy, was an outstanding champion of the *kolhoz* and had, on several occasions, publicly declared that if she was offered the finest individual allotment she would never return to individual farming, and that if all the peasants would join in and work honestly they would reap rewards, which, as individualists, they could never hope to enjoy? Ah, if Ulyana were only younger or if there were more like her! Again and again, after work hours, she would go around the barns and see that the horses were properly fed and watered and sheltered. Whenever she found any irregularity, she immediately set about to remove it and then searching out the man in charge of the stables, she chided him for his laxity with such vigor and eloquence that he felt shamed and crushed. There was a woman with a real social spirit, though she was so old and had never learned to read or to write. Was not Ulyana a living proof of the fact that there was something big in the *kolhoz* idea, which was getting into the very blood of people?

However, this was the first year of the *kolhoz* and I must always remember that all the members, from the chairman down to the herdsman, were only *mu-zhiks,* without culture, without experience in the opera-tion of large enterprises, and, save for agricultural ad-vice, they were not receiving the outside aid they needed. When the *kolhoz* first was started, one of their members, a *Komsomoletz,* twenty years old, with a talent for organization, gave promise of becoming the leader they required. Then the *raikom* on discovering his organizing abilities, transferred him to another *kolhoz,* which was made up of boys and girls from seventeen to twenty. They were not to blame, were they, if the Soviets didn't have enough leaders of talent and culture for all the *kolhozy?* They had to struggle along as best they could, but they were learning things. They were learning something about discipline from other *kolhozy.* In the *kolhoz* at P——, for example, a widow whose job was milking cows once came to the chairman and told him that she would quit work if she did not at once receive a pair of holiday shoes. She was the kind who loved to show off and had always worn her best shoes in the stables, while she was milking. The chairman did not hesitate to tell her that if she had not wasted her shoes on the cows, she would not have needed a new pair and that the coöperative store had none to spare. Exasperated, the widow walked away saying she wouldn't touch a milk pail until a new pair of holiday shoes had been sent to her. The chair-man didn't run after her; calmly he assured her that if she didn't want to work it was her affair and then, with the consent of the administration, he barred her from the supply store and suspended her from the *kolhoz* for a month. Immediately she experienced a change of heart and, with tears, promised the chairman that she never again would seek special privileges if she was allowed to return to her work. There was an example of real discipline of the kind that they needed to impose on some of their members. And they would impose it, too.

Such discipline, together with the system of piece work and political education, would solve a lot of their difficulties. They also hoped for some good results from the forthcoming division of the crops. Even the most hostile individualists had to admit that the *kolhoz* rye was vastly superior to their own. It could not have been otherwise, with the *kolhoz* enjoying the advantages of the tractor, the disk, the grain drill, the choicest seeds in the country and the council of an expert *agronom*. True, they were not so lucky with their spring crops. Lack of rain at the height of the growing season had stunted their barley and oats and flax, but their potatoes were superb. All in all, however, their harvest would enable them to pay their members a higher wage than the one they had set in the spring. They were all assured of bread, milk, potatoes, cabbage and of enough spare cash for some new clothes, herring, kerosene, soap, and other city products. With good luck in raising their pigs and their calves, they would also be enabled to increase their meat rations. All this, supplemented by the produce their members were deriving from their individual gardens, would enable all of them, and especially those who had a cow, a pig, hens and a few sheep of their own, to live in comfort during the ensuing year. Wouldn't I, therefore, agree, that in spite of all their deficiencies the results warranted faith in the future of the *kolhoz?* When the *kolhoz* first started, the individualists prophesied that it would collapse before their sowing and planting were finished and that by winter, all its members would be facing starvation. Yet, here it was, actually striking roots in the community. Some of their members, from among the *bedniaks,* never in the old days had raised enough grain to last them from harvest to harvest. By the time Easter arrived, and sometimes Christmas, they had to borrow grain for bread. But now they were assured of a decent living throughout the year. They felt, therefore, that nothing save a natural calamity, which would hit the individualist perhaps more severely than it would them, would stop their advance towards increasing comfort in their everyday life. In the villages of C—— and P—— they had successful *kolhozy.* Why then, couldn't they, in time, have a successful *kolhoz* in this village?

An unexpected visitor had come, Antosh, the fiery Young Communist, who was so impressive a figure in the community on my first visit in 1923. He had grown more stocky and appeared more mature. His hair was as frizzled and as abundant as formerly and fell in ringlets over his ears and temples. His eyes glowed with their old earnestness, but seemed void of their old impatience. Still taciturn, he seemed more subdued than in his younger years, or perhaps only more reflective and more tolerant. He informed me that he had been away from the village for six years, during which he had seen service in the Red Army, had attended an institute for political education and had held responsible posts in various parts of the country. No longer a *Komsomoletz,* but a full-fledged Party man, he was now secretary of a Soviet somewhere in the north. For the first time in five years he was allowed a vacation and had come home for a visit. But he was not resting — peasants would not let him. Because he was a Party man, they were bombarding him with complaints against local officials and he was making the rounds of village Soviets checking up and adjusting grievances. Evenings, when he was home, he would gather groups of young people in the *kolhoz* office, deliver lectures to them, read pamphlets, or conduct discussions.

One afternoon, while a cold shower was swishing over the village, he came to see me. The rain seemed to invigorate him, for he appeared fresh and cheerful. He immediately launched into a volley of the usual questions about the American proletarian, the American crisis and the possibility of an American revolution. Then he asked me for a frank appraisal of the *kolhoz* movement in Russia, and especially of the *kolhoz* in our village. Several members of the *kolhoz*, and a few other peasants who were present, followed me with their opinions of the *kolhoz*. A discussion ensued in which were repeated the arguments, presentiments, denunciations, that I had so often heard and have set down in preceding pages. However, as I listened to the words of some of the peasants, I couldn't help marvelling at the changed demeanor of Antosh. Severe as were the criticisms of the Party and the Soviets, he no longer flared into tirades and denunciations of the speakers. When someone flung at him the charge that his own father had left the *kolhoz*, he replied calmly enough, that his father's act was the best proof that he had been endowed with more than a generous share of stupidity. Then he launched into lengthy explanations of the shortcomings of the

Soviets, the Party and the *kolhoz* movement. These explanations differed but little from those of the numberless village Communists whom I had met in other places. All of them followed the lead of Moscow, and framed their thought to fit Moscow's latest formulas. I must add, however, that these peasant Party workers display a sense of reality and a human quality, which the more rigid-minded and bumptious city Communist seldom manifests. When arguments were at an end and the small group of peasants in the house had regained their composure, Antosh, growing expansive, proceeded with a further elucidation of the problems confronting the Soviets in their dealings with the village.

"I was a boy," he began, "when the German armies occupied this village but I remember well enough their way of dealing with our peasants. Do you suppose that when they wanted something done they would bother to make the rounds of houses, as we have been doing, knock at windows, and call peasants to mass meetings and take a chance on so few of them turning out that the meeting would have to be postponed? No, indeed. The Germans didn't bother to take the peasant into their confidence. They did not bother to make lengthy explanations and to engage in fiery discussions. They ordered things to be done and they saw to it that they were well done. Once they ordered our *muzhiks* to repair the roads and the roads were repaired. Again they ordered our *muzhiks* to build sidewalks and the sidewalks were built. Incidentally, do you know what happened to the sidewalks when the Germans left? They disappeared. The peasants tore them up. There now!"

He cast a sharp glance at his hearers, as if challenging them to a denial of his words. But no one murmured a word.

" Soon, however, our *muzhiks*, to escape tasks that they didn't like, resorted to their ancient trick — bribery. They began to bring ' gifts ' to the Germans — eggs, butter, pork, fruit and other things. At first the Germans scolded them and refused to accept the ' gifts.' But soon they experienced a change of heart. Lucky for them that they didn't remain here, else they would have become as corrupt as the old Czarist officials. Now, please understand, I am not blaming the peasant for making use of bribes when in difficulties with officials or superiors. Bribery was as much a part of the old régime as were uniforms. But I needn't tell you that it is a vitiating practice, and in the early days of the Revolution the peasant was as prodigal with bribes as he ever was under the Czar and he corrupted many an honest Soviet worker. I was at work once in this district Soviet, and all the time peasants would bring us eggs, meat, white flour, just as though we were Czarist officials. Once a peasant who had a law suit pending in the land court, brought our chairman a sack of pork, ' Just a gift,' he said, and the chairman in exasperation, turned the pork over to the children's home and sentenced the *muzhik* to jail for several days.

" At another time, a peasant came to the same chairman's home and called him outside to the barn, and what do you suppose he wanted? He shut the door, pulled out from a sack a flask of *samagon* and offered it to the chairman with the words, ' Take it, *tovarishtsh.* I've made it myself, excellent brew, you will like it.' The chairman grabbed an axe and smashed the flask to smithereens and fined the peasant. Of course, the peasants cursed and yelled when we punished them for what they regarded as 'acts of kindness' towards us. But we didn't mind. We were determined, in this district, to root out bribery and nowadays only a demented peasant would even think of presenting a bribe to an official.

" It is so with other things. If we had bothered to heed the peasants' outcries against innovations, we should never have made any advance. Is there anything, for example, more dreadful in our countryside than our roads? Look out of the window and see what happens after the rain. What you see in this street, you'll see on the highways. It is worse yet in the spring, when the snows thaw — the mud gets so deep that you can swim in it, and yet, you should have heard the peasants rail when we proposed that each household send a team and a worker for four days every summer to repair highways. If they all got together, they could easily pave the street and their yards and lay out sidewalks. But — there is so little public spirit in them, and I tell you, the only hope of developing such a spirit is to draw them into the *kolhoz*. The mud here will never disappear until the *kolhoz* gets busy and puts in pavements. Am I right, *tovarishtshui?* " He turned to his hearers. Several of them nodded in approval, and he with a smile of triumph continued.

" It is so easy to be misled by the peasant's wailing. He is so eloquent, that unless you know him, you feel that he has been grievously wronged. At one time, in this part of the country, the Soviets sought to break up the villages into homesteads. When the news of the new proposal reached our village, the peasants

were outraged. What sort of a life would it be, they
wailed, away from neighbors and cut off from the world
by snow in winter and mud in autumn, and so exposed
to attacks of bandits? Mass meeting after mass meeting was called to discuss the project, and then some
men ventured to take advantage of it. And do you
know, shortly afterwards, everybody wanted to be on a
homestead of his own! But the Soviets changed their
policy and instead of homesteading, advocated small
settlements with the land of the people blocked out
near their homes. Again the peasants protested. They
would have nothing but homesteads — settlements they
argued would only invite disaster. Once more we called
mass meeting after mass meeting, and finally they were
won over to the idea of small settlements. But before
the surveyors got around to break up this village into
settlements, the policy was again changed in favor of
the *kolhozy*, and, well — you have been around and you
have heard them talk and you know how they feel. But
I make this prediction. In two or three years they will
get so acclimated to the *kolhoz*, that they won't want
to change to anything else, and some day in the future,
when the Soviets decide to convert the *kolhozy* into
communes, they will again howl with indignation and
prophesy failure. And yet think what a boon the
kolhoz has been to the government. Take this *kolhoz*,
for example — it was supposed to sell to the Soviet co-
operatives one-eighth of its grain, but the crop proved
so good that at a recent meeting the members voted to
sell one-fifth. Yesterday, an order came for five hundred poods of potatoes for an army camp. Of their
own accord, they have doubled the order. Can you
imagine the energy we should have been required to

waste to collect these amounts of grain and potatoes from individualists? Can you imagine the meetings we should have had to call, the pledges we should have had to make, the threats we might have had to issue, to shake out of our *muzhiks,* at government prices, three thousand poods of rye and one thousand poods of potatoes? But with the *kolhoz* in control, there were no fuss, no excitement, no harangues. Of course, not all *kolhozy* have fulfilled their obligations to the Soviets as promptly as this *kolhoz,* but they all ought to and in time we hope they will."

" The trouble is," interposed a member of the *kolhoz,* " that somehow people don't work on the *kolhoz* as they do for themselves. They are not as interested. If you could only find some way of killing the urge for personal gain."

" That is because," Antosh flared back, " they are still dark and uncultured. What's personal gain for? What do people really want — ordinary people, who have not developed the *koolack* mania for hoarding? They want to live in comfort and in security, don't they, and well — the *kolhoz* has got to make them more comfortable and more secure than they were in their own households, else it will collapse. You can't offer a man a worse condition of life than he had and hope to succeed. It must be better. Supposing then that in the *kolhoz* a man works seven, eight, or six hours, and then comes home, washes up, perhaps changes his clothes, eats his evening meal, and goes out to the club-house to read something, or see a motion picture show, or a play, or participate in a game, or just stay around and chat with friends. Then he goes home to a clean and comfortable room and retires. What else does he need? His children are taken care of, and are like himself protected against all mishaps, and again I say what else does a man require? Must he indulge in personal gain, must he make profits? What for? "

Two days later I was to leave. All morning it drizzled but towards noon the skies cleared and the sun came out and stayed out. It was still chilly and people felt the need of warm clothes. The mud had turned into slush and stretched like a sparkling blanket from one end of the village to the other. Edward Deuss, an American journalist, happened to be with me on this trip. Taking advantage of the sun, we photographed the village, the *kolhoz,* and groups of peasants. Then bidding friends farewell, we drove off.

The fields were again humming with work. Peasants were getting ready for the winter sowing. Some of them were drawing manure in their little one horse carts. Others, mostly women and children, were scattering this manure with their bare hands. Others again were ploughing with wood framed ploughs that stirred up only a thin layer of earth, and still others were vainly trying to break up the lumps of soil with their toothpick harrows. These, of course, were individualist farmers, who from necessity more perhaps than from choice, were clinging to their ancient tools and their ancient methods of tillage. Across the road from their fields, was the *kolhoz,* spreading majestically to the horizon. No tractors or other machines were now at work, but the mere sight of it made one think of the huge steel mechanisms, which like a conquering army were marching onward and onward, all over the Russian countryside. It made one feel sorry for this plodding individualist, who cried out against the *kolhoz*, and whose weapons of warfare against it, both psychologically and mechanically, held out no promise of victory.

We passed two cabbage fields, one large and one small, and separated from one another by a narrow highway. The large field was marked up in rows, both ways, and the plants were set in squares, with the ground free of weeds. The heads were large, firm, clean, with even the outward layers of leaves unperforated by the chewings of worms. In the smaller field, the rows were uneven and the plants set close to one another. Weeds spread luxuriously in between the rows, and the heads of cabbage were small, soft, and laden with worms. The large field, the driver informed us, belonged to the *kolhoz*, and the other to an individualist.

We drove along at a leisurely pace. Deuss and I crouched in the back on straw, while our driver was in front hunched up on his knees. The cart was without a top, but the cumbrous coats which our host had provided for us were calculated to protect us against all emergencies. The weather however had steadied itself. Now and then the sun would slip under a cloud and a blast of wind would smite at our faces, but there was no rain, and we felt comfortable.

A quarter of a century earlier I had traversed the same road. We were then emigrating to America, all of us, mother, brothers, sisters. It was early autumn then as now and the weather was even more dismal — it drizzled without let-up and it was cold. Peasants followed us along in a mournful procession as at a funeral. At the cemetery our cart halted for a last round of farewells and for a fresh outbreak of loud crying.

America was so far away, in another world from which people never returned, and we felt sad. I was barely fourteen years of age and as we moved farther and farther away from the village I could not believe that I was actually leaving the old home. It seemed impossible that we would be separated forever from the surroundings and the people I had known so well.

Now I was likewise overcome with incredulity. This ancient countryside seemed like a legend. These *muzhiks* who fumed and railed, who wept and despaired or who thrilled and gloried, and all their new ideas and transformations, their dreams and conflicts, seemed too fantastic to be real. I knew these *muzhiks* so well in the old days. They were shut off from the tumult and excitement of the times. None of them ever read a newspaper or heard of foreign lands save America and perhaps Turkey. Very few of them ever saw a railroad train or heard of electricity or any of the machines that had been coming to the *kolhoz*. They trembled in the presence of officials and the landlord was to them the great master of the world. Their thoughts, their ambitions, their daily pursuits were bounded by their village and the nearby town bazaar. Nor could they escape from their antecedents. They were born *muzhiks*, they would always remain *muzhiks* and they would die *muzhiks*. That was their destiny and they could conceive of none other. They were all but buried in these ancient marshlands.

Yet now here they were all of them, the *koolack* and the revolutionary, the *bedniak* and the *seredniak*, and above all the children with their games of war between proletarians and *bourzhuis*, and the ten-year-old lad assuring me with astute self-confidence " that in this country we have stored away the word riches in the archives." A flood of new ideas was mercilessly beating down on them and a whole new world was rising before their very eyes. Whatever their future, their past with all its anchorages was fast breaking down. They could never again be what they had been throughout the ages, never!

" I suppose," asked the driver, " you are not expecting to come back so soon? "

" Not so soon," I replied.

" Don't stay away too long," he warned with good-humored expansiveness. If you do you may not see this village again. There is talk now of tearing down the half adjacent to the *kolhoz* and turning it into a school-park."

He jerked at the reins and urged the horse into a swifter pace. We had reached the end of our fields. The village had sunk from view, and out of the thickening haze there loomed only the freshly thatched roofs of the towering barns on the *kolhoz*.

RED BREAD

EARTH and sky, sky and earth, such is the Russian land, and never in history has it reverberated so mightily with the voice of the peasant. Hear this voice once and you never forget it. A shriek of wrath, a wail of despair, a cry of joy, it always overwhelms, for no man in Russia can plead with so sturdy a passion and frankness as the peasant. *Koolack* or revolutionary, middle peasant or poor man, for the *kolhoz* or against it, his words pour out a torrent of conviction.

Caught in the midst of a stupendous conflict he is overcome with bewilderment. Shall he remain on his own land and be an object of suspicion, and, in the event of material advance, a prey perhaps to brutal discriminations? Shall he join the *kolhoz* and forswear his independence and all that it implies in daily satisfactions and risk the guarantee of the modest security which individual landholding had always afforded him? The revolutionaries, of course, are promising him an earthly paradise in the *kolhoz,* but in these days of its beginning what assurance has he of the fulfillment of the promise other than their words, which he readily discredits? Always shunning chances, he is now called upon to make a plunge into what is to him the rashest venture he has ever known.

Yet he must make a choice, and quickly, for the

Revolution beats incessantly upon him. Event tumbles on event, crisis crowds on crisis, and whether he will or will not, he must decide which way to go. And whatever his decision, unless he has resigned himself to the demands of the Revolution or can respond with fervor to its call for social adventuring, he has no peace of mind.

It is this uncertainty of the peasant that gives rise to a host of ills on the *kolhoz,* to suspicion, jealousy, quarrels, to all manner of petty bickerings. The magnitude of the enterprise (and the tendency is to make the *kolhoz* larger and larger) adds to the peasant's discomfiture. He feels himself a small part of a big process, too big for his comprehension. His pride of workmanship wanes, and the *kolhoz* looms as something impersonal and sinister.

Let it be remembered, however, that the peasant's distrust of innovations, especially newly proposed innovations which touch the fundamentals of his life as intimately as does the *kolhoz,* is in part responsible for his recalcitrance. So is the haste with which the *kolhoz* is being promulgated, and even more so, the method of the promulgation. I am not referring to the barbarities which organizers perpetrated in the winter of 1929–30. These have been denounced and discarded. Communists, Stalin's staunchest supporters, admit that forcible methods in the villages pushed Russia to the brink of a holocaust. In their heart of hearts, however, they cherish no regrets, for in spite of the slaughter of live stock and other forms of destruction, when the tumult had subsided, one-fourth of the peasantry had remained in the *kolhoz.* That, they hold, was worth all the sacrifice that the venture cost. It imparted to the

movement the power and momentum it needed to push
it onward.

Indeed, if peaceable methods alone had been pursued and the principle of voluntary choice faithfully
observed, a decade or more might have been required
to bring the *kolhoz* to its present stage of development,
and time was precious. The city was threatened with
famine. A crisis might have been averted by acceptance
of the policy of the right opposition which counselled
compromise with private enterprise. But since this
policy was thrust aside, immediate and drastic action
was imperative. In Revolution, as in war, it is the objective that counts, and not the price, whether in gold
or in blood.

Other failings of the *kolhoz* are only too conspicuous.
The complexity of the enterprise demands the best of
leadership. The problems of personal relations and of
farm management would tax the ingenuity of the most
seasoned social worker and of the most brilliant agricultural expert. In Russia there is a scarcity of both.
Factory workers and peasants, with the aid of overworked *agronoms,* have been entrusted with the direction of the *kolhoz*. Naturally enough the blunders they
make strike the eye at every turn. Never, for example,
have I seen a threshing crew that did not resemble a
mass meeting, so many were the people assembled for
the job. The same is true of groups gathered for other
tasks that require bodies of workers. I have seen straw
handled five and six times between the threshing machine and the stack only a few rods away. Lack of
proper mechanical devices, the usual excuse of *kolhoz*
leaders, is only in part to blame for this waste labor.

Equally damaging is the reckless treatment of ma-

chinery on all the socialized lands, on the *sovhoz* as
well as on the *kolhoz*. True, the machine is a new thing
in Russia and the time has been too short to develop
in the peasant mechanical-mindedness and appreciation of its proper care. Yet that does not lessen the
damage resulting from abuse. With the exception of
girls, who are always more thoughtful in such matters,
one seldom sees a Russian tractor operator who, on his
way to and from work, does not race the tractor as
though it were an automobile. He glories in fast movement. The resulting breakage is colossal. Fleets of disabled tractors dot the Russian landscape; and what is
true of tractors is true of other machines. The abuse to
which they are subjected shortens substantially the
duration of their usefulness. Then, too, machines are
left with no cover over them in yards and in far away
fields, exposed to the devastation of wind, rain and
sun.

One could draw up a catalogue of failings, objective
and subjective, which would make the *kolhoz* appear
the most hopeless undertaking on earth. Yet the efforts
to overcome these failings and to exploit the advantages
that it makes possible are as dramatic a spectacle as
there is in the land of the Soviets.

All over the country special schools and courses have
been opened to develop capable leaders. Agricultural
institutes and colleges have never before been so
crowded with students who are seeking to make experts of themselves in farming. Specialization in every
field of endeavor has hit Russia harder even than
America. Propaganda on the vastest scale has been
launched to combat the peasant's unrest, and as an aid
to it, city products from soap to textiles, from hairpins

to cosmetics, have been rushed to the countryside. Again and again I found in village stores articles which I was unable to obtain in Moscow. Above all, a series of measures has been put into operation to bolster discipline and diligence.

In this respect the *kolhoz* is following the footpath of the factory. In the early days of the Revolution the self-exalted proletarian loafed on his job so blithely that he threatened an industrial collapse. Propaganda alone failed to move him. Other methods had to be devised to end his laxity. Equality of compensation was superseded by a graduated wage-scale. Wherever possible pay was based on piece work. Special rewards — a trip to some city, a rest house, a sum of money — were offered for meritorious service. Finally power was centered in a few hands, and now managers and directors are vested with personal responsibility. With the approval of the factory committee they may impose severe disciplinary measures on misbehaving workers, may not only issue reprimands, but fine them, suspend them from work for days, weeks, even months. Simultaneously, fresh and novel devices have been hit upon to rouse the proletarian to better effort through appeals to personal vanity and group pride. Shock brigades, socialist rivalry, public praise in the town press, in the wall-newspaper — these and other psychologic paraphernalia are in full sweep in the Russian factory.

Precisely the same processes of control are now being applied on the *kolhoz*. Piece work and premiums for special service are in wide use. Stern discipline is coming to the fore. Appeals to personal vanity and group pride, through public praise, socialist rivalry, shock brigades and other artificial stimulations are becoming an everyday experience.

These measures to make labor more productive would not have been of much account if the principle of the *kolhoz* had not possessed virtues of its own. *Its overpowering merit is its superiority to Russian individual agriculture as a method of production.* With one stroke it wipes out the stupendous wastes inherent in peasant farming. The strip system and all its attendant ills disappear. If there is no tractor available, there are enough horses on hand to make possible the use of modern implements from heavy plows to reapers. Indeed, these plows cut deep furrows; disk harrows break up the lumps and prepare a favorable seed-bed; grain drills sow evenly at a saving of one-fourth of the grain, and bury it deep enough so that crows cannot easily dig it out; the lumping together of the strips does away with needless travel; and, what is of greater consequence, the ridges and dead furrows, the chief sources of weed contamination, are obliterated.

These gains, colossal as they are, are reinforced by other advantages derived from the unified control of agriculture. With the peasant shying at innovations, the spread of anything new in farming under individualist control of the land, always encounters stiff opposition. Let the reader recall the incident with the peat in my own village. Though it was offered to the peasants without cost, they refused to avail themselves of it. They had never heard of mixing peat with straw for bedding and they were not disposed to bother about it. Only when they were threatened with a fine did they follow the suggestion. Equally informing is the incident of the incubator, when the peasants at first howled

down the very notion of a machine bringing forth
animal life. I happened to be among the Kuban Cossacks when the propaganda was launched for the introduction of cotton on their lands. Though more advanced than *muzhiks,* they fought strenuously against
the new crop, and only because it was new. I have attended meetings and institutes of peasants at which
modern methods of gardening and fruit-growing were
discussed at length, and yet on their return home these
peasants seldom ventured to make use of the information they had gained. That is why to this day in so
many sections peasants have little or no success in the
cultivation of cucumbers and cabbage, their favorite
vegetables. All over Russia, including the Ukraine, and
even among the Cossacks, it is seldom that one sees a
healthy orchard or fruits free of scabs and worms. Even
the *koolacks,* who agriculturally are the most progressive farmers in Russia, are slow to make use of new
methods. Witness their wretched homes, their windowless barns, their unpaved barnyards. At every turn in
the Russian village one stumbles upon needless waste,
incompetence and reluctance to heed the voice of the
laboratory and of the experiment station.

It is different on a *kolhoz.* The voice of the peasant
is not ignored. Final authority is vested in the mass
meeting; but it is easy to break down inertia and suspicion. The crowd cannot hold out against new ideas.
Nor can administrators delay action. They are constantly prodded by the *agronom,* the national and regional bureaus of agriculture, the Soviets, the Party.
When the building of a new type of house or barn is
proposed, or the cultivation of a new crop, or a new
process of tillage, the peasants on a *kolhoz,* unlike those

on individual farms, can be swung into doing something about it. If necessary their will can be overridden. It is easy to find legal excuses for such direct action. Equally significant is the fact that the acreage a person works on a *kolhoz* is larger than on a farm of his own, if only because of the use of machines. With all the drawbacks attendant on the first year of mass collectivization, this feature of the *kolhoz* is especially pronounced. Peasants who as individualists worked twenty-four million hectares, tilled twelve million more hectares in the *kolhoz*.

That on the *kolhoz* new ideas can easily be put into operation on a nation-wide scale has been eloquently demonstrated by the silo-building campaign. Russian peasants are notoriously ignorant of the science of stock feeding. Nor do they raise the needed fodder. To this day they make wide use of straw and chaff as food for cattle. The result is that in winter their cattle are poorly fed, give little milk and grow lean. In an effort to remedy this condition a campaign was started for the building of silos. I have been at meetings in villages at which this question was discussed, and it was pathetic to observe the distrust of peasants of the very idea of silos. Again and again the *agronom*, as if to strengthen his position, would call on me for a word of comment on what silos mean to the American farmer. If the project had been left to individual peasants, there would be few silos in Russia now. Yet there is hardly a *kolhoz* in the whole of the grain and grass growing regions but has several silos.[1]

Likewise, the orchards that many a *kolhoz* has set

---

[1] Because of a shortage of material, these are built, not above ground like those of American farmers, but in the ground — huge holes lined with cement.

out, and the gardens that have been started are new things in the Russian village. Also for the first time on a nation-wide scale, efforts are being made to weed out scrubby live stock and introduce the best available breeds, many of them imported from the United States, Canada, and South American countries and from various other agricultural lands. Then consider the amount of building, principally of barns and granaries, that has been achieved within the first year of mass collectivization. This in itself is eloquent testimony as to the possibilities of the *kolhoz*. From one end of the land to the other saws buzz, hammers clatter, logs are laid on logs and bricks are matched to bricks, and new barns, the largest and most modern which the peasants have ever known, are rising over the flat Russian landscape. There are no available statistics on the subject, but personal observation inclines me to the belief that more building has been achieved in the villages in the first year of mass collectivization than in all the preceding years of the Revolution.

Of course one must reckon the cost of all this, both in material substance and in human comfort. It has been prodigious. The breakage of machinery, the inability properly to organize time and labor are costly affairs in the Soviet Union. Reliable figures that cover every item of tangible and intangible expense are not as yet available. Those that are to be had can be variously interpreted. If one were to include the investment in the land, which Soviet bookkeeping never takes into consideration, it would not be difficult to prove on the basis of these figures that the cost of Russian agricultural production is the highest in Europe. Nor would it be difficult to prove the contrary.

It must, however, be emphasized that cost of production does not and cannot mean the same thing in present-day Russia that it does in a stabilized society. The Russian is engaged in a learning process. He is just discovering the machine. Therefore the machine serves a double purpose — productive and educative. The revolutionary tension in speeding up this education adds enormously to its cost. One of the chief causes of the breakage of machinery is the incessant drive for speed.

Yet from whichever angle it is approached, the *kolhoz* as a method of production has under Russian conditions indisputable and insuperable advantages. The individual peasant, even when ambitious and progressive, never would have dared to part with his ancient tools and his traditional methods of work as easily and swiftly as has the *kolhoz*. The sentiments and calculations that actuate a peasant play no part on the *kolhoz*.

The enforced parting with the past, as the reader has already learned from the preceding pages, has its tragic aftermath. It necessitates a break with old habits, old beliefs, old sentiments, and therefore perturbs and bewilders the peasant. It calls for a new faith, a new way of work, a new way of living, and thereby only adds to this perturbation and bewilderment. And there is none to whom the man in distress can turn for sympathy. There are no agencies ministering to hurt pride and dejected moods. There is nothing maternal in the mechanics and in the spirit of the Revolution, no more than in the mechanics and in the spirit of war, and one can escape from the one no more than from the other. Indeed, in a war the people who are not actively engaged in combat often can find refuge somewhere behind the lines. In Russia this is impossible. The territories behind the lines begin beyond the frontiers. Everywhere else there is only a battle front.

There is a parallel at least in some respects between the individualistically minded peasant in present-day Russia and the European artisan in the early days of the industrial revolution. He, too, stormed against the new system. He hated the machine. He cherished highly his independence and all the satisfactions that it afforded him, not the least of which was pride in the finished product. He, too, trusted to his own tool and his own method of work to provide daily sustenance and security against possible mishaps. Again and again he rose in masses and smashed the machine. But his resistance was of short duration. From the very beginning it was doomed, for his artisanry could not match the machine in productive capacity. The individual peasant in a Soviet society is facing a similar condition. He cannot rival the *kolhoz* in productivity.

One might speculate as to what would have happened in Russia had the Revolution followed in the footsteps of Stolypin, an astute Czarist minister, and allowed a homesteading act to work its way out on a national scale. One might speculate as to what would have been the outcome of some other plan for solving the perplexing agricultural problem of so backward a land as Russia. All such speculation at present is futile, if only because the Revolution has chosen its own course of action. It has appropriated the *kolhoz* as the sole way of coping with the existing difficulty, and one must judge Russian agriculture only in terms of the *kolhoz*.

Spectacular as is the agricultural revolution that the *kolhoz* is bringing to pass, the social revolution that it forebodes and is already in process of stirring is even more so. With the disappearance of the privately owned farm will come the disappearance of the individually inhabited home. The villages therefore will in time be torn down. The artel need not pass into a commune for this condition to eventuate. Peasant homes are notoriously unsanitary, uncomfortable, and are rapidly becoming dilapidated. Soon many of them will have to be rebuilt. Some of this rebuilding will follow along old models, but the plan which the *kolhoz* envisages will abolish them. The log or mud hut will be superseded by apartment houses. Many an older *kolhoz* has already begun to build such houses. More and more of them will do so, and in the end the age-old Russian village will give place to a new type of community, a rural township.

The *kolhoz* further promises to reduce appreciably Russia's birth rate. Because of the fall in the death rate from 30.5 per thousand in the pre-war days to 17.4 per thousand in the three years between 1926 and 1929, the population in Russia has been increasing more rapidly than in all of non-Russian Europe. In 1930 Russia boasted twenty million more people on the territories she is now occupying than in 1914. Were this increase to continue unchecked, the Russian revolutionaries, in spite of the Marxian doctrine which presupposes a sufficiency of material goods for uncontrolled growth in population, might eventually find themselves face to face with a serious problem.

Fortunately for them, the *kolhoz* promises to solve it automatically. Let it be remembered that for the peasant, as for all primitive people, large families are a form of insurance against the mishaps of life, especially old age. On the *kolhoz* the need of such insurance disappears. The aged and the disabled live at the expense of the community. Thus one of the primary motives for large families ceases to exist. Meanwhile, the women are gaining in sophistication. They have more leisure and greater opportunity for recreation and diversion. They enjoy the gatherings and the variety of entertainments which the *kolhoz* fosters. They begin to crave greater freedom, and no longer want to bear as many children as in the old days. The spread of birth control offers them the means of satisfying their wishes. The medical commissions which are making the rounds of collective farms usually hold sessions with the women on birth control. Of course there is still an acute shortage of physicians and trained nurses, and so the number of these commissions is small. In time, however, as fresh corps of graduates from medical schools swell the ranks of physicians, more and more such commissions will be sent out to the land.

Religion will suffer a fresh attack. Indeed, the *kolhoz* is on its way to becoming the staunchest foe of religion in the village. Let the reader recall the peasant who told the priest that on joining a *kolhoz* he would no longer christen his children because on a *kolhoz* there is no need for church, for God, for christenings. Unless he is a sectarian, especially a Baptist, an Evangelican, a Mennonite, the average peasant yields readily to atheistic influence. The example of others infects him. On the *kolhoz* the increased propaganda through everyday conversation, motion pictures, lectures, the constant emphasis that it is not God but the machine, not a supernatural power but science and nature that determine the productivity of the land, shatters the *muzhik's* mechanistic faith. In the building program of the *kolhoz* even as in that of the factory, church is accorded no place. Indeed, wherever the *kolhoz* becomes entrenched the church soon closes, is turned into a club-house, a granary, a school or a nursery. Only the sectarians who are the Russian Protestants are evincing religious vitality. Their numbers are comparatively few, and whether eventually they will triumph remains to be seen. Even they, however, are losing their younger adherents. Other religions, the Greek Orthodox, the Jewish and even the Mohammedan, are being submerged in the new social maelstrom.

The family, likewise, will feel the impact of the *kolhoz*. A nursery is among the first institutions to spring up on the new farms. Nurseries are spreading in the *kolhoz* more rapidly than in cities, and for obvious reasons. Building material and labor are easy of access, and food, especially milk, cereals and vegetables, is to be had in abundance. At present children stay in the nursery only in the daytime. Evenings they return to their parents. But this is viewed as a makeshift arrangement. When the *kolhoz* has become a full-blooded concern new nurseries are to be built, always in close proximity to the parents, to provide accommodations for children by day and by night. On the more advanced new farms such nurseries are already in operation. Children and parents visit each other constantly, but they live apart. Children receive training and inspiration chiefly outside the home and from non-parental sources. Community kitchens and dining rooms, in which children and adults eat their meals separately, are likewise spreading on the *kolhoz*. Under such conditions the family will no longer be the institution which it was when the peasant lived on his own land.

The disappearance of individual ownership of land, the coming of large-scale industrialized farming, the collapse of the village, the rise of rural townships, the growing sophistication of the peasant women and its effect on the nation's birth rate, the collapse of religion and the transformation of the individualistic family — these are the unmistakable guideposts of the approaching civilization in the Russian village. They are rooted in the very principle of the *kolhoz*, and as the *kolhoz* strengthens, they will strengthen.

There are further by-products of the *kolhoz* which are fraught with equally momentous potentialities. There is the peasant's changing standard of living. It began with the coming of the nep, when the peasant, because of loss of faith in money and lack of inducement to save, was beginning to keep for his own use more and more of his produce. Whenever he sold anything, it was chiefly for the purpose of buying something. He was reaching out for increasing amounts of manufactured goods. Boots, which in the old days conferred distinction on a man, now became a common article of wear. Rubbers, which were unknown except among youths who had spent some time in the city, became a common sight on Sundays and holidays. Handkerchiefs came into wide use. Collars and ties and even underwear were beginning to dribble in. Cosmetics followed. The quality of the bulk of these goods was and is low. But the peasant bought them and learned to enjoy them. His constant complaint was that they were not to be had in sufficient quantities. During 1929–30, owing to the so-called socialist of-

fensive, there came a disruption in the supply of manufactured goods more acute than at any time since the
coming of the nep. This socialist offensive had, indeed,
shaken down the peasant's standard of living all along
the line, even in food, though nowhere was he as seriously affected as the city person. The peasant has since
been grumbling loudly and volubly, but in the matter
of clothes he has as yet suffered no immediate or visible
distress. His purchases in the preceding years have
sufficed for current needs. On Sundays and holidays he
appears well dressed — better than at any time in his
history. *The Revolution has indeed enlarged his appetite for material enjoyment, and the* kolhoz *is destined
further to feed this appetite.*

It cannot be otherwise. Soviet organizers in their
effort to win him to the *kolhoz* have been promising
him all manner of material enjoyments. Since the harvest in the autumn of 1930, newspapers all over the
country have been busying themselves with dramatic
accounts of the increased productivity on the *kolhoz*
and with the resultant rise in the individual income and
in the purchasing power of its members. The peasant's
earthly appetites are indeed being constantly played
upon and expanded, and that alone is making him continually more demanding and self-assertive.

The growth of political-mindedness will give fresh
impetus to this self-assertiveness. Always an anarchist,
hating government as something evil and sinister, the
peasant is now slowly acquiring a new appreciation of
the meaning of political processes. In the old days he
could dismiss government with contempt, slink away
into his sequestered lair and be lost to the world. He
cannot do so now. Government is everywhere. Almost

everything he buys, everything he sells, reminds him of government. In the *kolhoz* all transactions are consummated through and with government institutions. Government is an all-pervading everyday experience, and the peasant has to face it openly and learn to deal with it as best he can. All these contacts with government are inculcating in him a fresh appreciation of its uses and functions. They are making him politically minded and are increasing his demands on government.

No less epochal is the idea of organization which the *kolhoz* is bringing to the peasant. A *kolhoz* implies a closely knit body. The continual mass meetings, their decisions and actions, cannot but impress him with the importance and possibilities of organization. As time goes on he will learn more and more to appreciate its value and its power.

As if in anticipation of such an eventuality, the proletarian rulers are seeking to gain ever increasing control of the *kolhoz*. Through their credit-giving organizations, their monopoly of manufactured goods, their transactions with the *kolhoz*, their political supervision, they are bent on holding the whip hand over the peasant. It is their boast that eventually they will convert him to their faith. Yet even if they do, and the peasant swears by Lenin and Marx as loquaciously as does the city proletarian, there is no guarantee that he will have no cause of his own to prosecute. Will he tolerate, for example, the disproportion of political representation that is now foisted on him? And supposing he remains only partially converted to the new dispensation?

Time alone can answer the question whether the *kolhoz* means an end to the incessant warfare between city and village, peasant and proletarian, or only the beginning of a fresh conflict, the most formidable that the Soviets have yet encountered.

Meanwhile the *kolhoz* with all its turmoil, all its agony, all its romance and all its promise, rolls on and on.